DATE

BROWNING AND THE MODERN TRADITION

BROWNING

AND

THE MODERN TRADITION

BETTY S. FLOWERS

Macmillan of Canada
Maclean-Hunter Press

First published 1976 by
THE MACMILLAN PRESS LTD
London and Basingstoke

First published in North America 1976 by
THE MACMILLAN COMPANY OF
CANADA LIMITED
Toronto

ISBN 0–7705–1418–9

Printed in Great Britain

For John

Contents

Acknowledgements

Most acknowledgements end with thanks to the author's spouse. I wish this to begin with thanks to my husband, John, first among my critics and deepest in my gratitude.

I am grateful, too, for the inspiration of the late Tom McMahon; for the kind guidance of Marjorie Thompson; for the helpful assistance of Tim Farmiloe; and for the careful and understanding criticism of Brian Southam.

And finally, I am indebted to Zulfikar Ghose, whose opinions, suggestions and encouraging words have supported me from the conception of this book to its publication.

The author and publishers wish to thank the following who have kindly given permission for the use of copyright material: The Bodley Head and Random House Inc., for an extract from *Ulysses* by James Joyce; Faber & Faber Ltd and Alfred A. Knopf Inc., for extracts from 'Notes Towards a Supreme Fiction: It Must Change', 'Sea Surface Full of Clouds' and 'The Idea of Order at Key West', from *Collected Poems* by Wallace Stevens; Faber & Faber Ltd and Farrar, Straus & Giroux Inc., for the poem '235' and an extract from '149', from *His Toy, His Dream, His Rest* by John Berryman; Houghton Mifflin Company for an extract from 'You, Dr. Martin' by Anne Sexton, from *To Bedlam and Part Way Back* (copyright © 1960 Anne Sexton and reprinted by permission of the publisher); New Directions Publishing Corporation, New York, for an extract from 'Picture of a Nude in a Machine Shop', from *Collected Later Poems* by William Carlos Williams (copyright 1948 William Carlos Williams and reprinted by permission of the publisher) and an extract from 'Portrait of a Lady', from *Collected Earlier Poems* by William Carlos Williams (copyright 1938 New Directions Publishing Corporation and reprinted by permission of the publisher); and Yale University Press for an extract from *Bee Time Vine and Other Pieces*, volume 3 of the Unpublished Works of Gertrude Stein.

Introduction

In many ways, Robert Browning seems an unlikely Victorian to be acknowledged as a major influence on modern poetry. The stereotypical image of Browning as a jolly dinner-guest with white hair and ruddy complexion is often reflected in the poetry itself with its atmosphere of hearty enthusiasm. For twentieth-century readers, this exuberance may seem insensitive, and is certainly contrary to what is usually taken to be the spirit of modern poetry. Browning, like his Victorian contemporaries, indulged his appetite for lengthy discussions of philosophy and religion in even lengthier poems. And although he offers the psychologically sophisticated reader detailed explorations of individual characters, these explorations lack the background sense of the forces of society on the individual so keenly presented by modern poets.

Given the great differences between these Victorian characteristics and much modern poetry, it is not surprising that many critics regard nineteenth-century French poets as being a greater influence on modern poetry than their English contemporaries, including Browning;[1] or that other critics regard Browning as being of very little importance at all. Hugh Sykes Davies, for example, while agreeing with Henry James's opinion that Browning is important to the modern novel, rejects Browning's influence as a poet: 'Because he has done so little, it seems, for modern poetry, modern poets have done nothing whatever for him.'[2]

Yet, surprisingly, of all the poetry of the nineteenth century, it is that of Browning which seems to be of greatest importance in the development of modern poetry. 'Und überhaupt ich stamm aus Browning. Pourquoi nier son père?'[3] Pound's acknowledgement of Browning's importance to his own poetry is particularly significant in that many poets have in turn acknowledged Pound as being a central figure in the development of modern poetry. In fact, in T. S. Eliot's view, Pound is 'more responsible for the xxth Century revolution in poetry than is any other individual. . . .'[4] And Pound is not the only poet Browning seems to have influenced. Browning has been mentioned in connection with such writers as: D. G.

Rossetti, Hopkins, Bridges, Chesterton, de la Mare, Gide, W. W. Gibson, Masefield, Auden, C. Day Lewis, Kipling, Frost, Hardy, Eliot, Pound, Lowell, Donald Davie, George Macbeth, Yeats, Robinson, Ransom, W. C. Williams, Crane.

As such a list indicates, Browning is certainly a familiar figure in the background of modern poetry; yet comparatively few attempts have been made to discover what aspects of Browning's poetry have been important to modern poetry, and exactly why modern poets such as Pound found Browning to be more interesting than any other Victorian poet.

Perhaps the central reason for this neglect in what is otherwise an abundance of Browning criticism is that the very pervasiveness of Browning's influence makes it difficult to study as a whole. The temptation is to isolate a few characteristics and to focus on them in detail, or to talk in general terms about 'Browning's Optimism' or 'Browning's Reputation as a Lover'.[5] The best studies have been those which explored particular aspects of Browning's style in relation to the general characteristics of modern poetry.[6] Of particular importance here is a 1954 essay by G. Robert Stange, 'Browning and Modern Poetry'.[7] Stange recognised the need for a detailed study of Browning's relation to modern poetry, a study to be based not on Browning's poetic thought or philosophical speculations, but on Browning as an influence on modern style. For surely it is here that the difference between modern poetry and Victorian poetry is most apparent; and it is the stylistic aspects of modern poetry which must be explored if we are to get any notion of Browning's importance to modern poetry.

In order to explore Browning's influence as fully as possible, and yet with an intensity of focus, I have isolated what I consider to be those characteristics of modern poetry which most clearly distinguish it from that of the nineteenth century: the emphasis on the poem as object, the approach to internal facts as the subject matter, the use of common diction, the dramatic method, the use of structures analogous to those of music, and the intermingling of prose and poetry. When explored in relation to each of these aspects, Browning's poetry takes on a new significance for twentieth-century readers.

1   The poem as object

The revolution in modern poetry which occurred early in this century
had at its centre an emphasis on the poem as object, and the creation
of the poem as an act similar to sculpting or painting in that it is
fundamentally concerned with craftsmanship rather than with any
sort of message to be conveyed. Browning's own use of painting and
sculpting as analogies to the art of writing poetry helps to illuminate
both his poetry and the relation of his experiments to the emphasis
put upon the visual arts by many modern poets. In Browning and
modern poets, the visual image is used not as decoration, but as a
central aspect of poetic structure. Modern poets seek not to legislate,
or to decorate, but to get to the 'bare bones' of poetry;[8] and in doing
so, they have devised methods of organisation which, like Browning's,
rely on principles of association.

2   Approach to the subject matter

For Browning, as for modern poets, the beauty of poetry lies in its
power to reveal the common facts of everyday existence in a new
light. Even though Browning sometimes uses unusual characters, he
is primarily interested not in the external aspects of these characters,
but in how they use words to make thoughts assume a different
shape. As Wilde said of him, 'it was not thought that fascinated him,
but rather the processes by which thought moves. It was the machine
he loved, not what the machine makes.'[9] The poetry of the process
of thought rather than the thought itself is one way to characterise
modern poetry. Browning's construction of forms appropriate to
process rather than product becomes even more significant in the
context of the forms exhibited by modern poets.

3   Common diction

In concentrating on the inner facts of the mind Browning uses the
diction of common speech, and in this use, provides an important
example for the poetic speech of the twentieth century. The diction
of modern verse is no longer that of the traditionally elevated poetic
speech, but takes on the characteristics of conversational speech. Yet
within this use of the rhythms of everyday speech, both Browning
and modern poets concentrate on individual words as centres of

meaning, and on the way in which a word interacts with its context, or on what happens when a word from one context is associated with words from an entirely different context.

4   Dramatic method

Like Browning, modern poets explore the function of masks and the way in which they are created through the manipulation of words. The poem itself becomes a mask for the poet, for although he speaks through it, he cannot be identified with its surface. Moreover, Browning's insistence that dramatic poetry is primarily poetry, and need not follow the conventions of drama, is echoed by modern writers whose poems, like Browning's, exhibit a freedom from the tyranny of conventions, whether poetic or dramatic.

5   Musical analogy

Within this freedom, poetic structure has assumed forms best explained by the use of a musical analogy. What is 'musical' about these structures is not their beauty of sound, but the use of syntax, rhythms and imagery to create a pattern of meaning which will have the power of music to express abstract emotion, while at the same time carrying the weight of words with their inescapable references to the concrete. In modern poetry, as in Browning's poetry, this attempt to give words the power of music has resulted in an organisation of poetic forms based on association rather than on a narrative or logical progression.

6   Prose and poetry

Finally, Browning's poetry exhibits the coming together of prose and poetry so characteristic of twentieth-century literature. The important distinction is no longer that between verse and non-verse, but that between art (the creation of word-objects, whether in poetry or prose) and speech (the use of words for utilitarian purposes). Poetry is 'that which gets lost from verse and prose in translation'.[10] Because modern novelists and modern poets express the same concerns, their arts often exhibit the same forms: the use of myth as underlying structure, for example, or the exploration of significant moments which illuminate the everyday world.

In relating Browning's poetry to modern poetry in general, rather than to any one poet in particular, I hope not only to emphasise those particular aspects of Browning's poetry which are significant to the development of modern poetry, but also to indicate the wide range of poetry in which Browning's influence is felt. Of course there are limitations inherent in this method – the most obvious being that the very generality of the subject will mean that the study is suggestive rather than exhaustive. Moreover, within the limits of English poetry, I have confined myself to a discussion of Browning, without attempting to trace other important influences in modern poetry, such as those of Whitman or Hopkins. And finally, I have concentrated my analysis of particular poems on those written earlier in this century, an approach which does not take into account the most recent developments in modern poetry. This concentration is deliberate, however, for it is in the poetry of the early part of this century that the aspects of modern poetry which constitute its difference from that of the nineteenth century first become apparent.

'The most individual parts of [a poet's] work', said Elliot, 'may be those in which the dead poets, his ancestors, assert their immortality most vigorously.'[11]

If Browning's poetry takes on a new significance in the light of the modern tradition, then an exploration of Browning should also result in a greater understanding of the modern tradition. It is my hope that the following study contributes to the understanding and appreciation of both.

I

The Poem as Object

Although lines of continuity can be drawn from poetry of the nineteenth century to that of the twentieth, and indeed from poetry earlier than the nineteenth century to what is called 'modern poetry', the movement centring around Ezra Pound in the years 1908 to 1920 was by nature more of a revolution than a continuing of the nineteenth-century tradition.[1] Imagism was the most clearly defined movement connected with the poetic revolution of the time, but it would be misleading to categorise all the poets experimenting with new forms as Imagist poets or to use Pound's Imagist doctrines as more than convenient simplifications for aspects of what was most remarkable in modern poetry.[2]

Even so, Pound spread his principles through the 'organisation' of the Imagists, through articles, and through his personal influence on poets not strictly in the Imagist group. This influence was acknowledged, for example, by T. S. Eliot who dedicated *The Waste Land* to 'il miglior fabbro', and referred to him as 'probably the most important living poet in our language'.[3] Pound had a similar effect on Yeats, serving as an important influence in his evolution towards a less romantic and abstract style of writing. William Carlos Williams admitted having 'borrowed' from Pound, adding that 'Everyone has who has followed him. Yeats especially.'[4] The list of those often mentioned as being indebted to Pound is long: Antheil, Eliot, Hemingway, Joyce, Marianne Moore, William C. Williams, Lowell, Ransom, Hardy, Beckett, Yeats, Masefield, Frost, Robinson, Olson, Ginsberg and others.

Pound's influence as theoriser and critic has often been acknowledged. More difficult to discuss is the importance of his role as populariser. It is not unfair to say that whatever engaged Pound's interest was enthusiastically shared with his friends. And certainly one of his early enthusiasms was Browning: 'Try Browning's Sordello', he says to one correspondent;[5] and to a translator: 'To ... get out of certain kinks whereinto you have been drawn solely by terza rima and the length of the lines, would it be any good your reading Browning's *Sordello*? Have you ever read it?'[6] Moreover, Pound's

literary essays do not merely praise Browning but often present him
as a poet of primary importance to English literature.[7]

The influence of Browning's poetry on poems such as 'Near
Perigord' and the early *Cantos* is obvious on first reading.[8] What is
not so obvious is how those attitudes fundamental to modern poetry,
many of which were made explicit by Pound, are implicit in
Browning's poetry. For example, a central Poundian idea is that of
the poet as craftsman. This does not imply that Tennyson and Arnold
and other nineteenth-century poets were not craftsmen or were
somehow deficient in poetic skills; rather that the concept of the
poet as craftsman was being emphasised with very specific and
significant connotations. Browning declared that his poetry was never
intended to be 'the solace of an afternoon cigar';[9] Pound insisted that
poetry was an art, not a pastime:

> It is certain that the present chaos will endure until the Art of
> poetry has been preached down the amateur gullet, until there is
> such a general understanding of the fact that poetry is an art and
> not a pastime; such a knowledge of technique . . . that the amateurs
> will cease to try to drown out the masters.[10]

And Eliot agreed, saying that 'Pound was original in insisting that
poetry was an art, an art which demands the most arduous applica-
tion and study; and in seeing that in our time it had to be a highly
conscious art.'[11]

To the nineteenth-century poet, the art of poetry involved knowledge of the traditional poetic forms and skill in rhyming and other
technical devices. As Browning put it, 'One should study the
mechanical part of the art, or nearly all that there is to be studied –
for the more one sits and thinks over the creative process, the more
it confirms itself as "inspiration," nothing more nor less.'[12] Pound's
emphasis is the same:

> Let the neophyte know assonance and alliteration, rhyme
> immediate and delayed, simple and polyphonic, as a musician
> would expect to know harmony and counterpoint and all the
> minutiae of his craft. No time is too great to give to these matters
> or to any one of them, even if the artist seldom have need of
> them.[13]

However, in modern poetry, this emphasis on the importance of
the poet's mastering the 'minutiae of his craft' has been expanded to

include the idea that, as William Carlos Williams says, 'the poem, like every other form of art, is an object, an object that in itself formally presents its case and its meaning by the very form it assumes.'[14] And it is this idea – the poem is an object – that has become one of the central aspects of the development of poetic forms which distinguished them from those of the nineteenth century.

Although 'the poem is an object' may seem like a rather obvious generalisation, the implications of the statement point towards the central differences between nineteenth-century poetry and that of the twentieth century. For example, the statement that a poem is an object stresses the resemblance of poetry to the plastic art of sculpture or the visual art of painting rather than the resemblance to an art such as music which involves the passing of time for its major effects. Even Eliot, noted for what might be called the 'musical' quality of his verse, insisted that 'Language in a healthy state presents the object, is so close to the object that the two are identified.'[15]

Thus, the poet as craftsman is seen as a maker of word-objects in the same way that a sculpture could be said to be a maker of statues. Charles Olson insisted that every element in a poem must be taken up 'just as solidly as we are accustomed to take up what we call the objects of reality...'[16] And Pound often spoke of a poem as if it were created from the same solid material as that a sculptor handles: 'It is as simple as the sculptor's direction: "Take a chisel and cut away all the stone you don't want." ???? No, it is a little better than that.'[17] Auden, also, used a sculptural analogy when discussing the difference between formal and free verse:

> The difference between formal and free verse may be likened to
> the difference between carving and modeling; the formal poet, that
> is to say, thinks of the poem he is writing as something already
> latent in the language which he has to reveal, while the free verse
> poet thinks of language as a plastic passive medium upon which he
> imposes his artistic conception.[18]

The analogy between poetry and the visual arts was carried even further by Wallace Stevens who believed there was 'a corpus of remarks in respect to painting, most often the remarks of painters themselves, which are as significant to poets as to painters.'[19]

Perhaps one reason that the relations between poetry, painting and sculpture were emphasised in the first quarter of the century was that poets began to see modern poetry as one aspect of a revolution which was occurring at the same time in all the arts. In 1915 the young E. E. Cummings gave an address on the 'parallel developments of the New Art in the fields of painting and sculpture, music, and literature'.[20] Pound, in publicising his idea of what modern poetry should be, included under 'vorticism' not only '"Imagismé" in verse', but also 'such and such painting and sculpture'.[21]

Not only have modern poets referred directly to specific modern paintings or artists in their poems, but also some have written on poetry and painting in prose essays (as, for example, Stevens's 'The Relations between Poetry and Painting').[22] Some modern poets have even been painters themselves. E. E. Cummings 'always painted more than he wrote'.[23] Williams in *I Wanted to Write a Poem* says that 'Under different circumstances I would rather have been a painter than to bother with these god-damn words.'[24] Although he did end up bothering with words, Williams firmly believed that the poets of his generation were more influenced by modern French painters than writers, and that 'their influence was very great'.[25]

The impact of the visual on the development of modern poetry is reflected even in the way the poem appears on the page. The words of the poem are often arranged deliberately to impress the eye before the sound, meaning or connotation can be apprehended. In Marianne Moore's poetry, for example, spaces are often used in conjunction with a strict syllabic scheme to create a formal structure which in earlier times might have been created by a regular metre and a strict rhyme scheme. And certainly the spacing of a poem such as Williams's 'Picture of a Nude in a Machine Shop' is immediately impressed upon the reader:

> and foundry,
>   (that's art)
>   a red ostrich plume
> in her hair:
>
> Sweat and muddy water,
> coiled fuse-strips
>   surround her
> poised sitting –
> (between red, parted
>   curtains)

the right leg
                    (stockinged)
up!

Of course the visual impression of the poem on the page was exploited as early as Herbert's 'Easter-wings'. In Herbert's case, however, the visual impact is primarily emblemistic; the lines are arranged to create an outline of wings on the page. By contrast, Williams's lines do not resemble a nude or any other image.

The use of spacing as part of the formal structure in modern poetry is complemented by experiments in creating visual and dramatic effects through different sizes of type or print. In *The Waste Land*, for example, Eliot puts a line in capitals to indicate a second voice:

> I didn't mince my words, I said to her myself,
> HURRY UP PLEASE ITS TIME
> Now Albert's coming back, make yourself a bit smart.
>
>   (II, 140–2)

And in 'O O O O that Shakespeherian Rag – /It's so elegant/So intelligent' (II, 128–30), the repeated 'O's' and the two short lines following suggest visually as well as aurally the syncopation of jazz rhythm.

The important role played by the visual rather than the aural aspect of the poem is illustrated in much of Pound's poetry. A reader who does not read Chinese, for example, would not be able to pronounce the ideograms which frequently appear in the *Cantos*. Pound also uses the ampersand as a variation for 'and', a variation which creates a different visual picture even though it does not affect the pronunciation.

The typographical or visual aspect of the poem emphasises sight over sound; also sight over the narrative content, or the 'prose' meaning of the poem. This is especially evident in the use of punctuation marks not to separate one clause from another, or to indicate something parenthetically, but primarily for their visual impact, as in the last line of Cummings's 'here's a little mouse) and':

> who   (look).   ,startled

In this line, the period and the comma do not function as servants of meaning, but have a prominent place in the visual arrangement of letters and spaces. Experiments such as these in typography and

spacing draw our attention to the page as a kind of spatial arrangement of black on white, a literal placing of pigment (ink) on canvas
(paper). Or, to use Valéry's analogy, 'typography can be compared
with architecture, just as, earlier on, reading might have brought to
mind melodic music and all the arts that espouse time.'[26]

Although Browning did not carry the idea of 'the page as picture'
to the point of exploiting typography to create a visual impression,
he did emphasise the visual aspect of poetry. Elizabeth Barrett
Browning pointed out, 'it is his way to *see* things as passionately as
other people *feel* them'.[27] Like Cummings, Williams and other
modern poets, Browning spent time painting and sculpting as well
as writing poetry. At one point he even referred to himself as
'SCULPTOR and poet'.[28] In 1859 Browning was drawing twice a
week at 'Mrs Mackenzie's'.[29] At one time, when he lived in Florence,
he spent six hours a day with the sculptor William Wetmore Story.
In later years Browning remembered this time and asked Story to 'tell
me what you can about the studio; let me smell the wet clay once
more...'[30] Later Browning said that all he wanted for himself was
'to be forgotten in some out of the way place in Italy or Greece, with
books, a model and a lump of clay & sticks...'[31] He once said to
Elizabeth Barrett: 'But I think you like the operation of writing as
I should like that of painting or making music, do you not?'[32] Even
later, in London, Browning kept close contact with sculptors and
painters. The sculptor Natorp was his most frequent correspondent
in three of the last six years of his life.[33]

Like modern poets, Browning often talked about the making of
poems as if he were a sculptor making a statue, or a painter painting
a picture. In his *Essay on Shelley*, Browning referred to the 'objective
poet' as 'the fashioner; and the thing fashioned, his poetry...' (p. 64)
And when writing to Elizabeth Barrett to point out the 'faults' in
her poetry, Browning shifted without pause, in the space of one
sentence, from talking of poetry to looking at the poetry as if it were
a painting:

> What 'struck me as faults,' were not matters on the removal of
> which, one was to have – poetry, or high poetry, – but the very
> highest poetry, so I thought, and that, to universal recognition: for
> myself, or any artist, in many of the cases there would be a
> positive loss of true, peculiar artist's pleasure ... for an instructed
> eye loves to see where the brush has dipped twice in a lustrous

colour, has lain insistingly along a favorite outline, dwelt lovingly in a grand shadow – for these 'too muches' for the everybody's picture are so many helps to the making out the real painter's-picture as he had it in his brain; and all of the Titian's Naples Magdalen must have once been golden in its degree to justify that heap of hair in her hands – the *only* gold effected now![34]

Even in his poetry, Browning uses the visual arts to image poetic creativity. In 'Charles Avison', for example, he chooses the image of tracing to describe the work of the artist:

> what lay loose
> At first lies firmly after, what design
> Was faintly traced in hesitating line
> Once on a time, grows firmly resolute
> Henceforth and evermore. (VIII)

At other times, as in *Sordello*, words are imaged as physical objects. The poet's art consists of

> – welding words into the crude
> Mass from the new speech round him, till a rude
> Armour was hammered out . . . (II, 575–7)

Years later, in *The Ring and the Book*, Browning expresses his hope that 'the rough ore', his verse, 'be rounded to a ring' (XII, 869). The ring imagery is also used by Browning in speaking of 'James Lee's Wife': 'I have expressed it all insufficiently, and will break the chain up, one day, and leave so many separate little round rings to roll each its way, if it can.'[35]

The tendency to represent poem-making as a kind of fashioning of physical material represents one facet of what might be called the 'sculptor's point of view'; another is revealed by the imagery within the poems. For example, some of the most characteristic of Browning's images are those which create a tangible and very particular artifact to represent an intangible process:

> And many a thought did I build up on thought,
> As the wild bee hangs cell to cell . . . (*Pauline*, 438–9)

Even music is described in terms of pieces of matter, that which is not merely heard, but also seen and touched:

> Her carols dropt
> In flakes through that old leafy bower . . . (*Paracelsus*, III, 29–30)

In addition to having the sculptor's feeling for creating tangible objects, Browning also had a painter's eye for colour. He himself confessed having a particularly intense joy for a vivid colour:

> But you should have seen the regimentals, if I could have so contrived it, for I confess to a Chinese love for bright red – the very names 'vermilion' 'scarlet' warm me, – yet in this cold climate nobody wears red to comfort one's eye save soldiers and fox hunters, and old women fresh from a Parish Christmas Distribution of cloaks. To dress in floating loose crimson silk, I almost understand being a Cardinal![36]

This love of colour is reflected in almost all of Browning's poems. In *Sordello*, for example, the particular colour of even an incidental object is often stated: 'yellower poison-wattles' (IV, 870), or a 'gold-flowered basnet' (IV, 740). Browning also uses colour to elicit associations. The colour grey, to take just one, is frequently associated with age or winter: a chill and grey heaven (III, 70), 'Grave and grey' men (I, 94), grey morning (V, 980), or 'A dullish grey-streaked cumbrous font' (I, 410). Here grey is not so much a detail as it is an element which emphasises a *quality* (such as 'age' or 'chill') of that which is being described (the men, or the cumbrous font).

In addition to the use of colour for descriptive effects, or as a means of eliciting associations, Browning also uses colours structurally, as if they were paints being laid on a canvas. In *Sordello*, for example, Browning uses three major strands of colour – black, white, and red.[37] Black, the colour of the night, forms the background to much of the action of the poem. Against this background move the characters, with their white skin and pale faces, and the events, etched with the red of flame and blood. Although white images are numerous and varied (white skin, marble, snow, ivory, pearl, alabaster, the moon), the colour red is used almost entirely in association with the one image of blood. In fact, it might be more appropriate to say of *Sordello* that it is tinged with black, white and blood.

With these three colours, Browning weaves a pattern on the level of imagery which embodies the action that is taking place so abstrusely on the syntactical level. Throughout the poem, Sordello, a 'pale' lean man of words, is faced with the dilemma of what to do in the world of action, a world in which blood and red flames move against the dark night. In book I, Sordello is introduced as 'A single eye' in a city teeming with men who 'gulped with a delirious glee/ Some foretaste of their first debauch in blood' (98–9), while sunset burns

> like a torch-flame turned
> By the wind back upon its bearer's hand
> In one long flare of crimson; as a brand,
> The woods beneath lay black. (I, 82–5)

Sordello has been associated with the woods, not with the flare of crimson and the bloody action of the Guelf–Ghibellin controversy. The pale visage of Sordello is described as moving in the white mist and white dust-clouds which 'overwhelm/The woodside' (III, 111–112).

The contrast of Sordello to this world of fire and blood is emphasised even in those scenes which seem to deal only with Sordello's private affairs rather than with the Guelfs and Ghibellins. For instance, in the description of Sordello's wooing of Palma, Browning reminds us of the background to the scene by using imagery reminiscent of the torch-flame revealing the black woods in Book I:

> 'Alive with lamp-flies, swimming spots of fire
> 'And dew, outlining the black cypress' spire (III, 105–6)

And Palma herself is associated with the colours which represent Sordello's conflict between being a man of action (blood) or a pale man of words. Palma is consistently described as white, with white, cool skin, not pale like Sordello, but white as marble. Yet this white is suffused with blood, with 'vein-streaks swollen' (I, 956), and further, the coolness of the white is contrasted with the warm gold of her hair, a colour which Browning invests with qualities of light and life ('gold-sparkling', for instance: VI, 382). Gold is used in connection with arrows ('gold shaft': I, 840, and 'golden quoits': IV, 610) and with the sun ('fierce gold fire': V, 939). Palma herself is called 'that golden Palma' (III, 586), and one weft of her hair is 'Golden and great' (II, 101).

Although red, white and black are stark, primary colours, Browning presents them as exotically sensual: the 'snowy birdskin robes' (III, 128), the red flickering torch in the night, the moonlight creeping through black vines, the pale ivory of Palma's skin. Combinations of these colours also create a sensual effect through the suggestion of one colour moving within another. The red blood suffuses the white skin in the same way that flame is usually described as flickering rather than burning.

Within the contrasting movements of these three colours is a fourth element, light. Although light is not a colour, in *Sordello* it is associated with both the whiteness of passivity and the redness of the flame of action, and in the image of flickering light, appears throughout the entire poem.

Using these colours as primary pigments, Browning has created an underlying structure which is essentially visual. The poem is not a statement about a subject but a structure of words used as objects; the elements of the poem are wielded as solid matter. In this way, Browning is very near to the sensibility of modern poets like William Carlos Williams who insisted that

> It is the making of that step, to come over into the tactile qualities, the words themselves beyond the mere thought expressed that distinguishes the modern, or distinguished the modern of that time from the period before the turn of the century. And it is the reason why painting and the poem became so closely allied at that time.[38]

Pound referred to the image as 'the poet's pigment'[39] and insisted that 'The point of Imagisme is that it does not use images *as ornaments*. The image is itself the speech. The image is the word beyond formulated language.'[40]

This emphasis on the image rather than the 'speech' was reflected in Pound's two principles of Imagism – 'Direct treatment of the 'thing' whether subjective or objective' and 'To use absolutely no word that does not contribute to the presentation'.[41] As Pound pointed out, the Imagist school had numerous followers who did 'not show any signs of agreeing with the second specification'.[42] Even some of the poets represented in the various Imagist anthologies were not strict followers of the Imagist principles. Thus, poems in the Imagist anthologies, rather than being embodiments of the principles, merely illustrate some of the characteristics of the Imagist movement.

Typical of the heterodoxy of Imagist poets was the fact that D. H. Lawrence was included in the *Some Imagist Poets* anthology of 1915 soon after appearing in Edward Marsh's popular anthology, *Georgian Poetry, 1911–1912*[43] – even though the poems which Marsh published exhibit those very characteristics against which Pound was formulating his principle of the image. For example, the first four lines of William H. Davies's 'Days too Short' illustrate the approach taken by many of the poets in Marsh's anthology: nostalgic descriptions of flowers and summer days in the country, frequent use of adjectives like 'small' or 'little', and use of predictable patterns of rhyme and metre:

> When primroses are out in Spring,
> And small, blue violets come between;
> When merry birds sing on boughs green,
> And rills, as soon as born, must sing . . .

And the opening lines of Rupert Brooke's 'The Old Vicarage, Grant-chester' serve as another example of the characteristics of the poems in *Georgian Poetry*:

> Just now the lilac is in bloom,
> All before my little room;
> And in my flower-beds, I think,
> Smile the carnation and the pink;
> And down the borders, well I know,
> The poppy and the pansy blow . . .

In contrast, Pound's 'The Garden' (1913) opens with a sharp image – 'Direct treatment of the "thing"':

> Like a skein of loose silk blown against a wall
> She walks by the railing of a path in Kensington
>   Gardens,
>   And she is dying piece-meal
>   of a sort of emotional anæmia.

And Eliot in 'Portrait of a Lady' seems to echo Brooke's opening line, but then goes on to develop a very different complex of imagery:

> Now that lilacs are in bloom
> She has a bowl of lilacs in her room
> And twists one in her fingers while she talks.
> 'Ah, my friend, you do not know, you do not know
> What life is, you who hold it in your hands';
> (Slowly twisting the lilac stalks)
> 'You let it flow from you, you let it flow,

And youth is cruel, and has no remorse
And smiles at situations which it cannot see.'
I smile, of course,
And go on drinking tea. (11)

By 1922 Marsh himself had taken notice of this new approach to
poetry, complaining that in its disregard of form, much of it seemed
like 'gravy imitating lava'. But, he added, 'Its upholders may retort
that much of the work which I prefer seems to them, in its lack of
inspiration and its comparative finish, like tapioca imitating pearls.'[44]
Marsh went on to say that he had 'tried to choose no verse but such
as in Wordsworth's phrase:

The high and tender Muses shall accept
With gracious smile, deliberately pleased.' [45]

In Georgian poetry, as well as in Wordsworth's, the image is often
used as a means of description, a way of setting a scene, and creating
a particular mood. For example, in Brooke's 'The Old Vicarage,
Grantchester', the lilac in bloom, the carnation and the pink, are not
in themselves what the poem is 'treating'. Except for effects on sound
and rhyme, it would make little difference if 'rose' were substituted
for 'pink'. The overall effect is created by accumulating similar
images, not by focusing on a particular thing:

'Twas summer, and the sun had mounted high:
Southward the landscape indistinctly glared
Through a pale steam; but all the northern downs,
In clearest air ascending, showed far off
A surface dappled o'er with shadows flung
From brooding clouds
(The Excursion, I, 'The Wanderer', 1–6)

Used in this way by Wordsworth and the Georgians, imagery is not
merely background decoration, but often serves as a reflection of the
poet's state of mind:

On Man, on Nature, and on Human Life,
Musing in solitude, I oft perceive
Fair trains of imagery before me rise . . .
(lines from The Recluse as printed in Wordsworth's
preface to the 1814 edition of The Excursion)

It is interesting that Wordsworth refers in this passage to 'Fair trains of imagery', because this use of imagery is aptly described as 'train-like' – one image following another, and the whole creating a mood through which the reader perceives the thought of the poet.

With the Imagists and other modern poets, however, the image does not so much provide a stage for the action, nor does it serve as a reflection of the poet or a vehicle for his musings; but it is itself the centre of the poem.

'Imagisme is not symbolism',[46] said Pound; it is not something standing for something else, or a means to decorate the poem, or a way to make the message palatable. In this he was emphasising a distinction between his practice and that of the Georgians and indeed of most nineteenth-century poetry. In Tennyson, for example, the image is often used as a summing up of the argument, a way to embody the thought in memorable terms: 'Nature, red in tooth and claw' (*In Memoriam*, LVI).

Yet within nineteenth-century poetry there is one example of a poet whose work demonstrates Pound's use of the image. The typical image in Browning is not personification or the embodiment of an idea, but the direct observation of the thing itself as perceived by the senses:

> Here you have it, dry in the sun,
>   With all the binding all of a blister,
> And great blue spots where the ink has run,
>   And reddish streaks that wink and glister
> O'er the page so beautifully yellow:
>   Oh, well have the droppings played their tricks!
> Did he guess how toadstools grow, this fellow?
>   Here's one stuck in his chapter six!
>
> ('Sibrandus Schafnaburgensis', VI)

It is almost as if Browning has focused the eye of a camera on each detail, rather than sketching in the general impressionistic effect. This attention to the detail as object rather than impression is evident even in the earliest of Browning's published poems, *Pauline*. Although *Pauline* reflects Shelley's 'Alastor' in theme, characterisation and even scenery, Browning has added a peculiarly sensuous effect in the details of imagery. For example, in both poems there is the description of a tranquil centre to a wild natural scene. In 'Alastor':

> It was a tranquil spot, that seemed to smile
> Even in the lap of horror. Ivy clasped
> The fissured stones with its entwining arms,
> And did embower with leaves for ever green,
> And berries dark, the smooth and even space
> Of its inviolated floor, and here
> The children of the autumnal whirlwind bore,
> In wanton sport, those bright leaves, whose decay,
> Red, yellow, or ethereally pale,
> Rivals the pride of summer. 'Tis the haunt
> Of every gentle wind, whose breath can teach
> The wilds to love tranquillity. (577–88)

In *Pauline*, Browning describes a small pool with tall trees:

> Breaking the sunbeams into emerald shafts,
> And in the dreamy water one small group
> Of two or three strange trees are got together
> Wondering at all around, as strange beasts herd
> Together far from their own land: all wildness,
> No turf nor moss, for boughs and plants pave all,
> And tongues of bank go shelving in the lymph,
> Where the pale-throated snake reclines his head,
> And old grey stones lie making eddies there,
> The wild-mice cross them dry-shod. (755–64)

The opacity of 'emerald shafts', 'tongues of bank', the dry-shod wild-mice, and the trees seen as strange beasts herding together gives Browning's description not necessarily more intensity than Shelley's but more immediacy. Browning's adjectives are closer to the eye – old, grey, emerald, pale-throated; while Shelley's are closer to the emotions – tranquil, dark, smooth, inviolated, wanton, bright, gentle.

Not only is Browning's imagery one of particulars rather than general impressions, but it is often presented in motion as well. This contrast in the use of imagery as stage backdrop against its use as an object for the eye of the camera is evident in Browning's description of a sunrise in *Pippa Passes*. Rather than describing the sun as in the sky, or as lighting the sky, Browning has it boiling and bubbling and breaking:

Day!
Faster and more fast,
O'er night's brim, day boils at last.
Boils, pure gold, o'er the cloud-cup's brim
Where spurting and suppressed it lay,
For not a froth-flake touched the rim
Of yonder gap in the solid gray
Of the eastern cloud, an hour away;
But forth one wavelet, then another, curled,
Till the whole sunrise, not to be suppressed,
Rose, reddened, and its seething breast
Flickered in bounds, grew gold, then overflowed
                                    the world. (Introduction, 1–12)

Browning's poetry has often been called 'grotesque'; and certainly
one of the characteristics from which the sense of the grotesque
emerges is Browning's emphasis on the image itself rather than on
what the image, as part of a larger comparison, is intended to convey.
As early as *Pauline*, Browning was juxtaposing a common poetic
image – 'Blue sunny air, where a great cloud floats' (785) – with a
highly specific and unusual image:

                a great cloud floats laden
    With light, like a dead whale that white birds pick,
    Floating away in the sun in some north sea. (785–7)

Except for the allusions to Browning as grotesque, the importance
of the image in Browning's poetry has often been neglected. Critics
writing on Browning's influence usually emphasise his thought or
his dramatic creation of character through the presentation of con-
flicting points of view. It is the dramatic aspect of his poetry which
has been most accessible to modern readers, and it is the didactic
aspect which has created in other modern readers the reaction to
Browning as a typical Victorian poet, one with a peculiarly old-
fashioned optimistic approach to life.

Of course this classification of Browning's poetry as either dramatic
or didactic is a radical simplification. However, these two modes can
be recognised almost immediately as typical of Browning. On the
one hand, we hear the lively voice of a character in the midst of a
drama which is indicated in the lines themselves:

> I am poor brother Lippo, by your leave!
> You need not clap your torches to my face.
> Zooks, what's to blame? you think you see a monk!
>
> (*Fra Lippo Lippi*, 1–3)

On the other hand, we hear Browning's philosophical voice, even if this voice is presented as belonging to a character in a dramatic monologue:

> Take one and try conclusions – this, suppose!
> God is all-good, all-wise, all-powerful: truth?
> Take it and rest there. What is man? Not God:
> None of these absolutes therefore, – yet himself,
> A creature with a creature's qualities.
> Make them agree, these two conceptions! Each
> Abolishes the other.
>
> ('A Bean-Stripe: Also Apple-Eating', 290–6)

In *Sordello*, the extensive use of imagery is obscured not by the dramatic or didactic aspects of the verse, but by the narrative framework which demands so much attention from the reader. Occupied with the struggles of the Guelphs and the Ghibellins, and having been assured in the beginning of the poem that Browning will be beside Sordello, 'pointing-pole in hand' (30), the reader is likely to miss the drama which occurs on what might be termed the lyrical level of the poem. On the narrative or dramatic level, *Sordello* is the story of a poet's confrontation with the necessity to act, a necessity for which he is not prepared. On a didactic or philosophical level, Sordello's story is linked with the theme of man's incompleteness and the virtual impossibility of achieving perfect wholeness. Sordello must choose, for he cannot unite the poet and the leader of men within himself. Woven between these two themes and central to the poem as a whole is the imagery.

The use of imagery in *Sordello* foreshadows not only Pound's insistence on the image as the poet's pigment but also Pound's further elaboration of the image as 'a radiant node or cluster; it is what I can, and must perforce, call a VORTEX, from which, and through which, and into which, ideas are constantly rushing.'[47]

Although *Sordello* is extensive and complex, perhaps one such 'radiant node' or vortex will serve as illustration. Within this strange poem which travels backwards and forwards in time is a scene which Browning recalls again and again: the room in Count Richard's Palace at Verona. This central passage begins with the image of a man who may be sleeping and 'whose brow/The dying lamp-flame sinks and rises o'er' (328-9). Then follows the introduction of Palma:

> What women stood beside him? not the more
> Is he unfastened from the earnest eyes
> Because that arras fell between! Her wise
> And lulling words are yet about the room,
> Her presence wholly poured upon the gloom
> Down even to her vesture's creeping stir. (I, 330-5)

So far the picture is an intertwining of several elements: the mood of sensuality and darkness, the presence of some sort of mysterious power centring in the woman, who stands while Sordello reclines, 'saturate with her' (337). Then comes an abrupt change in mood and imagery. When an 'outcry from the square beneath/Pierces the charm' (338-9), the verbs take on qualities of energy and action: Sordello 'springs up', breathes 'Above the cunning element', and 'shakes/The stupor off as (look you) morning breaks' (I, 339-42). But the scene ends in a most curious blend of the still, lulling atmosphere and Sordello's action:

> morning breaks
> On the gay dress, and, near concealed by it,
> The lean frame like a half-burnt taper, lit
> Erst as some marriage-feast, then laid away
> Till the Armenian bridegroom's dying day,
> In his wool wedding-robe. (I, 339-44)

Morning breaks on a gay dress, but the overall effect is very ambiguous – the lean frame of Sordello, the image of the half-burnt taper, the combined image of marriage and death, and the wedding robe which also serves as the burial garment. The half-burnt taper recalls the taper which flickered over the reclining Sordello.

This scene at Verona is echoed later in the poem (although earlier in chronological time) in the vault inside the castle at Goito (I, 381-444). Again, there is flickering light in a dark room. Instead of a Palma's 'wise/ . . . words . . . about the room' (332-3), there are the 'light-graven characters' of the 'Arab's wisdom everywhere' (396-7). And for Palma herself, there are not only 'sister-palms' (405), but

also Caryatides 'Of just-tinged marble like Eve's lilied flesh' (413).
Some of the Caryatides hang slack, looking as if they have 'once
drunk sweetness to the dregs' (427), recalling Sordello, reclining,
saturate with Palma. The time is sunset rather than sunrise, but the
sunset is described as 'cheerful' (433), an echo of morning breaking
on the 'gay dress' (340). Immediately after this description, Sordello
is introduced as a 'slender boy' (448) beside an arras, 'lifting in
both hands a light/Which makes yon warrior's visage flutter bright'
(455–6).

Not only do variations of this scene appear throughout *Sordello*,
but also individual images from the central scene are recalled again
and again – the flickering light, the lean frame, the setting and
rising of the sun, the poet within and the people without. These
images radiating from the central scene in turn form clusters of their
own. The flickering light of the taper, for example, itself becomes a
vortex 'from which, and through which, and into which, ideas are
constantly rushing'. In the first book alone, sunset burns in the
darkness 'like a torch-flame' (82), sunlight is tangled in scum on
water (222–5), sunbeams gleam over a haze, turning it to gold
(393–5), light shines 'by fits' through black shade about a ceiling
(406–8), Sordello's fancies wear a fluctuating halo (649), and a
light makes 'yon warrior's visage flutter bright' (456).

Only the stars are sources of pure, unflickering light, because only
they are the offshoots of the 'original' light:

> light had birth ere moons and suns,
> Flowing through space a river and alone,
> Till chaos burst and blank the spheres were strown
> Hither and thither, foundering and blind:
> When into each of them rushed light – to find
> Itself no place, foiled of its radiant chance. (I, 516–21)

The obstacle breaking up light on earth, that which causes light to
flicker, is the human condition, with all its impurities and imperfec-
tions. Sordello himself suffers from indecision, a condition which is
only occasionally pierced by light. Other poets who 'made pretence/
To strength not half his own, yet had some core/Within' (VI, 58–60)
are able to 'Amass the scintillations, make one star' of these glimpses
of truth they catch (VI, 69).

Yet the human condition which causes the pure, original light to flicker offers compensation in the form of beauty: 'light, thwarted, breaks/A limpid purity to rainbow flakes' (v, 605–6). It is the very imperfection of the human condition which is the source of beauty for the poet. Poetic creation, imaged by rainbow flakes, is one way to deal with imperfect, flickering light; another is action, imaged by flame. Flame is associated with blood and the battlefield, but it too can spread light in the darkness. It is when faced with the choice whether or not to act that Sordello becomes 'flushed/Out of his whiteness' (v, 841–2). And it is in making the decision to act that Sordello dies. Thus the 'flickering light' and others of Browning's images have indeed become radiant nodes; and it is this aspect of the modern use of imagery which Browning appears to exhibit, particularly in Sordello.

Wordsworth's 'fair trains of imagery' imply a linear progression, one image followed by another. But a 'radiant node' carries no such implication of temporal or narrative progression; one node is connected to another in space, rather than in time. In The Waste Land, for example, there is no logical narrative connection between 'children, staying at the arch-duke's' (I, 13) and 'Madame Sosostris, famous clairvoyante' (I, 42). The movement of the poem is from one node of imagery to another, each serving as a centre for the emotions and ideas of a particular section. One section is then connected to another by repeated images or by imagery which, although changing from section to section, evokes similar emotions.

Thus a series of images, or in Eliot's terms, objective correlatives, are connected by a meaning which would best be described as an emotional rather than a narrative or a dramatic one. Such a principle of connection is clearly seen in Browning's 'Childe Roland to the Dark Tower Came'. Although in both poems the reader is given what appears to be a story, certain important elements of the story are missing: for example, in The Waste Land, it is not clear who Stetson is ('You who were with me in the ships at Mylae!': I, 70); and in 'Childe Roland' the reader is never told explicitly what Childe Roland's mission is. In both poems, the strange, desolate landscapes resemble those in dreams: they are charged with undeniable significance, but a significance which is felt rather than understood. Also, as in dreams, objects are described in terms of the emotions aroused in the beholder rather than in terms of physical characteristics. In The Waste Land, 'April is the cruellest month' (I, 1); in 'Childe Roland', the horse is 'wicked' (XIV), the river 'spiteful' (XX).

In 'Childe Roland', as in *The Waste Land*, images are repeated and seem to be clustered around themes. For example, the prisoners, the victims, the cripple set to ensnare, and the disappearing road are images which all centre around the theme of 'traps'. Similarly, sickness, blindness and death are the centres of such images as skulls, bones, the setting sun, and the willows seen as a 'suicidal throng' (xx). Whatever meaning is to be found in the poem is not to be found in the narrative or didactic content, but suspended within the structure of imagery.

It is not surprising that 'Childe Roland' contains so much of what could be described as 'dream imagery'. Browning himself said that 'Childe Roland'

> came upon me as a kind of dream. I had to write it, then and there, and I finished it the same day, I believe. But it was simply that I had to do it. I did not know then what I meant beyond that, and I'm sure I don't know now. But I am very fond of it.[48]

The Waste Land, too, seems to operate through a sort of dream logic. One set of images fades into another, 'a public bar in Lower Thames Street' (III, 260) is followed by 'The river sweats' (III, 266) and then 'Elizabeth and Leicester/Beating oars' (III, 279–80).

According to Eliot, 'not only the title, but the plan and a good deal of the incidental symbolism' were suggested by Jessie Weston's *From Ritual to Romance* ('Notes on *The Waste Land*'). In the same notes, Eliot also acknowledges a general indebtedness to Frazer's *The Golden Bough*. The archetypes discussed in these books have been shown by some psychologists to be of major significance in many dreams. The modern discovery, or re-discovery, that certain images possess inherent power has been reflected in modern poetry. It is significant that Eliot sought a poetic technique which, as C. K. Stead puts it, would balance that part of the mind which rationalises and constructs with that passive part of the mind which 'independent of the will, negatively comprehends complexity, and provides images to embody it . . .'[49]

The radiant nodes or clusters of imagery, then, are connected by the subjective logic of the dream rather than the objective logic of narrative or rational idea; in Zukofsky's words, 'Emotion is the organizer of poetic form. The image is at the basis of poetic form.'[50] When the image is at the basis of form, the 'completed poem consists of large blocks of quite distinct material from which a common theme is intended to emerge; it is, that is to say, ideogrammic.'[51] The term 'ideogrammic' is taken from Pound's work on Fenollosa's notes concerning Chinese ideograms. According to Pound, the Chinese ideogram for red would be constructed by combining the symbols for rose, cherry, iron rust and flamingo.[52] Together, these create the general idea of 'red'; that is, that which is common to all the particulars. But in addition to the notion of redness, the ideogram also carries within it, to the discerning eye, the intimations of its origins in the particular things of which it is composed. Thus 'red', by carrying flamingo, rust, and so on, serves not merely as a definition, but also as a centre for feeling. The ideogrammic method involves setting images side by side. The images themselves are opaque; they are 'things' and have their own identities. The 'stiff blind horse' (XIII) and 'thin dry blades' of grass (XIII) in 'Childe Roland' do not merge with each other, but are merely seen one after another.

This dream-like placing of the things themselves in juxtaposition is one of the prime characteristics not only of modern poetry but also of the twentieth century's unique development in art – the film:

> In effect both Pound and Eliot began writing as imagist poets who developed a technique much like Eisenstein's in the film; for Eisenstein says he wanted to 'dismember' events into a montage of various shots, and 'by combining these monstrous incongruities, we newly collect the disintegrated event into one whole.'[53]

Eisenstein himself wrote an essay entitled 'The Cinematographic Principle and the Ideogram' (1929).[54] This principle of bringing together dismembered parts to form a whole was one which Browning felt to be at the heart of his poetic technique. According to Browning, one critique had been 'fair in giving the right key to my poetry – in as much as it is meant to have "one central meaning, seen only by reflexion in details".'[55] This technique is taken to its logical conclusion in The Ring and the Book where the entire structure is built up from different points of view, and where each point of view contains its own set of images.

The emphasis on the image as the poet's pigment and the juxtaposition of images as a poetic method are fundamental to modern poetry. Zukofsky, in An 'Objectivists' Anthology, characterised a poem as the 'desire for an inclusive object'.[56] The idea of the poem as a self-contained object like a painting or a sculpture is further defined in MacLeish's well-known statement that 'A poem should not mean /

But be' ('Ars Poetica'). From this point of view, poetry is a structure: like a painting, it is composed of concrete physical elements; like a sculpture, it exists as an object in space. It may be meaningful, but its primary meaning is found in its physical existence and not in whatever verbal message can be extracted from it.

Of course it has always been understood that a poem cannot be paraphrased without losing the very essence of what we value in the poem itself. Modern poets have carried this understanding further, insisting that the poem is an object rather than a metaphysical statement. The history of poetry then becomes not the history of thought, but 'a matter of technical discoveries'.[57] The best history of poetry, Pound suggested, would be 'a twelve-volume anthology in which each poem was chosen not merely because it was a nice poem or a poem Aunt Hepsy liked, but because it contained an invention, a definite contribution to the art of verbal expression.'[58]

This emphasis on the craft of the poem and the de-emphasis on philosophically meaningful subject-matter was one of the basic reasons why the Imagist and Objectivist poets often found the nineteenth-century poets so inimical to their own views of what poetry should be. A profound belief shared by many Victorian poets was that the message in a poem was vitally important, that, as Arnold said, 'More and more mankind will discover that we have to turn to poetry to interpret life for us, to console us, to sustain us'.[59]

In the case of Browning, many critics feel that one of the central reasons for the decline in his later verse was his conviction that the duty of the poet was to speak to the times, to serve as a prophetic voice, to teach and lead the multitude. While it is true that Browning emphasised the role of the poet as teacher, the way in which he felt the poet could best teach was through the creation of poetry rather than the exposition of any sort of message. In '"Transcendentalism"', Browning challenges the poet who speaks 'Stark naked thoughts', for "T is you speak, that's your error. Song's our art.' And then, characteristically, he concludes by saying 'You are a poem, though your poem's naught.' Ironically the later poems in which Browning does seem to offer 'stark naked thoughts' are often written in justification or explanation of his own approach to poetry. This approach was frequently misunderstood by the Victorian reading public who in many ways looked to their poets as thinkers rather than craftsmen, and who did not allow the role of the poet as 'legislators of mankind' to go 'unacknowledged'.

The idea that the poet is in any sense a legislator of mankind is fundamentally opposed by modern poets. Louis MacNeice insisted that in his view 'the poet is a blend of the entertainer and the critic or informer; he is not a legislator, however unacknowledged, nor yet, essentially, a prophet.'[60] And Auden made this point even more succinctly: '"The unacknowledged legislators of the world" describes the secret police, not the poets.'[61]

Modern poets objected not so much to the sentiments of the Victorian poets as to the emphasis placed on these sentiments, an emphasis which often resulted in a poetic structure based on paraphrasable content. When the message became the focal point, the poem became 'contaminated' as a formal object. Yeats, in defining his opposition to this Victorian characteristic, said:

> I saw ... that Swinburne in one way, Browning in another, and
> Tennyson in a third, had filled their work with what I called
> 'impurities,' curiosities about politics, about science, about history,
> about religion; and that we must create once more the pure
> work.[62]

Eliot complained that Tennyson 'is a very fair example of a poet almost wholly encrusted with opinion, almost wholly merged into his environment.'[63] And Pound emphasised 'Objectivity and again objectivity, and expression: no hindside-beforeness, no straddled adjectives (as "adled mosses dank"), no Tennysonianness of speech', adding that:

> Language is made out of concrete things. General expressions in
> non-concrete terms are a laziness; they are talk, not art, not
> creation. They are the reaction of things on the writer, not a
> creative act by the writer.[64]

All those impurities, the discursiveness, the history, the science and the talk, were to be excluded from modern poetry. Exactness was to be valued more than beauty. And, in fact, any 'decoration' which was not essential to the structure of the poem was considered as superfluous ornamentation. 'The essence of poetry with us in this age of stark and unlovely actualities is a stark directness', said Lawrence. 'Everything can go, but this stark, bare, rocky directness of statement, this alone makes poetry, today.'[65] It was this emphasis on the exact rather than the beautiful which early reviewers often criticised. Pound's *Personae* did not 'leave much room for beauty', one critic complained. 'Like Browning... he affects the eccentric and the obscure...'[66]

The charge that modern poetry was ugly and obscure was partially a result of the emphasis on what Eliot called 'poetry standing naked in its bare bones'.[67] Nothing was to be added to a poem for the sake of decoration. Furthermore, articles or pronouns, which served grammatical functions but carried no additional meaning in themselves, were often omitted.

This closing together of nouns and verbs without modifiers or connecting links results in a density of structure which is not only characteristic of much modern poetry, but is also one of the most vivid aspects of Browning's poetry. The often quoted 'Irks care the crop-full bird? Frets doubt the maw-crammed beast?' ('Rabbi Ben Ezra', IV) although a seeming parody of alliteration and the elliptical method of construction, finds an echo in Hopkins:

> Undenizened, beyond bound
> Of earth's glory, earth's ease, all; no one, nowhere,
> In wide the world's weal; rare gold, bold steel, bare
>   in both; care, but share care –
> This, by Despair, bred Hangdog dull; by Rage,
> Manwolf, worse; and their packs infest the age.
>
> ('Tom's Garland')

And later, Dylan Thomas uses a similar method in poems such as 'After the funeral' –

> After the funeral, mule praises, brays,
> Windshake of sailshaped ears, muffle-toed tap
> Tap happily of one peg in the thick
> Grave's foot, blinds down the lids, the teeth in black,
> The spittled eyes, the salt ponds in the sleeves...

This method of elliptical construction, while creating a density of structure, often proves exhausting to the reader. As an early reviewer of Browning's *Sordello* complained, 'We come to no places in *Sordello* where we can rest and dream or look up at the sky.'[68] Eliot, defending this method, says:

> any obscurity of the poem, on first readings, is due to the
> suppression of 'links in the chain', of explanatory and connecting
> matter, and not to incoherence, or to the love of cryptogram. The

justification of such abbreviation of method is that the sequence of images coincides and concentrates into one intense impression . . .[69]

But it was not merely density of structure which created difficulty for Browning's readers and for the early readers of modern poetry. Both Browning and modern poets were criticised for the use of uncommon words and allusions to obscure facts. *Sordello* contains many references to the complicated history of the struggles between the Guelfs and the Ghibellins. Without some knowledge of thirteenth-century Italian history, the reader will be puzzled about the action in passages such as the following:

> When the new Hohenstauffen dropped the mask,
> Flung John of Brienne's favour from his casque,
> Forswore crusading, had no mind to leave
> Saint Peter's proxy leisure to retrieve
> Losses to Otho and to Barbaross,
> Or make the Alps less easy to recross;
> And, thus confirming Pope Honorius' fear,
> Was excommunicate that very year.
> 'The triple-bearded Teuton come to life!'
> Groaned the Great League; and, arming for the strife,
> Wide Lombardy, on tiptoe to begin,
> Took up, as it was Guelf or Ghibellin
> Its cry: what cry?
>   'The Emperor to come!' (I, 193–205)

Many of the notes to Eliot's *The Waste Land* serve to enlighten the reader who might not have realised, for example, that 'shantih' was 'a formal ending to an Upanishad' corresponding to '"The Peace which passeth understanding"' (note to l. 433). Browning, however, refused to add notes on the ground that he had to 'choose between being historian or poet'.[70] As he explained to one of his readers:

> If you will only concern yourself with what is set down, –
> regarding a name as a name that explains itself, and a passing
> allusion to just an allusion and no more, you will find no difficulty
> but what is a fault *in the writer* . . .[71]

Perhaps the extreme instance of the allusion as method in modern poetry is to be found in Pound's *Cantos*. Pound's technique of using historical facts as integral to a poem's structure was influenced by his close study of *Sordello*. 'Ezra told me', said Pound's father, 'unless

I read Browning's "Sordello" I couldn't expect to understand the Cantos. So I waded through that. Ever read it? Well, I don't advise you to. I found it didn't help me much with Ezra's Cantos anyway.'[72] In the opening lines of an early draft of Canto I, Pound acknowledged what was considered by many critics to be the most obscure poem of the nineteenth century:

Hang it all, there can be but one *Sordello!*
But say I want to, say I take your whole bag of tricks,
Let in your quirks and tweeks, and say the thing's an art-form,
Your *Sordello*, and that the modern world
Needs such a rag-bag to stuff all its thought in . . .'[73]

The poem as rag-bag illustrates the other side of the emphasis on the 'bare bones' of poetry. On the one hand, poetry is stripped of the non-essential, or the nineteenth-century 'impurities' of science, history and religion. On the other hand, the stuff of which modern poetry is often composed, the material from which it is fashioned, is not so much meditations upon the nature of man as the artifacts themselves of man's world. The reader accustomed to nineteenth-century verse not only misses the pleasant pauses which allow him to 'dream or look up at the sky', but may also be confronted with the raw facts from the rag-bag:

Old standard of Araby, 9, 7, 9?
And out of Scanda in Colchis,
　　Getes had been in Cythera
　　(vide Pausanias, the Laconics)
2 doigts to a boodle, one bawbee: one sixty doigts,
Will they get rid of the Rooseveltian dung-hill
And put Capn. Wadsworth back in the school books?

(Canto XCVII)

Clearly, a new way of defining the craft of poetry must also take account of the reader, for the relation between the poet and the reader changes as soon as the view of the structure and purpose of the poem changes. Modern poetry, like Browning's poetry, may meet with resistance or criticism from the reader who expects something else. The difficulty of poetry, commented Eliot, 'may be due just to novelty: we know the ridicule accorded in turn to Wordsworth, Shelley and Keats, Tennyson and Browning – but must remark that Browning was the first to be *called* difficult . . .'[74]

Readers called Browning difficult throughout his entire career. Even to *Men and Women*, which contains some of the most understandable of Browning's poems, the response was one of bewilderment. Ruskin said to Browning that after having read *Men and Women*, 'I cannot write in enthusiastic praise, because I look at you every day as a monkey does at a cocoanut, having great faith in the milk – hearing it rattle indeed – inside – but quite beside myself for the Fibres.'[75]

But of course the most extreme reaction was to the poem which exhibited the most extreme use of many of Browning's characteristic techniques: *Sordello*. There are many anecdotes: Jane Carlyle, unable to tell whether *Sordello* was a man, a city, or a book,[76] or the dramatist Douglas Jerrold, who thought he was going mad until he was assured that no one else understood *Sordello*.[77] Tennyson was reported to have said that he understood only two lines – the first, 'Who will, may hear Sordello's story told', and the last, 'Who would has heard Sordello's story told' – and that both were lies.[78] One reviewer summed up the reaction of most of the early readers by saying, 'What this poem may be in its extent we are unable to say, for we *cannot* read it.'[79] Even Elizabeth Barrett objected to what she considered Browning's tendency 'which is almost a habit' of 'making lines difficult for the reader to read . . .'[80]

Although the obscurities of *Sordello* might justifiably be called 'premeditated',[81] Browning hoped that serious readers would overcome these difficulties. After the storm of criticism had greeted its initial publication, he revised the text, primarily in terms of punctuation. Commas are added or deleted, semi-colons are changed to dashes or full stops, parentheses are added or removed. Much indirect speech is made direct by the addition of quotation marks and changes from the third person 'one' or 'he' to the first person 'I', thus helping the reader to separate the fully dramatic speech from the author's commentary upon it. His attention to detail was noted by Carlyle: 'well, Browning, you have taught the English people one thing any way – you have taught them the value of punctuation.'[82]

Although these revisions help to clear up some of the surface obscurity, it is significant that they usually occur in the discursive sections or in the historical background, and not in the passages of imagery. Sensitive though Browning was to the criticism he received of *Sordello* – and the publication of *Sordello* resulted in his being neglected by the reading public for more than twenty years – he continued to defend what he considered to be his original intention: '. . . I lately gave time and pains to turn my work into what the many might, – instead of what the few must, – like: but after all, I imagined another thing at first, and therefore leave as I find it.[83]

Twenty years later, Browning wrote to Furnivall to say that the

> edition which I reprinted was the same in all respects as its predecessor – only with an elucidatory heading to each page, and some few alterations, presumably for the better, in the text – such as occur in most of my works: I cannot remember a single instance of any importance that is 'rewritten.'[84]

The elucidatory headings and the few lines added to the 1863 revised version illustrate Browning's attitude towards his uncomprehending readers as well as mirror some of his reactions to the criticism the poem had received. He hopes for a sympathetic, understanding audience ('Who will, may hear Sordello's story told': 1); at the same time, he seems to be prepared for disappointment, for often his comments sound like a reply to his exasperated readers. For example, at one point Browning says:

> But that's the story – dull enough, confess!
> There might be fitter subjects to allure . . . (III, 984–5)

But this concession is immediately followed by an admonition:

> Still, neither misconceive my portraiture
> Nor undervalue its adornments quaint:
> What seems a fiend perchance may prove a saint.
>
> (III, 986–8)

Perhaps the clearest example of Browning's ironic response to his critics is found in the running-titles added to the 1863 edition. These titles are extreme simplifications of the story, and exhibit Browning's response to the inadequacy of his readers and his awareness of their predictably negative reactions. Typical of this irony is the title which appears opposite the first line of the poem. 'Who will, may hear Sordello's story told', goes the line, to which the title responds, 'A Quixotic attempt'. After Sordello's death, towards the end of the poem, Browning hurriedly summarises the rest of the action in the running-titles: 'Salinguerra's part lapsing to Ecelin who with his brother, played it out, and went home duly to their reward' (a summary of over eighty lines). Then Browning adds: 'Good will – ill luck, get second prize: What least one may I award Sordello? This [a child sings Sordello's song centuries later] – that must perforce content him, as no prize at all, has contented me.' Browning's last comment – 'as no prize at all, has contented me' – does not summarise the closing lines of the poem; rather, it is offered as an indication to the reader that Browning is aware that he, like Sordello, will not receive recognition from his contemporary readers. As Elizabeth Barrett said of him: 'He will not die, because the principle of life is in him, but he will not live the warm summer life which is permitted to many of very inferior faculty, because he does not come out into the sun.'[85]

Browning himself not only recognised the difficulty of his poetry for his readers, but also seemed to regard this difficulty as an inevitable result of his poetic attempt to 'teach' by offering something new. To Ruskin he said:

> Do you think poetry was ever generally understood – or can be? Is the business of it to tell people what they know already, as they know it, and so precisely that they shall be able to cry out – 'Here you should supply this – that, you evidently pass over, and I'll help you from my own stock'?[86]

For Browning the task for a poet was to make something new. 'In Music, the Beau Idéal changes every thirty years', he told Elizabeth Barrett.[87] And in every art, what was once 'sufficient fare' needs to be 'cooked again in rhyme,/Dished up anew in paint, sauce-smothered fresh in sound,/To suit the wisdom-tooth, just cut, of the age' (Fifine, XCII).

In this attempt to offer something new, the past exercises a form of tyranny. In poetry, for example, readers expect the continuation of forms with which they are familiar, an attitude which prompted T. E. Hulme to declare himself 'in favour of the complete destruction of all verse more than twenty years old'.[88]

While Browning did not go this far, he did attempt to warn his reader, even as early as Pauline, that his poetry, being new, was not merely an offering to the reader of what had already been tried and therefore of what he was sure to like, but a creation which demanded the full engagement of the reader and a sympathy of mind and spirit. In Pauline, Browning conveyed this to his audience in the form of a warning to those

whose minds are weak [and] who are unable to accept my
genius. . . . Let them beware that it not shake their understanding
out of them. But if you who come to its perusal with
unprejudiced minds will exercise as much discernment and
prudence as bees in gathering honey, then read with safety. For I
think you will receive not a little of instruction and a great deal of
enjoyment.[89]

And in *Paracelsus*, Browning made a much more straightforward
acknowledgement of the importance of the reader's 'discernment',
saying that 'a work like mine depends more immediately on the
intelligence and sympathy of the reader for its success' (1835 preface).

By the time of *Sordello*, Browning was being explicit about the
aspects of his poetry which might create difficulty for those who did
not come to the reading of the poem 'with unprejudiced minds'. His
elliptical method he defended to a friend who wanted a passage in
Sordello 'cleared up':

one does not like serving oneself as a certain 'Watson' served
Horace in a translation I have: e.g. Book 1, Ode 1. Lines 1 and 2:
'O Mæcenas, descended from Kings (*Tuscan, that is Etrurian*)
your Ancestors, (*O you who have proved yourself to be*) both my
patron (*since you kindly reconciled me with Augustus*) and a
sweet honor to me (*by your Quality and politeness to poor me
whose father was nothing but a Freedman*) etc. etc. etc.[90]

Within *Sordello* itself, Browning continued this justification of his
method. At the end of the poem, Browning holds an imaginary
conversation with his 'friends', the readers. First he asks them to
wake up and then states that if, as he suspects, his readers are left
with a 'bad odor' after reading his poem, it is only because they
don't know how to approach a 'savour' so rare:

> Friends, be frank! ye snuff
> Civet, I warrant. Really? Like enough!
> Merely the savour's rareness; any nose
> May ravage with impunity a rose:
> Rifle a musk-pod and 't will ache like yours!
> I'd tell you that same pungency ensures

An after-gust, but that were overbold.
Who would has heard Sordello's story told.
(VI, 879–86)

Yet in spite of the irony directed against his readers, Browning also
takes pains to explain himself to them in the course of the poem.
Some of the comments which Browning added when revising his
poem emphasise the comparison he draws between himself and
Sordello. For example, in the original 1840 version, there is a suggested comparison of Sordello, the speaker of the following lines,
with Browning, the poet who in writing *Sordello* has 'cast external
things away':

> I boast! Man's life shall have yet freer play:
> Once more I cast external things away
> And Natures, varied now, so decompose
> That . . . but enough!

In the revised version, this implied comparison has been made
explicit by the addition of Browning's comment on Sordello's speech:

> 'Man's inmost life shall have yet freer play:
> 'Once more I cast external things away,
> 'And natures composite, so decompose
> 'That' . . . Why, he writes *Sordello!* (V, 617–20)

In casting external things away, Browning claimed for himself
the freedom from restrictions of arbitrary conventions and of the
expectations of his readers. As he told Ruskin, 'I cannot begin writing
poetry till my imaginary reader has conceded licenses to me which
you demur at altogether.'[91] Modern poets have echoed this insistence
on the freedom from the old, no matter what difficulties the novelty
of poetic techniques might cause for poet and reader alike. Eliot told
readers of poetry:

> If you complain that a poet is obscure, and apparently ignoring
> you, the reader, or that he is speaking only to a limited circle of
> initiates from which you are excluded – remember that what he
> may have been trying to do, was to put something into words
> which could not be said in any other way, and therefore in a
> language which may be worth the trouble of learning.[92]

It was Browning's 'new language' which created at the same time
difficulty for his own readers and an impetus for the development of

certain aspects of modern poetry. Pound said that when he began as a poet, 'Browning was the one thing to go on from – the only live form.'[93] And in Canto I, Pound made more explicit the exact nature of Browning's challenge to poets after him:

> So you worked out new form, the meditative,
> Semi-dramatic, semi-epic story,
> And we will say: What's left for me to do?[94]

In Browning's own words, this working out of new form was a process of 'welding words', of concentrating on the poem as an object of art rather than as a vehicle for ideas:

> He left imagining, to try the stuff
> That held the imaged thing, and, let it writhe
> Never so fiercely, scarce allowed a tithe
> To reach the light – his Language. How he sought
> The cause, conceived a cure, and slow re-wrought
> That Language, – welding words into the crude
> Mass from the new speech round him, till a rude
> Armour was hammered out, in time to be
> Approved beyond the Roman panoply
> Melted to make it . . . (Sordello, II, 570–9)

2

The Approach to the Subject

When Browning, speaking to Ruskin, insisted that he could not begin writing poetry until his imaginary reader had 'conceded licenses to me which you demur at altogether',[1] he was pointing to a problem which he faced throughout his writing career – that of a public expecting something from his poetry which he refused to give, and through this expectation, being blind to that which was peculiarly his own to give. Through his introductions and through pointed remarks in the texts, Browning attempted to warn his reader to expect the unusual, or at least to approach his work with as few prejudices as possible. 'I am anxious', he said in introducing *Paracelsus*, 'that the reader should not, at the very outset – mistaking my performance for one of a class with which it has nothing in common – judge it by principles on which it was never moulded, and subject it to a standard to which it was never meant to conform.'

Unfortunately, readers of Browning's poetry did subject it to contemporary standards to which 'it was never meant to conform'. Criticisms of Browning's style bear witness to the general lack of appreciation:

> The story is most elliptically constructed, full of breaks and leaps; the syntax of quite an unusual character, a mass of perplexity and obscurity; the versification is harsh and knotty; the language, instead of being throughout 'English undefiled,' is larded with many fantastic and arbitrary invertions [sic], and the whole set together in a ricketty, hysterical, capricious style, producing the most startling and repulsive effect.[2]

Browning's reputation, unlike that of Tennyson, developed very slowly. Tennyson's popularity came as early as 1843, with the second edition of his *Poems*, while it was not until 1864, with *Dramatis Personae*, that a Browning work achieved a second edition. Browning was called 'the Columbus of an impossible discovery', and a work such as *Sordello* labelled, 'a promised land . . . if ever so rich and rare a chaos can be . . . wrought into a shape that will fit the average mental vision.'[3]

Although many of Browning's readers eventually seemed to come to terms with his dramatic style and with his 'harsh versification', these same readers never quite came to accept his subject-matter. As Browning became more popular with the reading public, the criticism concerning his style diminished, while that directed toward his subject-matter increased. Of course this change in the direction of criticism is partially due to the fact that Browning himself changed his emphasis. In the earlier poems, Browning experimented with language and poetic forms, using historical or Shelleyan themes as subject-matter. But, as he said in a later introduction to *Pauline*, 'I have since written according to a scheme less extravagant and scale less impracticable...' In the later poems, Browning's language seems to be a continuation or sometimes even a caricature of his early style, while the main emphasis, as in *The Ring and the Book*, falls upon the treatment of subject-matter.

The criticisms levelled at Browning's choice of subject-matter were different in kind from those directed against Tennyson. Tennyson had been accused of escaping to the past when he dealt with King Arthur's Round Table. Even Browning criticised Tennyson's choice of subject-matters as being unsuited to an age of railways:

> I am sorry to hear of poor Tennyson's condition – the projected book, – title, scheme, all of it, – *that* is astounding; – and fairies? If 'Thorpès and barnes, sheep-pens and dairies – this maketh that there ben no fairies' – locomotives and the broad or narrow guage must keep the very ghosts of them away...[4]

In Browning's case, criticism was not directed against his subject-matter as being irrelevant, but as being unnecessarily disagreeable. When *The Inn Album* appeared, the *British Quarterly Review* advised: '...to all save students of literature, whose duty it is to read and to study morbid developments and their relations to literature, we say, pass *The Inn Album* by, and devote yourself to what is purer...'[5] Earlier, when *Red Cotton Night-Cap Country* was published, Browning was criticised not merely for studying morbid developments, but for not giving 'any true poetic excuse for telling a story so full of disagreeable elements. When told, it fails to purify, as tragedy should, "by pity and by fear".'[6]

Thus, it was not for choosing morbid subject-matter that Browning was criticised, but for not providing the reader with any redeeming moral value in the treatment of that subject-matter. The reading public, after all, had given its blessing to Dickens, notorious for dealing with the shadowy underside of Victorian life. (Browning even parodied Dickens's subject-matter in an aside in 'Bishop Blougram's Apology' – "'The Slum and Cellar, or Whitechapel life / 'Limned after dark!'") Elizabeth Barrett Browning's *Aurora Leigh*, with such 'sordid' matter as the heroine's protection of an abandoned mother and her illegitimate child, ran into a second edition within two weeks of its initial publication.[7] Moreover, the criticism of Tennyson implied that perhaps he was not devoting the attention he should to subject-matter appropriate to an age less beautiful than that of the spires and turrets of Camelot.

In Dickens, the redeeming value of the emphasis on sordid subject-matter was made clear. A villain was clearly a villain and received a villain's just deserts. Sikes's murder of Nancy in *Oliver Twist* is 'redeemed', when the reader's expectation of Sikes's own downfall is fulfilled. Moreover, Dickens bridged the gap between respectable reader and sordid character by giving even the scoundrels a lovable quirk, or a vivid and comic trait of behaviour. Elizabeth Barrett Browning, as well as Dickens, made sordid subject-matter acceptable through pathos. When the abandoned girl describes her state after she has been seduced, the reader is guided to feel pity:

'I was mad,
How many weeks I know not, – many weeks.
I think they let me go when I was mad,
They feared my eyes and loosed me, as boys might
A mad dog which they had tortured.' (*Aurora Leigh*, VI)

Browning, however, did not often attempt to reach his readers through the subject-matter in the ways that Dickens and Elizabeth Barrett Browning did. In a poem such as *Red Cotton Night-Cap Country*, the gap between reader and main character is very large indeed. Far from focusing on the dramatic pathos of a man who is so tortured in spirit that he burns off his hands, Browning takes a narrative stance at a distance from the character, and even makes jokes about poor Miranda's condition:

There was no washing hands of him (alack,
You take me? – in the figurative sense!) ... (III, 3106–7)

Whereas *Aurora Leigh* might have aroused sympathetic emotions,

Red Cotton Night-Cap Country, in contrast, is not related to emotions at all. The Victorian reader was given no clue as to what he should feel for Miranda – pity? sympathy? disgust? Hence, he was likely to agree with the critic who said that there was no 'excuse for telling a story so full of disagreeable elements'.

If Browning provided no clear direction for the reader's emotions, the reason was that he was not so much interested in making the reader sympathise as in making him see what he called 'the facts', and through seeing these facts, to understand. When one of his friends criticised him for his choice of subject-matter in *The Ring and the Book*, he admitted, 'I believe I do unduly like the study of morbid cases of the soul. . . . But here', he went on to say,

> – given the subject, I cannot but still say, given the treatment too: the business has been, as I specify, to explain *fact* – and the fact is what you see and, worse, are to see. The question with me has never been, 'Could not one, by changing the factors, work out the sum to better result?' but declare and prove the actual result, and there an end.[8]

Browning's insistence on the facts was at the heart of the misunderstanding he encountered from his readers. Many readers could sympathise with a concern for truth, but saw truth as having more to do with beauty, or great ideas, or significant actions, than with ugly facts and commonplace actions. If facts were used at all, they were to be tied to the spiritual in such a way that a clear moral could be drawn. As Elizabeth Barrett Browning expressed it:

> Natural things
> And spiritual, – who separate those two
> In art, in morals, or the social drift,
> Tears up the bond of nature and brings death,
> Paints futile pictures, writes unreal verse,
> Leads vulgar days, deals ignorantly with men,
> Is wrong, in short, at all points. (*Aurora Leigh*, VII)

Browning, however, refused to make any explicit connections between the facts and whatever moral could be drawn from them. For him, the facts themselves were significant and should be allowed to stand alone. He criticised Victor Hugo's *La Légende des Siècles* because Hugo would not 'let truth be truth, or a number of remarkable poetical pieces speak for themselves, without assuring you that he

meant them to join Man to God, with the like pleasant practica-
bilities.'⁹

One of the dangers, as Browning saw it, of using poetry as a
platform for philosophising was that the ordinary life of men and
women was despised by the poet who puts 'mankind well outside
himself' in order to instruct. In *Prince Hohenstiel-Schwangau*, Browning analysed the relation of poet to audience which followed from
the use of poetry as sermon rather than fact:

> 'O littleness of man!' deplores the bard;
> And then, for fear the Powers should punish him,
> 'O grandeur of the visible universe
> Our human littleness contrasts withal!
> O sun, O moon, ye mountains and thou sea,
> Thou emblem of immensity, thou this,
> That, and the other, – what impertinence
> In man to eat and drink and walk about
> And have his little notions of his own,
> The while some wave sheds foam upon the shore!'
> First of all, 't is a lie some three-times thick:
> The bard, – this sort of speech being poetry, –
> The bard puts mankind well outside himself
> And then begins instructing them: 'This way
> I and my friend the sea conceive of you!
> What would you give to think such thoughts as ours
> Of you and the sea together?' (517–33)

Of course, when the bard leaves Bond Street, he

>   cares not to ventriloquize,
> But tells the sea its home-truths: 'You, my match?
> You, all this terror and immensity
> And what not? Shall I tell you what you are?
> Just fit to hitch into a stanza . . .' (540–4)

For Browning, the object of poetry was not to deal with the
'grandeur of the visible universe' and other such topics, but to explore the common life of men and women, and in so doing, seek to
find the truth in the facts. Browning's readers would have to 'con-
tinue patient', as Prince Hohenstiel-Schwangau put it, 'while I
throw,/Delver-like, spadeful after spadeful up,/Just as truths come.'

To the listener he said, 'your object, – just to find,/Alike from handlift and from barrow-load,/What salts and silts may constitute the earth' (96–101). At the end of the process, the 'crude truths' would be left, 'bare for poetry' (107):

> But truth, truth, that's the gold! and all the good
> I find in fancy is, it serves to set
> Gold's inmost glint free . . . (The Two Poets of Croisic, CLII)

That truth was to be gleaned from unadorned fact was a view of poetry so revolutionary as to meet with misunderstanding even among the greatest of Browning's poetic contemporaries. Tennyson admitted to not having 'the courage' to read The Ring and the Book, adding that although Browning was

> a great friend of mine . . . it does not follow that I should put up with obsolete horrors, and unrhythmical composition. What has come upon the world that it should take any metrical (?) arrangement of facts for holy Poesy?[10]

Although Browning's approach to the facts sometimes dismayed Victorian readers, it was just this approach which modern poets recognised as meaningful to their own art. As Robert Lowell expressed it, 'there is almost nothing Browning couldn't use . . .'[11] Poets were no longer to be restricted to treating great actions, the beauties of nature, or other such subjects fit for 'holy Poesy'. These traditional subjects began to seem inadequate for many of the modern poets. In a letter to William Carlos Williams, Pound argued that there was no point in writing traditional poems, no matter how popular they might be – 'Why write what I can translate out of Renaissance Latin or crib from the sainted dead?' He went on to stress the need for new subject-matter in humorous fashion, sending Williams a list of 'topics on which I and 9,000,000 other poets have spieled endlessly'. The list included such subjects as 'Spring is a pleasant season. The flowers, etc. etc. sprout bloom etc. etc.' and 'Love, a delightsome tickling. Indefinable etc.'[12]

'What excited me about the modern movement', said Stephen Spender, 'was the inclusion within new forms, of material which seemed ugly, anti-poetic and inhuman.'[13] Eliot and others had begun to experiment with subject-matter which was explicitly banal:

> I grow old ... I grow old ...
> I shall wear the bottoms of my trousers rolled.
>> ('The Love Song of J. Alfred Prufrock')

Like Browning, many modern poets considered poetry which was 'merely' beautiful to lack the 'sap/Of prose-experience which provides the draught/Which song-sprouts, wanting, wither' ('Jochanan Hakkadosh', 488–90). Only the facts, not the embellishment and beauty of song, could give the poem substance and make it live. If a poem missed what Browning called the 'test of truth',

> though flowers allure

> The goodman's eye with promise, soon the pact
> Is broken, and 't is flowers, – mere words, – he finds
> When things, – that's fruit, – he looked for.
>> ('Jochanan Hakkadosh', 495–8)

Eliot's emphasis on facts rather than the beautiful as the subject-matter of poetry prompted him to disagree with Matthew Arnold's contention that 'no one can deny that it is of advantage to a poet to deal with a beautiful world'. It might be an advantage for mankind in general to live in a beautiful world, said Eliot. 'But for the poet is it so important?'

> We mean all sorts of things, I know, by Beauty. But the essential advantage for a poet is not, to have a beautiful world with which to deal: it is to be able to see beneath both beauty and ugliness; to see the boredom, and the horror, and the glory.[14]

Here the poet is viewed not as a singer of beautiful songs, or a speaker of noble truths couched in memorable images, but as one who sees beneath the surface to the life and truth within. And the beautiful poem is one which gives the reader, if even for a moment, this same experience of viewing old facts in a new light. Pound was fond of relating an experience which illustrated this view of the poet's function. A Russian correspondent who labelled one of Pound's poems as a 'symbolist poem', was corrected by the poet: 'and having been convinced that it was not symbolism, said slowly: "I see, you wish to give people new eyes, not to make them see some new particular thing."'[15] Pound's anecdote echoes Browning's description of the poets who, seeing, 'Impart the gift of seeing to the rest'

(*Sordello*, III, 868). In other words, the poet was to show man what he fails to see in what is around him:

> we're made so that we love
> First when we see them painted, things we have passed
> Perhaps a hundred times nor cared to see . . .
>
> (*Fra Lippo Lippi*, 300–2)

Giving people new eyes involved going back to the facts of common experience, even if these facts had nothing beautiful or philosophically elevating about them. Before one could 'presume/To teach heaven legislation', he must 'learn earth first' ('Christopher Smart', IX):

> I found
> Somehow the proper goal for wisdom was the ground
> And not the sky, – so, slid sagaciously betimes
> Down heaven's baluster-rope, to reach the mob of mimes
> And mummers. (*Fifine*, CVIII)

Browning's view of the poet as one who makes people see has a background in Shelley's notion of poetry which 'turns all things to loveliness. . . . it strips the veil of familiarity from the world, and lays bare the naked and sleeping beauty, which is the spirit of its forms' ('A Defense of Poetry', pp. 55–6). For Browning and many modern poets, the idea of poetry as stripping the veil of familiarity from the world is an important one. But the crucial difference between these later poets and Shelley, as it is reflected in modern poetry, is the emphasis on 'the world' rather than on 'the spirit of its forms'. In his *Essay on Shelley*, Browning made this emphasis clear:

> For it is with this world, as starting point and basis alike, that we shall always have to concern ourselves: the world is not to be learned and thrown aside, but reverted to and relearned. The spiritual comprehension may be infinitely subtilised, but the raw material it operates upon, must remain. (p. 67)

The poet presents, as best he can, the object or fact from the everyday life of prose experience. 'Ultimately all we can do', said William Carlos Williams, 'is to try to understand something in its natural shapes and colors.'[16]

However simple and straightforward this task appears to be, understanding something in its natural shapes and colours is, as

Browning himself noted, very difficult to do. Art, even at its most perfect, can never be as complex and 'whole' as life. Browning was continually aware of 'Artistry's haunting curse, the Incomplete!' (in both *The Ring and the Book*, XI, 1561, and 'Beatrice Signorini', 38). The Queen of *In a Balcony* is described as living in a picture gallery where 'there's a life/Better than life, and yet no life at all' (104–5). The artist must take care not to 'confound the knowing how/And showing how to live (my faculty)/With actually living' ('Cleon', 281–3). Browning was so persistently aware of the inadequacy of art in this respect that he seems never to have been tempted by any vision similar to Tennyson's 'Palace of Art'.

The inadequacy of art in relation to life is particularly evident when the poet attempts to use the 'raw' facts as material for his art. As Browning so clearly recognised, a fact was only a facet of the truth. Although a scientist might be satisfied with examining one aspect of the truth, for a poet who insisted that 'Man's inmost life shall yet have freer play' (*Sordello*, V, 617), finding the whole truth by seeing individual facets, one by one, seemed an enormous task. This direct approach to the individual facts was not common to most other nineteenth-century poets, who chose to approach the truth as a whole. Browning envied Elizabeth Barrett for just that:

> ... your poetry must be, cannot but be, infinitely more to me than mine to you – for you *do* what I always wanted, hoped to do, and only seem now likely to do for the first time. You speak out, *you*, – I only make men & women speak – give you truth broken into prismatic hues, and fear the pure white light, even if it is in me . . .[17]

Years later, however, Browning's approach to the truth was still very different from that of his wife. As Browning put it, Elizabeth Barrett Browning would not have 'dirtied her hands for any scientific purpose'.[18] Although he had professed to admire her direct approach to the truth, within his own poetry, he offered many reasons for concentrating on the facets rather than the whole. The primary reason was that, as Browning saw it, man himself is so structured that he is incapable of comprehending the whole. Therefore the best that a mortal man can do is to examine the truth from as many points of view as possible. In contrast to his admiration of his wife's poetry based on her direct approach to the truth, Browning complimented another writer using words similar to those he applied to his own poetry: 'It is very subtle, very beautiful, – a jewel raying out truth from many facettes.'[19]

As Browning recognised, sense and sight

> take at best imperfect cognizance,
> Since, how heart moves brain, and how both move hand,
> What mortal ever in entirety saw?
>
> (*The Ring and the Book*, I, 826–9)

The best a poet could hope to do, if he insisted on staying close to the ground, was to ray forth facets of the whole rather than to approach the 'pure white light' directly. All poetry, Browning wrote to Ruskin, is 'a putting the infinite within the finite'.[20] *Sordello* Browning described as a poem which was 'modified by the impulse to "thrust in time eternity's concern" – *that*, or nothing.'[21]

When the finite, in the form of the facts at hand, is made to carry the infinite, the load may sometimes distort the language which carries it. Browning himself recognised the tendency for the outer, in struggling to represent the inner, to become grotesque:

> – the face, an evidence
> O' the soul at work inside; and, all the more intense,
> So much the more grotesque. (*Fifine*, XCVI)

One of the common devices used by poets to represent the intangible is that of allegory. Human situations familiar to the readers are used as analogies to a divine situation which cannot be apprehended by the earthly senses. Browning also employed extended analogy as a way of putting the infinite into the finite, but unlike *Everyman* or *Pilgrim's Progress*, his work places the analogy within the context of a strong emphasis on factual details. In *Sordello*, for example, Browning compares what 'an interval of vain discursive thought' has come to, with an Ethiopian slave stopping at a river:

> just to this was brought
> That interval of vain discursive thought!
> As, shall I say, some Ethiop, past pursuit
> Of all enslavers, dips a shackled foot
> Burnt to the blood, into the drowsy black
> Enormous watercourse which guides him back
> To his own tribe again, where he is king;
> And laughs because he guesses, numbering
> The yellower poison-wattles on the pouch
> Of the first lizard wrested from its couch

> Under the slime (whose skin, the while, he strips
> To cure his nostril with, and festered lips,
> And eyeballs bloodshot through the desert-blast)
> That he has reached its boundary, at last
> May breathe; – thinks o'er enchantments of the South
> Sovereign to plague his enemies, their mouth,
> Eyes, nails, and hair; but, these enchantments tried
> In fancy, puts them soberly aside
> For truth, projects a cool return with friends,
> The likelihood of winning mere amends
> Erelong; thinks that, takes comfort silently,
> Then, from the river's brink, his wrongs and he,
> Hugging revenge close to their hearts, are soon
> Off-striding for the Mountains of the Moon.
>
> (*Sordello*, IV, 862–85)

The imagery is delightful in itself; but it becomes grotesque because it is not sufficiently abstract to bear the meaning of that which it is intended to represent; the very abundance of detail gives the analogy a life of its own, apart from that which it is trying to explicate.

Elsewhere, it is not the *abundance* of detail but the very *intensity* of detail which creates a certain grotesque effect. In the beginning of Book IV of *Sordello*, Browning compares Ferrara to a lady being fought over by a pair of suitors:

> Meantime Ferrara lay in rueful case;
> The lady-city, for whose sole embrace
> Her pair of suitors struggled, felt their arms
> A brawny mischief to the fragile charms
> They tugged for – one discovering that to twist
> Her tresses twice or thrice about his wrist
> Secured a point of vantage – one, how best
> He'd parry that by planting in her breast
> His elbow spike – each party too intent
> For noticing, howe'er the battle went,
> The conqueror would but have a corpse to kiss.
>
> (IV, 1–11)

The analogy does not fail to convey its point – that whoever wins the city will have a prize which has been destroyed in the process of the fighting. Yet the picture of the lady and her suitors is painted so explicitly that the reader, caught up by the plight of the poor lady with elbows planted in her breast, is likely to lose sight of the fact that it is Ferrara that is being described, and that the lady is merely a figure of speech.

Browning's use of explicit imagery in such a way that an analogy takes on a tinge of the grotesque is evident not only in cases in which the analogy is that of abstract with concrete, but also in descriptions comparing one concrete aspect with another. A familiar example of this characteristic is found in the introduction to *Pippa Passes*, where a sunrise is compared with a liquid boiling over the brim of a cup – 'O'er night's brim, day boils at last' (3). The use of the very specific verb 'boil' to describe a sunrise which, although it is evident to the eyes, is not so specifically an action as it is a *process*, is a characteristic device of Browning which modern poets have frequently used. For example, Louis MacNeice in 'Ode' refers to 'slowly ladled clouds', and Edith Sitwell in 'Aubade' describes the morning light as 'creaking'.

> Jane, Jane,
> Tall as a crane,
> The morning light creaks down again . . .

Readers of modern poetry have come to expect these juxtapositions of the abstract with concrete images, images which are not only intensely specific, but often shockingly familiar:

> Viciousness in the kitchen!
> The potatoes hiss.
> It is all Hollywood, windowless,
> The fluorescent light wincing on and off like a terrible migraine,
> Coy paper strips for doors –
> Stage curtains, a widow's frizz. (Sylvia Plath, 'Lesbos')

Browning's readers, however, in their expectation of straightforward narrative, regarded the 'digressions' and 'grotesque' images as further instances of Browning's obscurity. What many of them failed to see was that the subject-matter of *Sordello*, for example, was not the story of a poet, obscurely told, but the delineation of the development of a soul, an attempt to 'thrust in time eternity's concern'. Thus Browning felt that the charges of obscurity called down upon *Sordello* were particularly unfair. It was not, after all, that Browning was unconcerned with clarity. He told Elizabeth Barrett that 'I am almost inclined to say that clear expression should be his [the artist's] only work and care.' He went on to say, 'what ever *can* be clearly spoken, ought to be: but "bricks and mortar" is very easily said – and some of the thoughts in "Sordello" not so readily even if Miss Mitford were to try her hand on them ...'[22]

That in *Sordello* which was not so readily expressed as 'bricks and mortar' was the attempt to deal with what Browning called 'perception', as opposed to emotions or thoughts. 'Perception' was defined in *Paracelsus* as being

> unexpressed,
> Uncomprehended by our narrow thought,
> But somehow felt and known in every shift
> And change in the spirit, – nay, in every pore
> Of the body, even,) – what God is, what we are,
> What life is ... (Book v, 638–43)

The major difficulty in dealing with a process uncomprehended by thought becomes immediately apparent: the poet must use words, and words themselves are products of thought. Browning described the inevitable failure of a poet like Sordello (and of course, himself) who attempted this. Although Sordello succeeded in 'welding words' until 'a rude/Armour was hammered out', when he attempted to use the new armour,

> Piece after piece that armour broke away,
> Because perceptions whole, like that he sought
> To clothe, reject so pure a work of thought
> As language: thought may take perception's place
> But hardly co-exist in any case,
> Being its mere presentment – of the whole
> By parts, the simultaneous and the sole
> By the successive and the many. Lacks
> The crowd perception? painfully it tacks
> Thought to thought, which Sordello, needing such,
> Has rent perception into: it's to clutch
> And reconstruct – his office to diffuse,
> Destroy: as hard, then, to obtain a Muse
> As to become Apollo. (Book II, 588–601)

Sordello has rent perception into thought in order to create his armour. But the words clothing the 'perception whole' are necessarily pieces, and so the poet is faced with a dilemma: how can he represent 'the whole/By parts, the simultaneous and the sole/By the successive and the many'? This dilemma is the obstacle against which Browning's experimentation operated. It is from this new welding of words, the trying of the *stuff* that holds the imaged *thing*, that the difficulties of reading and understanding *Sordello* originated.

This same realisation of the inadequacy of words to express aspects of the soul directly as perceived rather than through the medium of thought became a common theme of twentieth-century poetry. In the *Four Quartets*, Eliot echoes Browning's description of the armour breaking away piece by piece:

> Words strain,
> Crack and sometimes break, under the burden,
> Under the tension, slip, slide, perish,
> Decay with imprecision, will not stay in place,
> Will not stay still. (v)

Thus the artist is doomed to frustration. If he merely expresses that which can be expressed, he becomes, like Andrea del Sarto, a faultless craftsman whose art in being 'silver-grey/Placid and perfect' (98–9) misses the soul of the true artist whose 'reach should exceed his grasp' (97). Browning complains about 'tools so rude/To execute our purpose' (*Paracelsus*, II, 499–500), and exclaims 'Had we means/ Answering to our mind!' (*Paracelsus*, II, 509–10). Words, the outer expression of the inner perception, are paradoxically barriers to the very truth that they attempt to convey:

> But, do your best,
> Words have to come: and somehow words deflect
> As the best cannon ever rifled will.
>
> (*Prince Hohenstiel-Schwangau*, 2132–4)

Browning recognised that not only are words inadequate for the complete expression of the perception, but that if an artist were merely aiming for a representation of external facts, this very representation, if at all accurate, would point out that life itself seldom illustrates the artistically complete contours provided by much nineteenth-century poetry. The poem ends arbitrarily and far short of the complicated reality of the facts. Thus, Browning, in attempting to approach truth, was faced with a double dilemma: first, that of dealing with the 'nether-brooding loves, hates, hopes and fears,/Enwombed past Art's disclosure' ('Charles Avison', VIII); and second, that of dealing with the 'whole' when art can present only a facet. Even to begin to look at an experience as a whole, one must approach it from many different directions. But when an experience is seen from these different points of view, it sometimes appears to be a different experience from each viewpoint.

As Browning saw it, truth is always more complicated than appearances. In *Red Cotton Night-Cap Country*, for example, Browning examined an incident which took place in Normandy and developed from the facts a point of view that what appeared to be a suicide was really something far more complex. The title itself was inspired by Anne Thackeray's remark that that area was a 'White Cotton Night-Cap Country' (Book I). Browning's response was that all was not as tranquil as it appeared, and the 'white' could be seen as 'red' (I, 331 ff.).

Browning was acutely aware of the limited nature of looking at something from a single point of view. His disagreement with the treatment of the subject-matter in Tennyson's *Enoch Arden* was based on his insistence that the facts should be seen from several different points of view. 'I still see that fault in Enoch Arden', he said, and then described how he would have written the poem. What Browning disagreed with was the conclusion of the poem in which the dying Enoch Arden leaves messages for his family – 'tell her that I died/Blessing her . . .'

> So past the strong heroic soul away.
> And when they buried him the little port
> Had seldom seen a costlier funeral. (909–11)

For Browning, 'the concluding touch in the poem about the fine funeral – which Tennyson gave me to understand was a very pregnant one – strikes me as ambiguous and unlucky . . .'[23] Browning would have had Enoch Arden 'confirm himself in his resolution "never to let her know", and only admit those other fancies of her learning the truth after his death, and of his children seeing their father once again – as impossible luxuries, to be put down *as* fancies . . .' After Enoch Arden had quietly died 'in his hole', Browning would not have ended the poem with three lines about a costly funeral, but would have continued to describe the family's ironic

speculations concerning the pauper's funeral they have come across
on their nutting excursion:

> The young man, with the sagacity of his age, should divine that
> the poor devil could be no other than that odd, disreputable-looking
> and suspicious character who used to skulk about the ale-house, as
> if he had reasons enough for avoiding the constable, and – telling
> on his fingers – wonder whether it could be Giles the Poacher, or
> Jack the Gypsy that had to do with setting the barn on fire – or
> peradventure George the Tinker that decamped from his wife and
> children, leaving them a present to the parish? Thereupon should
> the Miller, whose thumb is proverbially made of gold – he should
> 'improve' the occasion, by inculcating on the young ones the evil
> consequences of self-indulgence – how man is made to conquer his
> riotous desires, not yield to them 'like this publican', while the
> Mother, the faithful Annie, though setting a proper example by
> turning up the white of her eyes, should treat herself to a little
> retrospective thankfulness – acknowledging that after a little
> roughness things had come satisfactorily round, and that, worst
> coming to the worst, dear Enoch's brave death in the storm – was
> it not better for him, and these beloved ones, than that he should
> ... who can tell? ... have lived on, even for such an end as this!
> And so they should proceed to their nutting, and Enoch, by a
> series of jolts, to his harbour in the churchyard – and we, to the
> considerations appropriate to one more view of this world.[24]

Browning's rewriting of the ending of *Enoch Arden* illustrates
some of the differences between his approach to the facts and that
of his more popular contemporary. In Tennyson's poem, an emo-
tionally satisfying conclusion is reached in that Enoch eventually
receives what is presented as the recognition due his years of self
sacrifice. The justice meted out in heaven is brought to earth by the
poet. Enoch Arden himself enjoys a foretaste of his own fame
through imagining his family's reaction when they come to know of
his sacrifice. In contrast, Browning is more interested in the facts–
the man who makes sacrifices here on earth is not likely to get an
earthly reward in the form of a costly funeral. In fact, he is more
likely to be misunderstood and even to suffer for his own good deeds.

Browning's most obvious successor in this approach to the facts
was Hardy. Like Browning, Hardy was unlikely to leave the story
at the point where all happy stories end or where, in unhappy stories,

the hero's fame is assured, and the villain has been punished. In fact, Hardy would have been more likely to begin where *Enoch Arden* ends. The character in "'Ah, are you Digging on my Grave''' is already dead and buried. Her assumptions that lover, kin or enemy is digging on her grave are each shown to be false; only a dog is digging on her grave, and even he has forgotten her and is merely burying a bone 'in case/I should be hungry near this spot/When passing on my daily trot.'

In Browning's version of *Enoch Arden*, the recognition scene, so loved by Victorian readers, never comes to pass. What is 'recognised' is the irony of a situation in which the characters who credit themselves with superior insight or understanding do not even see the facts. And this recognition takes place not within the narrative of the poem, but on the level of what might be termed the author–reader relationship. The author and reader are at a distance from the characters in the poem. This distance brings with it a certain objectivity in which the reader does not so much sympathise with the characters, but analyses them.

Presenting a character as a subject for analysis rather than sympathy is perhaps an inevitable result of Browning's concern with the facts. When the truth is approached through different facets, it is likely that one point of view will conflict with another. In many of Browning's dramatic monologues, the character presents the facts one way, the auditor within the poem apparently sees the facts from another point of view, or perhaps sees facts the narrator neglects to mention, and the reader, analysing both these points of view, synthesises a third.

Like Bishop Blougram, Browning's 'interest's on the dangerous edge of things./The honest thief, the tender murderer' (395–6). When Browning used mythical or historical persons, or lovers or knights as characters, he usually did not treat them as, for example, Tennyson treated his figures in *Idylls of the King*. A lover like Browning's Don Juan, although not true to his love, is not merely false; nor is he, like Tennyson's Lancelot, 'falsely true'. Don Juan, in Browning's poem, embodies a point of view from which falseness in love can be seen as a higher good than faithfulness. In other words, the very definition of 'lover' is seen from an ironical point of view. Other characters include a lover who strangles his beloved in order to have her near forever, a medium who both is and is not a fake, and a painter whose very perfection is at the root of his failure

– as if Browning delighted in exposing the fallacies of what is taken to be true.

This approach to the hero – or anti-hero as it has come to be called – is one of the attitudes of mind in which Browning is most like modern poets. And, like them, he was also aware of the inner dynamics of rationalisation, the mental processes which may change 'bad' to 'good'. For example, through his characters Browning explored the human tendency to present the facts in a light favourable to oneself. The speaker in a dramatic monologue may know the facts, but because of his wish to present himself as favourably as possible, he does not draw the apparent conclusion from the facts, but constructs a false logic of his own. The reader is often depended upon to analyse the bias of the speaker so that objective fact can be separated from subjective interpretation. Consequently, the viewpoint of the reader, like that of the poet, is superior to that of the speaker. In a monologue like 'Caliban upon Setebos', this superiority is obvious, and Caliban's quick retraction of his musings when the storm begins seems ironic from the reader's point of view. However, in 'Bishop Blougram's Apology', the logic constructed by the character is not so easily separated from the facts – at least Browning must have thought it sufficiently convincing to warrant a note to the reader at the end of the poem:

> certain hell-deep instincts, man's weak tongue
> Is never bold to utter in their truth
> Because styled hell-deep ('t is an old mistake
> To place hell at the bottom of the earth)
> He ignored these, – not having in readiness
> Their nomenclature and philosophy:
> He said true things, but called them by wrong names.
>
> (990–6)

The distancing between character and reader in a dramatic monologue is different from that of Browning's version of the narrative poem *Enoch Arden*. In *Enoch Arden*, Browning would have given the readers facts which the characters did not possess; but in a dramatic monologue the character has the same facts as the reader, and the reader can seldom be completely sure which half of what he speaks the character believes and which half he merely shapes for 'argumentatory purposes'. The distance between character and reader here is an analytical distance. The reader steps back to judge the character's motives and through this judgement, to separate the character's 'true' words from those he is using as a mask to fend off criticism. At the end of the poem, the reader, like a good psychologist, understands the character better than he appears to understand himself.

In *The Ring and the Book*, Browning experimented with another method of approaching the facts from different points of view. In the individual monologues, the reader is again in the position of having to separate objective fact from subjective bias; but after he has done this, he is confronted with the monologue of another character. Using this additional data, he synthesises a new point of view which leads him not only to see the original monologue in a different light, but also to revise his analysis of the facts. He then approaches the third monologue with, on the one hand, the analysis of the facts gleaned from the previous two monologues, and on the other hand a dual outlook through having experienced the facts from two different points of view. At the end of the twelfth book, the reader has seen the facts from many facets, each reflecting all the others.

Browning's many-sided approach to the facts has not only evolved into a specific concern of modern poets ('Thirteen Ways of Looking at a Blackbird') but has also initiated a further development: the centring of the multi-faceted approach to the facts in the consciousness of the character-narrator. In Eliot's 'Prufrock' the character looks at his own situation with the insight which in Browning's monologues is reserved for the reader. He is not making a case for himself, but, through the use of allusions, presents himself in the light of many other situations – 'No! I am not Prince Hamlet ...'

One aspect of this development is that what was disconnected in Browning's dramatic monologues – the objective facts as the reader perceived them, and the subjective view of the facts as presented by the character – has been brought together in the poetry of Eliot and others. In 'Prufrock', the 'facts' are subjective perceptions. Even so objective a statement as 'My necktie rich and modest' says less about the objective situation than it does about Prufrock's perception of himself. The fact that the tie is rich and modest is not as important as the fact that Prufrock has chosen to remark on his tie. Of course we catch a glimpse of the character through this detail; but it is not the same 'kind' of fact as that which Andrea del Sarto presents in his musings about 'that long festal year at Fontainebleau' (150). In Eliot's poem, the tie is 'rich' for the reader because Prufrock has said it is; in Browning's, however, the reader comes to different conclusions about whether "'twas right', as Andrea del Sarto asserts (167), for him to leave the French King because his wife grew restless.

Although there are more similarities than differences between modern dramatic monologues and those of Browning, the difference in the approach to facts is a basic one. For Browning, the more facets one could examine, and the more facts that could be brought into play, the closer one could be to the truth. Although the discussion of objective facts about the Bible had upset the religious convictions of many nineteenth-century people, the validity of *facts* themselves was not called into question. But with the advent of twentieth-century science, the nature of a fact was seen to be less 'objective' than the Victorians had imagined. For example, modern scientists began to emphasise that the 'laws of nature' are merely statistical laws, and not accurate or rigid descriptions of the individual cases encompassed by the law. Furthermore, scientists such as Heisenberg discovered that in observing small particles, for example, 'the interaction between observer and object causes uncontrollable and large changes in the system being observed', and that therefore, 'every experiment performed to determine some numerical quantity renders the knowledge of others illusory . . .'[25]

A layman's reactions to Heisenberg's discoveries might be to regard the objective data – the facts – as being 'contaminated' by the subjective. But another way of looking at this new relativistic background – again a layman's response – might be that in linking the object to the subject, the 'merely subjective' is given a new importance. It is interesting to note that one of the fundamental developments of what might be called the twentieth-century mentality was that of psychology. Mental illness, which in previous eras had been thought to be the product of a demon seizing the soul, or of a brain 'fever', was shown to be a development from within the subjective nature of the individual. The illness, although perhaps a *response* to the outside, was no longer regarded as an *invasion* from the outside. This twentieth-century turning towards the subjective as an object for analysis was a major influence on modern poetry, and indeed on literature in general.

Of course nineteenth-century poets had been interested in the nature of man also. However, this interest was in accordance with nineteenth-century views of science. For example, Tennyson was one of those very much concerned with the place of the individual in the context of evolution. If natural selection was ultimately purpose-less, man might become merely a fossil record, one of many species which Nature had produced and abandoned:

> 'So careful of the type'? but no.
> From scarpèd cliff and quarried stone
> She cries, 'A thousand types are gone:
> I care nothing, all shall go.' (*In Memoriam*, LVI)

As Tennyson questioned, what was the meaning of an individual life in a context in which man as a species no longer seemed of cosmic significance? Tennyson's fear – that in the overall scheme of things, man is very similar to those extinct fossils, and not likely to outlast them indefinitely – has largely been taken for granted in the twentieth century. For modern poets, the task now seems to be the attempt to focus on the individual, or the 'I' in the given context of meaninglessness.

The explorations of the 'I' have taken many forms, but one of the major ones, that of the dramatic monologue, is largely based on developments of that form made by Browning. Of course Browning was not focusing on the 'I' in the context of a meaningless universe – in fact, his firm conviction was that imperfection always aimed towards perfection. Now that the twentieth-century background no longer includes this teleological view of the universe, and natural selection is regarded as having been, in many cases, the result of chance rather than the product of any master design, Browning's conviction and its influence on his poetic technique does not seem very relevant to modern poetry.

Yet although Browning is not peculiarly modern in either the way he regarded facts as an approach to an objective truth, or in the way he saw his art and all man's endeavours in a context of imperfection aiming at perfection, he is a forerunner to the modern movement in the kinds of facts he selected for observation. Although a Browning monologue may be filled with narrative statements of facts, such as Andrea del Sarto's musings about his year with the French King, the real subject-matter of the poem is not a narrative of facts, but an exploration of the painter's inner life. As Wallace Stevens puts it:

> The subject-matter of poetry is not that 'collection of solid, static objects extended in space' but the life that is lived in the scene that it composes; and so reality is not that external scene but the life that is lived in it. Reality is things as they are.[26]

In 'My Last Duchess', for example, the subject of the poem is apparently the Duchess, for more facts are given about her than about anything or anyone else. However, the focus of attention in the poem, and the subject with which the poem is really concerned, is the psychology of the Duke. What might be called the objective facts of the case – what has happened to the Duchess – are ultimately ambiguous. However, although the reader never discovers what exactly has happened to the Duchess, he does finish the poem with a very vivid picture of the Duke, even though few direct facts have been given about him.

What the reader discovers about the Duke are psychological 'facts', deductions from the way the Duke talks about his last Duchess. Thus, when the Duke says, 'I choose/Never to stoop', the reader does not take it as a fact at its face value – that the Duke is merely proud – but connecting it with other facts, comes to the conclusion that the case is not one of mere family pride, but paranoid jealousy. Browning thus directs his reader to gather the clues which will help to create an understanding of the Duke on what would be called in modern terms, the subconscious level. As Bishop Blougram points out, every man has a dreaming life as well as a waking one and these two lives are often contradictory.

Browning's interest in the subconscious level of his characters results in an emphasis not so much on what the character does, but in why he does it. The 'Roman murder case' in *The Ring and the Book* is not a detective story or even a murder mystery. Browning tells his readers the entire plot in the first few lines of the poem. Moreover, he comes to the same conclusion as that of the original judges concerning who is guilty and who is innocent; thus Browning is no more a prosecutor or judge than he is a detective. Yet, in a sense, he is something of both in respect to the subconscious: a detective of the motivations of the characters, and a judge as to the purity of these motivations. As Aprile, speaking of the poet, remarks in *Paracelsus*:

> I would live
> For ever in the thoughts I thus explored,
> As a discoverer's memory is attached
> To all he finds . . . (II, 560–3)

An explorer of thoughts, like the explorer of a new land, would attempt to report exactly what he discovers. Once again, in doing this, Browning presented unpleasant facts to his readers. One objection, for example, was to Guido's reported wickedness. Browning replied to this objection with a remarkably Freudian insight:

> We differ apparently in our conception of what gross wickedness can be effected by cultivated minds – I believe the grossest – all the more, by way of reaction from the enforced habit of self denial which is the condition of men's receiving culture.[27]

With this interest in subconscious as well as consciously apparent data, Browning was obviously looking forward to the twentieth century, rather than back to a golden age of art which so many Victorians attributed to classical Greece. To demands for 'Greek Art and what more wish you', Browning replied:

> 'To become now self-acquainters,
> 'And paint man man, whatever the issue!'
>
> ('Old Pictures in Florence', XIX)

The resulting criticism of obscurity was also directed towards modern poetry in which, as one critic complained, advances in psychology had emphasised the part played by the 'unintelligible'.[28] Because of the attention paid to the subconscious, 'a writer whose aim is to reproduce a modern consciousness will spend much of his time conducting his readers through a sort of wonderland.'[29]

The twentieth-century emphasis on psychology has resulted in a kind of self-consciousness on the part of artists. One form of this self-consciousness is that poetry itself is frequently the subject-matter of the poem. Of course poets have talked about poetry for centuries. But previously this concern has been with such ideas as, for example, the poem as a way to preserve the memory of a person:

> Yet do thy worst, old Time: despite thy wrong,
> My love shall in my verse ever live young.
>
> (Shakespeare, Sonnet 19)

However, modern poets seldom regard the poem as a way to preserve a precious thing, but rather regard it as a way to approach reality. The obvious example of a poet concerned with poetry as the subject-matter of a poem is of course Wallace Stevens:

> The poem goes from the poet's gibberish to
> The gibberish of the vulgate and back again.
> Does it move to and fro or is it of both

> At once? Is it a luminous flittering
> Or the concentration of a cloudy day?
> Is there a poem that never reaches words
>
> And one that chaffers the time away?
> Is the poem both peculiar and general?
> There's a meditation there, in which there seems
>
> To be an evasion, a thing not apprehended or
> Not apprehended well. Does the poet
> Evade us, as in a senseless element?
>
> (*Notes Toward a Supreme Fiction*, 'It Must Change', IX)

The relationship between the poet, the poem and reality which Stevens explores was also a significant theme in Browning's poetry. Each of Browning's first four major poems dealt in some manner with the role of the artist. In *Pauline* Browning attempted a psychological study of the young poet, struggling with creative emotion. In *Paracelsus* he was concerned with the search for knowledge, and the relationship of truth or science to beauty or poetry. *Sordello* represents the artist's struggle with creative form. At one point Browning even has the character Sordello speak about poetry in a way that refers to the poem *Sordello*:

> 'Man's inmost life shall yet have freer play:
> 'Once more I cast external things away,
> 'And natures composite, so decompose
> 'That' ... Why, he writes *Sordello!*' (Book V, 617–20)

And finally, in *Pippa Passes*, the theme is approached through the voice of Jules ('One may do whate'er one likes/In Art' (II, 308–9).

In *Sordello*, after discussing the problem of expressing perceptions through words, and the whole through mere fragments, Browning exclaims:

> 'For the rest,
> 'E'en if some wondrous vehicle expressed
> 'The whole dream, what impertinence in me
> 'So to express it, who myself can be
> 'The dream!' (Book II, 61–5)

Yet, in spite of this 'impertinence', Browning maintains that

> from true works (to wit
> Sordello's dream-performances that will

> Never be more than dreamed) escapes there still
> Some proof, the singer's proper life was 'neath
> The life his song exhibits, this a sheath
> To that ... (Book III, 622–7)

Although Browning refused to consider biographical facts as necessary to the understanding of his poetry, he did admit the closeness of the poet himself to the 'life his song exhibits'. Modern poets such as Robert Lowell and Sylvia Plath have expanded the use of the singer's life as a source of poetry. Facts of the writer's inner experience have formed the basis of much modern poetry. In addition, daily experiences, trivial or commonplace, such as that described in Sylvia Plath's 'Cut', are used as centre-points around which are clustered thoughts and feelings which make the experience itself a complex image:

> What a thrill –
> My thumb instead of an onion.
> The top quite gone
> Except for a sort of a hinge ...

One aspect of modern culture which further influences modern poets to look inward for subject-matter is the lack of a common background. Even as late as the nineteenth century, a poet could assume that he and his readers shared a certain religious and national heritage, and that however broad this common experience was it could be used as a subject-matter immediately familiar to the audience. Arnold, in writing a poem entitled 'Empedocles on Etna', could assume that most of his educated readers would be familiar with the general background of the story and thus appreciate what he had done with it. Neither modern poets nor Browning, however, use this common background – modern poets because there is no longer a public with a common religious or educational heritage, and Browning because his own education was unusual, and he discovered early in his career that his assumptions that his audience would know certain things familiar to him – the origin of the title 'Bells and Pomegranates', for example – would very likely prove mistaken.

This lack of common or shared experience coupled with the turning toward subjective data as the material for poetry has increased the possibility that a reader will have difficulty in understanding the poem. One critic complained that the modern poet offers to his reader 'raw pieces of himself, and the reader is expected to accept without understanding them, by some unintellectual process of assimilation, much as St. John in the Apocalypse was given a book and told, not to read it, but to "eat it up."'[30]

If, like Browning, the modern poet attempts to express 'perceptions whole', the emphasis would fall on attempting to represent the inner experience rather than in creating an intellectually intelligible set of words. At this stage, as Eliot described it, the poet

> is not concerned with making other people understand anything. He is not concerned, at this stage, with other people at all: only with finding the right words or, anyhow, the least wrong words. He is not concerned whether anybody else will ever listen to them or not, or whether anybody else will ever understand them if he does.[31]

Poets of another age might have thought that finding the right words does involve the reader, and that in fact, the right words are precisely those words which the reader will understand. Eliot argues, however, that the right words have little or no necessary connection with the reader's understanding. The emphasis is on finding the right words for the subjective experience, rather than attempting to communicate this experience 'objectively' at the cost of distorting the subjective nature of the facts.

Considering such an emphasis and considering the absence of any common set of symbols to which the poet can refer, it is not surprising that Eliot thought a poet was

> right, very right, in looking for a set of symbols which should relate each of his poems to the others, to himself, rather than using in each poem symbols which should merely relate it to other poems by other people.[32]

Although this emphasis on the importance of the poet behind the poem can perhaps be traced back to the Romantics' view of the poem as the expression of the poet rather than as a mirror of the world,[33] there is a fundamental difference. The modern poet is much more self-consciously aware of his own voice as a point of view, and one of many in a universe in which no point of view can with certainty be labelled the right one. Consequently, the poet stresses the development of the voice or the point of view rather than a description of the outside world. The formal results can be seen in Harry Crosby's

Transit of Venus, in which, as Eliot points out, the poems are related to 'the others' and 'to himself', or in John Berryman's *77 Dream Songs* and *His Toy, His Dream, His Rest*, in which the point of view of a character named 'Henry' is carried through 385 poems in two volumes.

At first glance, this emphasis on the subjective might seem to contradict modern poets' interest in the objective 'facts' of existence. Yet, as Browning seemed to foresee through his own approach to the facts, the primary interest is in the relationship of the subjective with the objective.

For Browning, this relationship was seen as that between facts themselves and the poet's soul. Facts are dead and meaningless unless infused with experience, in this case, the poet's own experience and feelings, his soul:

> For clay, once cast into my soul's rich mine,
> Should come up crusted o'er with gems.
>
> (*Paracelsus*, II, 565–6)

Browning's use of the ring metaphor in *The Ring and the Book* is an illustration of his concern with the relation between the outer and the inner. As Browning explained, the Old Yellow Book provided the facts, the material for his poem, but the poem itself is not merely a reporting of the facts, but the representation of the truth obtained when the facts have been fused with his soul (pure gold with the alloy):

> such alloy,
> Such substance of me interfused the gold ...
>
> Something of mine which, mixed up with the mass,
> Made it bear hammer and be firm to file.
>
> I fused my live soul and that inert stuff ...
>
> (Book I, 681–2, 463–4, 469)

Yet Browning, in emphasising the place of the subjective in animating inert stuff, did not go to the length of declaring the poet's fancy to be the primary ingredient in the production of truth. The poet mediates between the extremes of objective fact and subjective fancy by the use of a third term – the 'fact unseen':

> but somehow fact
> Has got to – say, not so much push aside
> Fancy, as to declare its place supplied

> By fact unseen but no less fact the same,
> Which mind bids sense accept. ('Gerard de Lairesse', VI)

In a sense, the 'fact unseen' is the opposite of empirical fact in that it is obtained not from the mind's grasping of the data of the senses, but from the acquiescence of the senses to the 'insight' of the mind. If twentieth-century poetry often seems to be radically anti-scientific in spirit, the cause is probably to be found in this stress on the inner fact rather than in the spirit of earlier poets who bewailed what science had done to humanitarian values. This view of the relationship of inner and outer relies neither on logical necessity (the poet's drawing of a moral conclusion based on facts), or on traditional poetic correspondences (the association of a physical object like a rose with, for example, an inner or emotional idea like love). Thus the realm of facts, which had seemed to be the province of science, came to be appropriated in a peculiar way by poetry, and a humanistic poetry at that. 'The only human value of anything, writing included', said Zukofsky, quoting William Carlos Williams, 'is the intense vision of the facts, add to that by saying the truth and action upon them – clear into the machine of absurdity into a core that is covered.'[34]

Thomas Hardy, greatly influenced by Browning, carried this emphasis on the 'fact unseen' into his novels. He described *Tess of the D'Urbervilles* as 'an attempt to give artistic form to a true sequence of things.'[35] Yet, like Browning, Hardy approached this 'true sequence' with an artistic soul rather than with journalistic objectivity, as the subtitle of his novel testifies: 'A Pure Woman Faithfully Presented.' Hardy's conclusion that Tess was a 'Pure Woman' was reached in much the same way that Browning reached the 'truth' in *The Ring and the Book*: through letting the material impress itself on the soul of the artist. 'A novel is an impression, not an argument', said Hardy in his preface to later editions of *Tess of the D'Urbervilles*.

Thus, the artist–soul deals with facts in two ways: from the mere facts of existence, he gleans truth; and in the common facts of everyday life, he reveals beauty:

> So, then, if Nature's defects must be looked in the face and
> transcribed, whence arises the *art* in poetry and novel-writing?
> which must certainly show art, or it becomes merely mechanical
> reporting. I think the art lies in making these defects the basis of a

hitherto unperceived beauty, by irradiating them with 'the light that never was' on their surface, but is seen to be latent in them by the spiritual eye. (Thomas Hardy, 1877 diary)[36]

Seeing with 'the spiritual eye', like Browning's fusion of 'live soul and inert stuff' in order to get at 'fact unseen but no less fact the same', calls for a different poetic technique, especially in the realm of imagery. Although there is no clear distinction between imagery of the outer fact and imagery of the inner fact, a comparison with the more easily accessible imagery in painting might illustrate the difference between the two approaches.

In representational painting, the object is to mirror the outer facts, the reality a camera might record. An example of what might be termed representational imagery can be found in Tennyson's *Enoch Arden*:

> For cups and silver on the burnished board
> Sparkled and shone; so genial was the hearth:
> And on the right hand of the hearth he saw
> Philip, the slighted suitor of old times,
> Stout, rosy, with his babe across his knees;
> And o'er her second father stoopt a girl,
> A later but a loftier Annie Lee,
> Fair-haired and tall, and from her lifted hand
> Dangled a length of ribbon and a ring
> To tempt the babe, who reared his creasy arms,
> Caught at and ever missed it, and they laughed;
> And on the left hand of the hearth he saw
> The mother glancing often toward her babe,
> But turning now and then to speak with him,
> Her son, who stood beside her tall and strong,
> And saying that which pleased him, for he smiled.
>
> (738–53)

The available space is filled, and the picture is even framed, for Enoch Arden views the scene through a window.

In modern painting, the emphasis is on the external representation of the internal state of mind. Picasso's 'Guernica', for example, does not objectively depict the wounded people, the shell craters, the torn flesh of the horses; it does not depict these outer signs of the event, but expresses the inner pain, the agony of soul. Of course these two approaches to imagery are extremes along a continuum.

There is a sense in which Tennyson's framed picture of the family mirrors the inner well-being of the household just as Picasso's painting has within it recognisable objects of external reality. The point of difference lies in the emphasis given to the inner or the outer facts, and it is this difference which Browning saw as a major one between himself and Tennyson:

> Well, I go with you a good way in the feeling about Tennyson's new book: it is all out of my head already. We look at the object of art in poetry so differently! Here is an Idyll about a knight being untrue to his friend and yielding to the temptation of that friend's mistress after having engaged to assist him in his suit. I should judge the conflict in the knight's soul the proper subject to describe: Tennyson thinks he should describe the castle, and effect of the moon on its towers, and anything *but* the soul.[37]

That modern poets were essentially in agreement with Browning is illustrated by Eliot's referring to Tennyson's long poems as being 'always descriptive, and always picturesque'.[38]

For Browning, the object of the image was to express the inner state of the individual regardless of the outer circumstances. This difference between Tennyson's approach to imagery and that of Browning is especially evident when one compares the *Idylls of the King* with Browning's dramatic monologues. For example, the imagery of autumn is found throughout both 'Andrea del Sarto' and 'The Last Tournament'. But whereas in Tennyson, the imagery provides an atmosphere of decay surrounding the last days of Arthur's Round Table, in 'Andrea del Sarto' the autumn images do not so much create an atmosphere, but operate in the dialectic movement of Andrea del Sarto's self-examination. The silver of declining day and the 'autumn in everything' (45) which the painter sees are contrasted with the gold of Lucrezia's beauty (especially her golden hair). The imagery provides the outer representation of the inner realisation that 'All is silver-grey/Placid and perfect with my art' (98–9) because he has forsaken the 'golden look' of his benefactor in order to paint for the gold coins demanded by his wife. Although Andrea del Sarto approaches regret on the conscious level ('A good time, was it not, my kingly days?': 165), he never quite allows himself to admit the truth of his failure ('I regret little, I would change still less./Since there my past life lies, why alter it?': 245–6). Yet it is here that the imagery operates on the inner level, for by the end of the poem, the weight of autumn imagery, of the silver-grey end of the day which Andrea del Sarto describes, reveals the truth which the soul feels, but which the conscious mind cannot admit to itself.

This difference in the use of imagery is perhaps most clearly seen when Tennyson is using images directly to describe an inner state. Section XCV of *In Memoriam* describes Tennyson's mystical reunion with his dead friend:

> So word by word, and line by line,
>   The dead man touched me from the past,
>   And all at once it seemed at last
> The living soul was flashed on mine,
>
> And mine in this was wound, and whirled
>   About empyreal heights of thought,
>   And came on that which is, and caught
> The deep pulsations of the world,
>
> Æonian music measuring out
>   The steps of Time – the shocks of Chance –
>   The blows of Death. At length my trance
> Was cancelled, stricken through with doubt.
>
> Vague words! but ah, how hard to frame
>   In matter-moulded forms of speech,
>   Or even for intellect to reach
> Through memory that which I became ...

In Tennyson's poem, the experience is precise, but the imagery used to depict it is vague or general: 'empyreal heights of thought', 'Æonian music', 'steps of Time – the shocks of Chance –/The blows of Death.' For Browning, however, the imagery most often chosen to represent those inner experiences which seem to elude 'matter-moulded forms of speech' is that of outer objects modified by the inner impression. Thus, to an excited hero in 'The Patriot', 'The house-roofs seemed to heave and sway'. Unlike Tennyson's use of vague imagery to describe a precise experience, in a poem such as 'Childe Roland to the Dark Tower Came', the images are very precise indeed, but what the experience is remains in doubt, although laden with particular feelings. These feelings are conveyed through adjectives which are not objective descriptions of the objects they modify, but subjective descriptions of the reactions to the objects. Thus the horse is 'wicked and hated', the cripple is 'hateful', the earth is 'desperate', the river is 'petty' and 'spiteful' and the tree is 'threatening'. As discussed in Chapter 1, Browning's imagery in this poem is very similar to that of dreams. In dreams, imagery is precise, and the feeling surrounding the image is strong, although not always reasonable; but the meaning of the dream is not immediately clear. In dreams and in poems such as 'Childe Roland to the Dark Tower Came', there is a sense that a meaning is suggested, and that it is something other than that which arises directly from the situation or images explicitly described.

The use of 'dream imagery' is common to modern poetry, and is one of the primary reasons for the fact that modern poetry is often not immediately understood. The exact nature of Tennyson's mystical experience may have been obscure to the reader, but he could at least understand why it came about, what it meant to the poet, and what results come of it in the poem. But many readers experiencing Eliot's *The Waste Land* for the first time, could not make sense of images like the corpse planted in the garden, even though the image itself was precise.

One way of looking at Tennyson's imagery in contrast, for example, to that of the Imagists, would be to see Tennyson's struggle with 'matter-moulded forms of speech' as an attempt to communicate his experience to the reader, or at the least, to make it possible 'for intellect to reach ... that which I became ...' For Pound and his followers, however, the struggle with words was not to produce an image which the intellect could reach, but one which exactly expressed the inner feelings of the poet, whether or not anyone, including the poet, understood the image intellectually – 'the author must use his *image* because he sees it or feels it, *not* because he thinks he can use it to back up some creed or some system of ethics or economics.'[39]

Eliot's idea of the objective correlative was so popular partly because it summarised what many felt to be peculiar to modern poetry in its approach to imagery:

> The only way of expressing emotion in the form of art is by finding an 'objective correlative': in other words, a set of objects, a situation, a chain of events which shall be the formula of that *particular* emotion; such that when the external facts, which must terminate in sensory experience, are given, the emotion is immediately evoked.[40]

To be the formula of a *'particular'* emotion, imagery must be very precise in its effect. It could be said that this is the purpose of imagery in any age. But what made it new and produced different types of imagery, was again the emphasis on the subjective as the major source of subject-matter. As Spender said, 'Poetry was a use of language which revealed external actuality as symbolic inner consciousness.'[41] It no longer created 'a special world in which the poet enjoys Keatsian imaginings shutting out the real wor[l]d'; nor was the poet

> a kind of shadowy prophet behind the throne of power, Shelley's unacknowledged legislator of mankind. Instead, he was now a translator of the world which man projects around him through the actions of his will, back into language of the inner life of dreams and phantasy which has projected this materialistic external actuality.[42]

From this point of view, the image or the objective correlative could be seen as the mediator between the outer world of objective facts and the inner world of subjective facts. The mediator is a 'direct' one in that it does not need to go through the interpreting apparatus of the conscious mind in order to make its effect. Perhaps this directness was what Eliot was referring to when he said that the 'meaning' of the poem, in its ordinary sense, was merely used to 'satisfy one habit of the reader, to keep his mind diverted and quiet, while the poem does its work upon him: much as the imaginary burglar is always provided with a bit of nice meat for the house-dog.'[43]

In '"Transcendentalism"' Browning also points out the value of the image or the thing created as opposed to the 'thought' which 'grown men want' in verse. Another Boehme, Browning says, might write a book with 'subtler meanings of what roses say', but a 'Mage' like John of Halberstadt, 'made things Boehme wrote thoughts about':

> He with a 'look you!' vents a brace of rhymes,
> And in there breaks the sudden rose herself,
> Over us, under, round us every side,
> Nay, in and out the tables and the chairs
> And musty volumes, Boehme's book and all, –
> Buries us with a glory, young once more,
> Pouring heaven into this shut house of life.

The idea that the poet makes things rather than talks about them, that he is closer to the craftsman than to the prophet or legislator, is an idea which has been expressed by many modern poets. In a sense it seems paradoxical to say that the poet creates, if what he insists that he is doing is dealing with facts, inner or outer. In one poem Browning's image of poetry is the 'sudden rose' breaking round on every side; but in another poem, Browning will insist that he is merely using the facts of the case already established; or he presents an image of poetry as the 'Poet's word-mesh', bringing up prizes from the sea ('Charles Avison', VIII).

From one point of view, to bring up fish from the sea is to bring the fish into being, to 'create' the fish. The fish in the net are different from the unseen, unheard, unfelt fish in the sea, just as the everyday scene framed in a picture is different from the ordinary scene man passes 'Perhaps a hundred times nor cared to see' (Fra Lippo Lippi, 302). In Wallace Stevens's 'Anecdote of the Jar', the poet places 'a jar in Tennessee,/And round it was, upon a hill'. The jar on the hill, without creating one new thing in the wilderness around it, takes 'dominion everywhere'. The wilderness sprawls around it, 'no longer wild'. It becomes the central fact, even though

> It did not give of bird or bush,
> Like nothing else in Tennessee.

Browning's concern with the peculiar nature of artistic creation led him to wonder:

> Are means to the end, themselves in part the end?
> Is fiction which makes fact alive, fact too?
> (The Ring and the Book, I, 704-5)

Browning went on to say that although man cannot give life, through the artist, 'something dead may get to live again' (729). The artist sends out his soul which

> May chance upon some fragment of a whole,
> Rag of flesh, scrap of bone in dim disuse...' (752-3)

The artist enters, 'spark-like', and like Elisha, breathes life into a corpse (755 ff.).

Poets 'are fain invest/The lifeless thing with life from their own soul' (Sordello, I, 490-1) until 'Visibly through his garden walketh God' (504). Not only does the poet breathe life into dead matter, but he also embodies the idea, gives flesh to the spirit so that it can be seen by the world. 'Poetry', said Browning, 'if it is to deserve the name, ought to create – or re-animate something – not merely reproduce *raw* fact taken from somebody else's book.'[44] Marianne Moore called for 'the poets among us' to be '"literalists of/the imagination"', and to present '"imaginary gardens with real toads in them"' ('Poetry'). Yeats carried this modern point of view about the nature of 'created reality' to its logical although extreme conclusion when he said that 'The only real *Imagist* was the Creator of the Garden of Eden'.[45]

In regarding poetry as creation rather than imitation, Browning was of course acting within the framework of the Romantics. But in experimenting from this point of view, Browning became one of the primary influences in the change from a stress on 'a great human action' as subject-matter (as Arnold advised)[46] to an emphasis on the subject as *means*:

> The subject exists for the poem, not the poem for the subject. A poem may employ several subjects, combining them in a particular way; and it may be meaningless to ask 'What is the subject of the poem?' From the union of several subjects there appears, not another subject, but the poem. (Eliot)[47]

Browning's influence on this fundamental shift in emphasis can be summarised as involving two important aspects. First, stressing the facts of experience rather than whatever conclusions can be drawn from the facts, Browning utilised subject-matter which was not necessarily 'poetical' or of primary interest in itself. In his dramatic monologues, Browning constantly reminds the reader that someone is talking, that a 'real' person is eating and drinking, or dying, or trying to defend himself in the presence of a listener who is also 'real' in that he is made particular and concrete. With Browning's emphasis on 'real' people talking and listening, it followed that the subject-matter was often drawn from real life and not from speculations about the past. If the scene is set in the past, the characters are revealed with peculiarly modern psychologies, and talk about problems bothering the modern man of Browning's own day. Even among the least ordinary of Browning's characters, such as Caliban, the real subject-matter is shown to be not that of a primitive man poking around on an island looking for insects to eat and playing God in his spare time, but the steps a mind takes when speculating about the unknown, and the futility of a speculation which relies on reason to reach God.

In addition to emphasising facts as the subject-matter of poetry, Browning stressed the personal nature of the facts. In the framework of a dramatic monologue, for example, the reader is reminded that the point of view is only that of the character involved, not that of the omniscient poet, legislator of mankind. But from another viewpoint, the process of the character's musings, and the outcome of his struggle with himself, is a 'fact', even though the character himself is a fictional creation, for the results have been 'proved' in the artist's soul. The nature of poetic truth, as Browning presents it, is experiential rather than didactic. Subject-matter is different because the subject is no longer the object of the poem, but the image for the object – and the object involves a reality not approached by the senses:

> Why take the artistic way to prove so much?
> Because, it is the glory and good of Art,
> That Art remains the one way possible
> Of speaking truth, to mouths like mine at least.

> But Art, – wherein man nowise speaks to men,
> Only to mankind, – Art may tell a truth
> Obliquely, do the thing shall breed the thought,
> Nor wrong the thought, missing the mediate word.
> So may you paint your picture, twice show truth,
> Beyond mere imagery on the wall ...
>
> (*The Ring and the Book*, XII, 841–4, 858–63)

3

The Use of Common Speech

'Every revolution in poetry is apt to be ... a return to common speech', said Eliot.[1] The revolution in twentieth-century poetry with which Eliot was so closely involved was no exception to this generalisation. In fact, one of the most immediately noticeable differences between twentieth-century poetry and most poetry of the nineteenth century is the modern emphasis on common diction. For readers accustomed to the diction of Tennyson – 'Dost thou look back on what hath been' (*In Memoriam*, LXIV) – Eliot's poetry might have seemed more like prose:

> we stopped in the colonnade,
> And went on in sunlight, into the Hofgarten,
> And drank coffee, and talked for an hour.
>
> (*The Waste Land*, I, 9–11)

Of course the revolutionary nature of Eliot's poetry involved more than the use of common diction – after all, Hardy had used the diction of prose conversation in many of his poems. Yet Hardy had set these common words within the context of an immediately noticeable poetic metre:

> 'A woman never agreed to it!' said my knowing friend to me,
> 'That one thing she'd refuse to do for Solomon's mines in fee:
> No woman ever will make herself look older than she is.'
>
> ('The Elopement')

In contrast, Eliot often used not only the diction of common speech, but also its rhythms and tones.

This aspect of the twentieth-century revolution in poetry can also be seen in the development of Yeats's poetry. The early poems exhibit regular iambic rhythms and end-stopped lines, while in the later poems, Yeats often speaks with a conversational rhythm or employs traditional poetic forms in a self-consciously elevated manner. The difference becomes immediately apparent when lines from a well-known nineteenth-century poem are compared with lines from a much later poem:

When you are old and grey and full of sleep,
And nodding by the fire, take down this book,
And slowly read, and dream of the soft look
Your eyes had once, and of their shadows deep ...

(from 'When You are Old', *The Rose*, 1898)

Pythagoras planned it. Why did the people stare?
His numbers, though they moved or seemed to move
In marble or in bronze, lacked character.

(from 'The Statues', *Last Poems*, 1936–9)

What both Eliot's poetry and that of the later Yeats reveals is a fundamental change in the nature of diction, a revolution which involved a 'return to common speech'. Yeats said that he 'tried to make the language of poetry coincide with that of passionate, normal speech', and claimed that 'in this English poetry has followed my lead...'[2] Yet, as Eliot recognised, modern poets were not the first to call for such a revolution. In the preface to *Lyrical Ballads* (1800), Wordsworth had said that his principal object was 'to choose incidents and situations from common life, and to relate or describe them, throughout, as far as was possible in a selection of language really used by men...'[3]

Whatever Wordsworth's object, his own poetry did not always exhibit what twentieth-century readers would consider 'the language really used by men'. The revolution in early nineteenth-century poetry did not result in a language similar to that spoken by the man on the street. What the revolution did accomplish was the loosening of established poetic forms which had come to seem habitual and confining.

By the middle of the nineteenth century, both Tennyson and Arnold were criticising Wordsworth's style. Tennyson said, 'I used to weary of the hopelessly prosaic lines in some books of "The Excursion"...'[4] Arnold claimed that Wordsworth had 'no assured poetic style of his own.... When he seeks to have a style he falls into ponderosity and pomposity.'[5] At the beginning of the twentieth century, the nineteenth-century revolution in diction seemed very far away. Yet when the modern poets began to establish a new diction in poetry, they were in part building on the earlier revolution. What the twentieth-century revolution did was to carry the nineteenth-century departure from rigid *poetic* forms to its logical end – an approximation to *prose* rhythms and diction.

In one sense, then, the twentieth-century revolution in poetry is a linear descendant of the Romantic revolution. But there is another sense in which modern poets can be seen as operating on one end of a continuum containing two poles. Keeping in mind the distortions inherent in such vast generalisations, one can thus see the history of English poetry as a movement of language between these two poles: on the one side, 'at the extreme limit from prose',[6] as Eliot put it, is a line running from Spenser through Milton, Keats, Tennyson and the Georgians; at the other pole, using a diction 'assimilated to cultivated contemporary speech' with the 'virtues of prose' are most of the modern poets, descendants of Donne, Butler and – the most important immediate predecessor – Browning.

Of all the nineteenth-century poets, it is Browning who comes closest to the modern revolution in poetic diction. Eliot said that Browning was the only poet of the nineteenth century 'to devise a way of speech which might be useful for others', and that this was done primarily through his 'use of non-poetic material' and his insistence on 'the relation of poetry to speech'.[7] It is not surprising to find that Pound, who valued Ford Madox Ford's emphasis on contemporary spoken language as one of the four most important things he had learned in London,[8] agreed with Ford's comment that the only English poet who mattered 'twopence' was Browning.[9] When Browning is compared with other nineteenth-century poets, it is his common diction and conversational rhythms which immediately distinguish his poetry from that of his contemporaries.

Very early in his career Browning was aware of the difference between his poetry and that of his predecessors 'at the extreme limit from prose'. In Sordello, Browning wards off Shelley's spirit as well as 'the silver speech/Of Sidney's self' not because he does not admire them, but because 'this is no place for thee!' (I, 60–9). Instead, he found Donne and Shakespeare to be the poets most congenial to his style, however much he might admire Shelley's spirit.

Browning's championship of the 'revered and magisterial Donne!' (Two Poets of Croisic, CXIV), although perhaps not beginning the modern appreciation of Donne as one critic asserted, certainly had much to do with it.[10] In fact, a major nineteenth-century edition of Donne was dedicated 'to Robert Browning ... knowing how much his poetry, with every abatement, is valued and assimilated by him'.[11]

Browning's championship of Donne was sometimes considered

eccentric in the nineteenth century. Yet it is understandable that
Browning would be drawn to a predecessor whose voice and tone bore
so much resemblance to his own. Donne's conversational immediacy
– 'For Godsake hold your tongue, and let me love' ('The Canoniza-
tion') – had few successors until Browning – 'Now, don't sir! Don't
expose me! Just this once!' ('Mr Sludge, "The Medium"', 1). And
through Pound – 'Damn it all! all this our South stinks peace./You
whoreson dog, Papiols, come! Let's to music!' ('Sestina: Altaforte') –
this manner entered much of modern poetry. This is not to say that
most poems begin with startling exclamations, but that the pervading
tone is that of a man talking with the accents he would use in
ordinary conversation.

It is just this sense of unpremeditated speech that modern poets,
looking back at their Victorian predecessors, did not find – except in
Browning. And even Browning presents a contradiction in that he
sometimes chose to employ the dominant poetic voice of the day, a
voice emphasising the speaker as 'Poet' rather than man. In the first
poem Browning published, he claimed to have 'nought in common'
with Shelley's spirit while at the same time employing Shelleyan
diction and imagery to a very large extent. It has been generally
recognised that Shelley's *Alastor* was in fact the model for Browning's *Pauline*.

At first glance, it might appear that Browning's style changed
abruptly beginning with his *Dramatic Lyrics* in 1842. Here it is, in
such dramatic monologues as 'My Last Duchess', that Browning
takes his characteristically dramatic approach, an approach very
different from that exhibited in the *Pauline* of 1833. However, there
is no clear-cut development of Browning's style, no obvious progression from Shelleyan imitator (1833) to apprenticeship to the stage
(1836–46), and ending finally with the dramatic monologues exhibiting common diction and the rhythms of everyday speech (1842–89).
As one complication, the dramatic 'Porphyria's Lover' was written
only a year after *Pauline* was published and eight years before the
publication of *Dramatic Lyrics*. Another stumbling block to any
clear line of development 'from Shelley to Pound' is the large body
of verse written late in his career and exhibiting very pronounced
traditional rhythms:

> I – 'NEXT Poet?' No, my hearties,
>   I nor am nor fain would be!

> Choose your chiefs and pick your parties,
> Not one soul revolt to me!
>
> ('At the "Mermaid"', 1)

While Browning, of course, did develop in his treatment of the
dramatic monologue, there was throughout his career the continual
use of two primary styles of writing: what might be termed the
'conventional', in which Browning's poetry often exhibits the
characteristics of other nineteenth-century poetry; and the dramatic,
in which the techniques peculiarly his own are more easily seen.
These two styles were used from the beginning to the end of
Browning's career.

The importance of Browning's diction in the evolution of modern
poetry from its Victorian forebears has usually been noticed only in
connection with the development of the dramatic monologue. The
diction of ordinary speech is of course an important characteristic of
the dramatic monologue, but most attention has been focused on
other aspects: for example, the difference between what the speaker
says about himself and what is revealed in the course of the poem,
the dramatic setting, and the use of an implied audience within the
framework of the poem. However when attention is focused on these
characteristics, then Tennyson certainly must be acknowledged as an
important influence in the evolution of the dramatic monologue
form. His 'St. Simeon Stylites' was written in 1833, several years
before Browning's first dramatic monologues appeared. Yet when this
dramatic monologue is set next to a Browning dramatic monologue,
an important difference immediately becomes obvious:

> O my sons, my sons,
> I, Simeon of the pillar, by surname
> Stylites, among men; I, Simeon,
> The watcher on the column till the end;
> I, Simeon, whose brain the sunshine bakes;
> I, whose bald brows in silent hours become
> Unnaturally hoar with rime, do now
> From my high nest of penance here proclaim
> That Pontius and Iscariot by my side
> Showed like fair seraphs. ('St. Simeon Stylites', 157–66)

> Well, well, there's my life, in short,
> And so the thing has gone on ever since.

> I'm grown a man no doubt, I've broken bounds:
> You should not take a fellow eight years old
> And make him swear to never kiss the girls.
>
> (*Fra Lippo Lippi*, 221–5)

'St. Simeon Stylites' exhibits a dramatic situation, a narrator, an implied audience, and other characteristics of the dramatic monologue; but its syntax and rhythm is that of poetically heightened speech. The repeated pattern of 'I, Simeon of the pillar', 'I, Simeon,/ The watcher on the column', 'I, Simeon, whose brain the sunshine bakes' forms a sort of chant which, it might be argued, is an accurate rendering of the inflation of self which the saint is experiencing; but which, on the other hand, exhibits the careful construction and rhetorical devices of poetic speech 'at the extreme limit from prose'.

The difference in the two approaches – Tennyson's emphasising the rhythms of poetry, Browning's the rhythms of common speech – was noticed by W. M. Rossetti as he listened to the two poets reading 'dramatic poems':

> [Tennyson's] deep grand voice, with slightly chaunting
> intonation, was a noble vehicle for the perusal of mighty verse. On
> it rolled, sonorous and emotional.

> After Tennyson and *Maud* came Browning and *Fra Lippo Lippi* –
> read with as much of sprightly variation as there was in Tennyson
> of sustained continuity.[12]

When Hopkins said that Browning had 'the air and spirit of a man bouncing up from the table with his mouth full of bread and cheese and saying that he meant to stand no blasted nonsense',[13] he was reacting to the almost aggressively dramatic quality of much of Browning's verse. This quality is often apparent not only when Browning's characters speak, but also when Browning himself speaks directly to the reader. In *The Ring and the Book*, for example, Browning says:

> Well, British Public, ye who like me not,
> (God love you!) and will have your proper laugh
> At the dark question, laugh it! I laugh first. (Book I, 410–12)

The speech of everyday conversation is a speech of contractions, pauses for thoughts and colloquial expressions such as 'no doubt' and 'at any rate'. A man speaking without premeditation often uses an expression such as 'well . . . ' – a word used not for its meaning, but as a sound to fill a silence while the mind organises its as yet shapeless thought. This groping for words is a major characteristic of the spoken language in contrast to the written. But Browning exploited these pauses, giving to his poetry the tone of the speaking voice rather than that of the singing or poetic voice:

> She should never have looked at me
> If she meant I should not love her!
> There are plenty . . . men, you call such,
> I suppose . . . she may discover
> All her soul to, if she pleases,
> And yet leave much as she found them . . .
>
> ('Christina', 1)

Unlike the spoken word, the written word exhibits only its final form. But when a man speaks, his corrections and revisions stand along with his original utterance.

> And gained a grave, or death without a grave.
> I was at Rhodes – the isle, not Rhodes the town . . .
>
> (Balaustion's Adventure, 10–11)

Browning clarifies which Rhodes he is talking about here not by 'rewriting' the line so that the intention is perfectly clear, but by adding an afterthought. The speaker is thus made to correct herself as she would in ordinary conversation.

'Rhodes – the isle, not Rhodes the town' is a fairly straightforward example of a characteristic which pervades much of Browning's poetry. What Browning presents is not the completed thought in its final version, but the working out of the thought in the speaker's mind. Bishop Blougram's analogy of the ship's cabin is worked out in detail only in the process of his conversation with Gigadibs. Don Juan in Fifine creates his argument partly out of thoughts suggested by his surroundings:

> How quickly night comes! Lo, already 't is the land
> Turns sea-like; overcrept by gray, the plains expand,
> Assume significance; while ocean dwindles, shrinks
> Into a prettier bound: its plash and plaint, methinks,
> Six steps away, how both retire, as if their part
> Were played, another force were free to prove her art,

> Protagonist in turn! Are you unterrified?
> All false, all fleeting too! And nowhere things abide,
> And everywhere we strain that things should stay, – the one
> Truth, that ourselves are true! (LXXXIV)

The effect is one of immediacy. What the speaker says, he seems to have just thought. Browning emphasises this sense of the immediate by using punctuation as a sort of stage direction, giving the reader not only words, but also the manner in which the words are spoken. For example, the dash is used quite often for purposes of dynamic expression, like the rests and crescendo notations in a musical score:

> What is gone
> 'Except Rome's aëry magnificence,
> 'That last step you'd take first? – an evidence
> 'You were God: be man now! Let those glances fall!
> 'The basis, the beginning step of all,
> 'Which proves you just a man – is that gone too?'
> (*Sordello*, V, 94–9)

> OTTIMA.   – Me!
> Me! no, no, Sebald, not yourself – kill me!
> Mine is the whole crime. Do but kill me – then
> Yourself – then – presently – first hear me speak!
> I always meant to kill myself – wait, you!
> (*Pippa Passes*, I, 269–73)

Often within the space of only a few lines Browning uses a variety of punctuation marks to produce distinctive dramatic effects. In the following, the colon is used as a dramatic pause, the dash as the announcement of an interruption, and the parenthesis as an indication that action accompanies the speaker's words:

> Listen: my plan will please you not, 't is like,
> But you are little versed in the world's ways.
> This is my plan – (first drinking its good luck) –
> I will accept all helps . . . (*Paracelsus*, IV, 232–5)

To further intensify the dramatic effects of his poetry, Browning uses sound effects. For example, the choking of Mr Sludge is recorded in dramatic pauses and words resembling sounds:

> Go tell, then! Who the devil cares
> What such a rowdy chooses to . . .

Aie – aie – aie!
Please, sir! your thumbs are through my windpipe, sir!
Oh – oh! (15–18)

'Soliloquy of the Spanish Cloister' begins with an expression of sheer
animus: 'GR-R-R – there go, my heart's abhorrence!' And later in the
same poem, Browning shows the monk snickering under his breath:
'(He-he! There his lily snaps!)', III.

What makes Browning's use of implied stage directions so distinctive is not only the number of varied devices he uses, but also the
frequency with which he uses them:

It is a lie – their Priests, their Pope,
Their Saints, their . . . all they fear or hope
Are lies, and lies – there! through my door
And ceiling, there! and walls and floor,
There, lies, they lie – shall still be hurled
Till spite of them I reach the world!

('The Confessional', I)

In these lines, the dramatic pauses are used so often that the poetic
metre underlying the lines is not immediately evident. It is not until
the last line that the metre becomes apparent to the ear, conveying
a sense of completion.

The tendency of modern poetic metres to be obscured – or made
more subtle – is a direct result of the emphasis on common diction
and the rhythm of conversational speech. The speaking voice does
not flow smoothly, but halts, pauses, turns around in its tracks,
interjects thoughts in the midst of other thoughts:

Your knees
are a southern breeze – or
a gust of snow. Agh! what
sort of man was Fragonard?
– as if that answered
anything. Ah, yes – below
the knees, since the tune
drops that way, it is
one of those white summer days,
the tall grass of your ankles
flickers upon the shore –
Which shore? –

the sand clings to my lips –
Which shore?
Agh, petals maybe. How
should I know?
Which shore? Which shore?
I said petals from an appletree.
        (W. C. Williams, 'Portrait of a Lady')

Thus, with the human voice so emphasised, not only are diction and rhythm affected, but also the metrical base of poetic form. Until the twentieth century, the length of the line was usually dictated by a given number of feet. There were of course variations from line to line, but the underlying pattern was apparent. Some modern poets, however, felt that the rhythms of common speech could not always be cut to fit a line based on a pattern of feet. William Carlos Williams said:

A minimum of present new knowledge seems to be this: there can no longer be serious work in poetry written in 'poetic' diction. It is a contortion of speech to conform to a rigidity of line. It is in the newness of a live speech that the new line exists undiscovered.[14]

It seems to be that the 'foot' being at the bottom of all prosody, the time has come when that must be recognized to have changed in nature. And it must be seen to have changed in its rhythmical powers of inclusion. It cannot be used any longer in its old-time rigidities. Speech for poetry is nothing but time – I mean time in the musical sense. That is where the real battle has been going on.[15]

As early as 1913, Pound had advised poets not to 'chop your stuff into separate *iambs*. Don't makes each line stop dead at the end, and then begin every next line with a heave.'[16] Essentially what Pound was asking for was a closer approximation to the rhythm of the speaking voice. Rather than pausing when the required number of stresses had been reached, modern poets were to pause when the speaking voice would pause.

Many poets began to carry this emphasis on the rhythm of the speaking voice even further by regarding the line as a unit indicating duration in time – a time which might include pauses, and one which could not be measuered by the metronome of stresses and feet. 'I think I read my poetry more by length than by stress', said D. H. Lawrence, ' – as a matter of movements in space than footsteps

hitting the earth.'[17] Marianne Moore, also, began to use the line from
a highly individual point of view:

> A Roman had an
> artist, a freedman,
>   contrive a cone – pine cone
>   or fir-cone – with holes for a fountain. Placed on
>   the Prison of St. Angelo, this cone
>   of the Pompeys which is known
>
> now as the Popes', passed
> for art. ('The Jerboa')

Here the prose movement of the rhythm is set within a very rigid,
although highly individual line arrangement. Corresponding lines of
succeeding stanzas have exactly the same number of syllables, regardless of the number of stresses in the line. This gives the poem a
distinctively formal look. Yet, if printed in paragraph form, the
underlying rhythm becomes apparent – a rhythm based on the
speaking voice, delicately heightened by repetition of particular
words and of dactyllic feet:

> A Roman had an artist, a freedman, contrive a cone – pine-cone or
> fir-cone – with holes for a fountain. Placed on the Prison of St.
> Angelo, this cone of the Pompeys which is known now as the
> Popes', passed for art.

This is a very different effect from that obtained when lines from a
poem such as Tennyson's *In Memoriam* are printed in paragraph
form:

> Strong Son of God, immortal Love, Whom we, that have not seen
> thy face, by faith, and faith alone, embrace, believing where we
> cannot prove; Thine are these orbs of light and shade; Thou madest
> Life in man and brute; Thou madest Death; and lo, thy foot is on
> the skull which thou hast made. (Prologue, 1–8)

Eliot, in searching for a method of versification for his play *The
Family Reunion*, was trying to find

> a rhythm close to contemporary speech, in which the stresses could
> be made to come wherever we should naturally put them, in
> uttering the particular phrase on the particular occasion. What I
> worked out is substantially what I have continued to employ: a

line of varying length and varying number of syllables, with a
caesura and three stresses.[18]

Eliot's choice of versification was partly a response to what he
considered a failure of nineteenth-century poets. When Victorian
poets wrote for the theatre, they largely used a strict blank verse
which, as Eliot saw it:

> ... after extensive use for nondramatic poetry, had lost the
> flexibility which blank verse must have if it is to give the effect of
> conversation. The rhythm of regular blank verse had become too
> remote from the movement of modern speech.[19]

At the same time, Eliot thought that the most interesting non-
dramatic verse had been written either by taking a form like iambic
pentameter and 'constantly withdrawing from it', or by 'taking no
form at all, and constantly approximating to a very simple one'.[20]
With this principle in mind, Browning's poetry can be seen as a step
from the strict use of the iambic pentameter found in much nineteenth-century verse, and a step toward the modern habit of approximating the form, rather than allowing oneself to be confined within
it. Moreover, in Browning – and this distinction becomes significant
when Tennyson's masterly variations within traditional forms are
taken into consideration – the principle of deviation from the underlying form is based on the characteristics of the speaking voice. When
Fra Lippo Lippi says: 'Remember and tell me, the day you're hanged,/
How you affected such a gullet's-gripe!' (19–20), the iambic is modified 'to give the effect of conversation'.

In speaking of Browning as using common diction and as largely
basing his principle of versification on the pattern of the speaking
voice, one apparent contradictory characteristic must be pointed out
– Browning's frequent employment of words so unusual that they
belong neither to common diction nor to any other aspect of everyday
speech:

> Didst ever touch such ampollosity
> As the monk's own bubble, let alone its spite?
>
> (*The Ring and the Book*, XII, 647–8)

In *Paracelsus* alone, the reader finds: 'riveled' (I, 481), 'arch-geneth-
liac' (II, 25), 'fire-labarum' (II, 265), 'sudary' (III, 437), 'rear-mice'
(III, 391), 'tetter' (IV, 630), 'morphew' (IV, 630), 'furfair' (IV, 630),
'fane' (V, 299), 'bale' (V, 388), 'phares' (V, 386) and 'dorrs' (V, 673).

This attraction to uncommon words is not primarily because these words suggest meanings which no simpler words could convey. Browning could have substituted 'bats' for 'rear-mice' or 'temple' for the lesser-known 'fane'. Rather, the fascination with these words is a sensuous fascination, a delight in the physical qualities of the words almost as if they were objects which could be touched and tasted. This sensuous appreciation of words is in the same spirit as the appreciation of food which Browning's Englishman displays:

> Meantime, see the grape bunch they've brought you:
>   The rain-water slips
> O'er the heavy blue bloom on each globe
>   Which the wasp to your lips
> Still follows with fretful persistence:
>   Nay, taste, while awake,
> This half of a curd-white smooth cheese-ball
>   That peels, flake by flake,
> Like an onion, each smoother and whiter;
>   Next, sip this weak wine
> From the thin green flask, with its stopper,
>   A leaf of the vine;
> And end with the prickly-pear's red flesh
>   That leaves thro' its juice
> The stony black seeds on your pearl-teeth.
>
>   ('The Englishman in Italy', 101–15)

This delight in the individual characteristics of physical objects extends to a delight in the unique characteristics of a particular word. As Roma King has pointed out, in Fra Lippo Lippi there are 'forty words that occur nowhere else in Browning's poetry'.[21] From this point of view, a synonym is impossible as a substitution – the meaning might remain intact, but the physical properties of the individual word would be lost. W. M. Rossetti, remembering an incident in which Browning advised him to visit a certain local museum, said, 'I can still hear the gusto with which he pronounced the name of "Beccafumi."'[22]

A love of words, and even a love of words for the sake of their physical properties, is probably characteristic of most poets. What makes Browning's fascination with words significant is firstly, the intensity with which he displayed his fascination, and secondly, the concentration on words which were not necessarily beautiful. Behind many of the complaints concerning Browning's harshness was the willingness on his part to ignore regularity of rhythm if in so doing a particular word received the attention he desired for it.

Modern poets have followed Browning in regarding the word itself as worthy of emphasis rather than treating the word primarily as a servant of meaning or beauty. William Carlos Williams insisted, 'It's the words, the words we need to get back to, words washed clean...'[23] This emphatic highlighting of the word itself is perhaps reflected in its most extreme form in the poetry of Gertrude Stein:

> He had.
> She had.
> Had she.
> He had nearly very nearly as much.
> She had very nearly as much as had had.
> Had she.
> She had.
> Loose loosen, Loose losten to losten, to lose.
> Many.
> If a little if as little if as little as that.
> If as little as that, if it is as little as
> that that is if it is very nearly all of it, her dear
> her dear does not mention a ball at all. ('New')

A nineteenth-century reader – and many twentieth-century readers as well – might have approached 'New' with the question: 'But what does it mean?' Stein might have responded to this question with the words: 'My writing is clear as mud, but mud settles and clear streams run on and disappear...'[24]

To compare writing with mud and to point out that mud settles is to emphasise the nature of words as objects in themselves. Through repetition, Gertrude Stein calls attention to the physical nature of the word and examines how the word acts in different contexts. The reader is not allowed to 'look through' the word to the meaning, but must regard the word as the centre of attention in its own right. William Carlos Williams compared Gertrude Stein's emphasis on individual words with the point of view of certain modern painters who directed the viewer to see the paint itself as the subject of the painting:

> I for one believe that it was Gertrude Stein, for her formal
> insistence on words in their literal, structural quality of being

words, who had strongly influenced us. . . . It all went with the
newer appreciation, the matter of paint upon canvas as being of
more importance than the literal appearance of the image
depicted.[25]

This same interest in all the different facets of a word is exhibited
by Browning in, for example, his fondness for creating compound
words. When two words are welded together in this way, a new
entity or word is created through the process of the mutual illumina-
tion:

> What then? does that prevent each dunghill, we may pass
> Daily, from boasting too its bit of looking-glass,
> Its sherd which, sun-smit, shines, shoots arrowy fire beyond
> That satin-muffled mope, your sulky diamond? (*Fifine*, XXX)

When Browning refers to a diamond as a 'satin-muffled mope', the
particularity of the epithet seems to suggest the later Hopkins who
looked for that '"individually-distinctive" form (made up of various
sense-data) which constitutes the rich and revealing "oneness" of
the natural object':[26]

> shéer plód makes plough down sillion
> Shine, and blue-bleak embers, ah my dear,
> Fall, gall themselves, and gash gold-vermilion.
>
> ('The Windhover')

With both Hopkins and Browning, the compound words are not
inevitable, in the sense that the compound words of Milton and
Keats are often inevitable (and therefore 'right'). Rather, there is a
surprising quality about the new word – it makes itself felt as
distinctive.

Because of Browning's emphasis on the word as thing, it is not
surprising that he should refer to the poet's 'word-mesh' ('Charles
Avison', VIII), or that he should use the image of welding to describe
the poetic activity (*Sordello*, II 575). With both Browning and many
modern poets, there is a sense of play involved in this handling of
word-objects. The poet singles out words, turns them over in his
hands, and remarks on them, or points them out to the reader –
whether with delicate but self-conscious understatement, as in
Auden, or with the gusto exhibited in Browning's thumping rhymes:

> For poems, dolphin-graceful as carts from Sweden,
> our thank-you should be a right

good salvo of barks: it's much too muffled to say
'how well and with what unfreckled integrity
it has all been done.' ('A Mosaic for Marianne Moore')

He harangued on the faults of the Bailiwick:
'Red soon were our State-candle's paly wick,
If wealth would become but interfluous,
Fill voids up with just the superfluous;
If ignorance gave way to knowledge
– Not pedantry picked up at college
From Doctors, Professors *et cœtera* –
(*They* say: '*kai ta loipa*' – like better a
Long Greek string of *kappas, taus, lambdas*,
Tacked on to the tail of each damned ass) –
No knowledge we want of this quality,
But knowledge indeed – practicality
Through insight's fine universality!
If you shout '*Bailiffs, out on ye all! Fie,*
Thou Chief of our forces, Amalfi,
Who shieldest the rogue and the clotpoll!'
If you pounce on and poke out, with what pole
I leave ye to fancy, our Siena's
Beast-litter of sloths and hyenas –'
(Whoever to scan this is ill able
Forgets the town's name's a dissyllable) . . .

(*Pacchiarotto*, xv)

This sense of playfulness, of the exploration of the word for its own sake, persists even in the context of traditionally exalted subject-matter. Many twentieth-century poets have rejected the lofty platform of the Romantic poets. With common diction and conversational rhythms, modern poets speak to the readers as men to men, rather than as teachers or prophets to an audience in need of enlightenment. As Auden pointed out: 'The characteristic style of "Modern" poetry is an intimate tone of voice, the speech of one person addressing one person, not a large audience; whenever a modern poet raises his voice he sounds phoney.' ('The Poet and the City').[27] Nineteenth-century poets, however, even if mourning the death of an intimate friend, retained the diction appropriate to a *public* speaker. In grieving for the loss of Hallam, Tennyson expressed hopelessness, despair and all the weakness of a suffering human being – but always with the dignity and reserve inherent in an elevated diction:

> Be near me when my light is low,
>> When the blood creeps, and the nerves prick
>> And tingle; and the heart is sick,
>> And all the wheels of Being slow. (*In Memoriam*, L)

In contrast, when a modern poet such as Berryman writes a series of poems expressing grief for the death of a friend, the tone is at the opposite pole from that of the public speaker:

> This world is gradually becoming a place
> where I do not care to be any more. Can Delmore die?
> I don't suppose
> in all them years a day went ever by
> without a loving thought for him. Welladay. ('149')

For Browning, the tone of preacher or prophet was like a robe to be donned on special occasions. A lofty subject often elicited a tradition-ally elevated tone and diction. For example, Browning ends Book One of *The Ring and the Book* with a section addressed to his wife ('O lyric Love', 1391):

> – Never conclude, but raising hand and head
> Thither where eyes, that cannot reach, yet yearn
> For all hope, all sustainment, all reward,
> Their utmost up and on, – so blessing back
> In those thy realms of help, that heaven thy home,
> Some whiteness which, I judge, thy face makes proud,
> Some wanness where, I think, thy foot may fall!
>> (1410–16)

Immediately after this begins Book Two:

> What, you, Sir, come too? (Just the man I'd meet.)
> Be ruled by me and have a care o' the crowd:
> This way, while fresh folk go and get their gaze:
> I'll tell you like a book and save your shins.
> Fie, what a roaring day we've had! (1–5)

When Browning writes 'O lyric Love' in the accepted poetic style, he is using the language as a means of dignifying the subject. In the next section, the tone is conversational, that of one man talking to another.

This strict division between the elevated and the common which Browning sometimes exhibits has been rejected by many modern poets. For one reason, the modern viewpoint seldom accords respect to that which is dressed in traditional robes. For another, the relativism of the twentieth century has made the words common to an elevated tone peculiarly suspect. Abstract nouns such as 'truth' or 'honour' are seldom seen except in a context which undercuts them. Pound had advised his followers to 'Go in fear of abstractions', saying that 'the natural object is always the *adequate* symbol'.[28] Yet Pound himself did use abstractions and 'poetic words', but in such a way that they were deflated by the diction of conversational speech:[29]

> the case presents
> No adjunct to the Muses' diadem.
> ('E. P. Ode Pour L'Election de son Sepulchre', 1)

The juxtaposition of the elevated and the mundane is also seen in Eliot:

> Time for you and time for me,
> And time yet for a hundred indecisions,
> And for a hundred visions and revisions,
> Before the taking of a toast and tea.
> ('The Love Song of J. Alfred Prufrock')

In *The Waste Land* this juxtaposition is present in the rhythm as well as in the diction:

> I remember
> Those are pearls that were his eyes.
> 'Are you alive, or not? Is there nothing in your head?' But
> O O O O that Shakespeherian Rag –
> It's so elegant
> So intelligent . . . (II, 124–30)

Thus Eliot uses the juxtaposition of formal poetic rhythms with rhythms of ordinary speech and of jazz to great effect, emphasising the debasement of a civilisation by calling to mind earlier, less cynical cultures.

Because the traditional rhetoric of poetry is now seldom used in a straightforward way, the conversational language of everyday occasions is made to bear the weight of elevated occasions as well. That a colloquial diction, rhythm and tone can bear this weight is one of the 'discoveries' important to modern poetry.

This dignifying of common speech is seen in, for example, Auden's 'In Memory of W. B. Yeats'. The beginning of the poem exhibits the quiet, conversational tone common to the modern poet:

> He disappeared in the dead of winter:
> The brooks were frozen, the airports almost deserted,
> And snow disfigured the public statues . . .

But in the last section of the poem, the rhythm changes abruptly to that of a formal elegy:

> Earth, receive an honoured guest;
> William Yeats is laid to rest:
> Let the Irish vessel lie
> Emptied of its poetry.

The formality of this diction, rhythm and tone is still not of the traditional order, for it allows within its stately tempo, the bluntness of lines such as 'Time that is . . ./indifferent in a week/To a beautiful physique'.

In one sense, this mixture of formal and informal styles reflects the modern awareness that human speech itself exhibits a paradoxical impropriety: the deepest expressions of sorrow can slide into comic bathos; and the highest moments of serious thought can be brought to earth by trivial interruptions. Thus, the common speech of modern poetry is closely linked with a willingness to reflect every aspect of feeling and experience, and the inexorable way in which the lowest of man's characteristics mingle with the highest of his dreams.

The nineteenth-century roots of this willingness to reflect the mingling of high and low, sacred and profane, lie most firmly in the poetry of Browning. Speaking in his own voice, Browning may put on the ceremonial robes of tradition. But speaking through a fictional character, Browning often reveals the indiscriminate way in which the mind brings together thoughts from different spheres. The Bishop ordering decorations for his tomb is not merely exhibiting Renaissance taste when he asks for Pan and Moses in the same breath:

> The Saviour at his sermon on the mount,
> Saint Praxed in a glory, and one Pan

Ready to twitch the Nymph's last garment off,
And Moses with the tables ...

('The Bishop Orders His Tomb', 59–62)

Browning clearly saw life's comic mixture of sacred and profane, and his tone and diction often mirrored this perception. Years before Eliot and Pound were exploiting the juxtaposition of abstract with concrete, 'visions' with 'toast and tea', Browning was startling his readers with his quick changes from high-sounding phrase to debunking image and back again. In *Pacchiarotto* Browning describes God as a dramatist, men as actors. The lines summing up this analogy exhibit a characteristic use of sacred idea and mundane context:

> *Things rarely go smooth at Rehearsal.*
> *Wait patient the change universal* ... (XXII)

Like modern poets, Browning also subjects abstract words like 'immortal' to a relativistic point of view:

> 'Dust and ashes, dead and done with, Venice spent
>   what Venice earned.
> 'The soul, doubtless, is immortal – where a soul
>   can be discerned.

('A Toccata of Galuppi's', XII)

The word 'immortal' is undercut by the accompanying 'doubtless'. But abstract words are not the only victims of ironic juxtaposition. Browning also observed the transformation undergone by images when brought into an alien context. The world traditionally associated with a kiss is romantic, filled with moonlight, young lovers, and ethereal beauty:

> What Psyche felt, and Love, when their full lips
> First touched; what amorous and fondling nips
> They gave each other's cheeks; with all their sighs,
> And how they kissed each other's tremulous eyes;
> The silver lamp – the ravishment – the wonder –
> The darkness – loneliness – the fearful thunder ...

(Keats, 'I Stood Tiptoe upon a Little Hill', 143–8)

Browning's absurd context, however, jars the kiss from the Romantic world and the elevated language surrounding it to quite another one:

> Twitt'st thou me
> Because I turn away my outraged nose
> Shouldst thou obtrude thereon a shovelful
> Of fertilizing kisses? ('Plot-Culture')

And in *Fifine*, the associations usually called forth by the word 'grace' are hobbled in advance by a decidedly graceless adjective: 'sympathize/With gastroknemian grace' (LX).

This exploration of the way a word changes from context to context, and the willingness to bring the abstract word down to earth, are intimately bound up with, on the one hand, the poem regarded as object and, on the other, the use of everyday experience as subject-matter. 'As to twentieth-century poetry', said Pound,

> I mean it will not try to seem forcible by rhetorical din, and luxurious riot. We will have fewer painted adjectives impeding the shock and stroke of it. At least for myself, I want it so, austere, direct, free from emotional slither.[30]

Modern poets, in using common diction and the rhythms of everyday speech, have largely fulfilled Pound's expectations. The old rhetorical stance of the poet as prophet has given way to the intimate tone of a man in conversation with other men; and the informal language accompanying this approach has been shown to be just as finely tuned and delicate an instrument as the traditional poetic speech. Long before Pound and Eliot called for a revolution in poetic language, Browning had recognised that:

> 't is but brother's speech
> 'We need, speech where an accent's change gives each
> 'The other's soul ... (*Sordello*, v, 635–7)

4

The Dramatic Method

On those rare occasions when Browning discussed the nature of his own poetry, he usually referred to it as being essentially dramatic. 'Robert Browning, you writer of plays' he said of himself nearly a decade after the publication of his last play:

> Well, any how, here the story stays,
> So far at least as I understand;
> And, Robert Browning, you writer of plays,
> Here's a subject made to your hand!
>
> ('A Light Woman', XIV)

Even the titles of his books reveal his preoccupation with the dramatic: *Dramatic Lyrics*, *Dramatic Romances and Lyrics*, *Dramatis Personæ*, *Dramatic Idyls*. It is not surprising, then, that one of the primary approaches to Browning's poetry has been the examination of his dramatic method; and that the poems which have received the most critical attention have been the dramatic monologues.

In addition to Browning's own emphasis on the dramatic nature of his poetry, there is another reason for focusing on the dramatic monologues. Modern poets have so often used the dramatic monologue form that critics, noticing these dramatic characteristics and looking for their sources, have turned to studies of the dramatic monologue in the history of English poetry. Of all the possible nineteenth-century models for twentieth-century dramatic monologues, Browning's poems seem to be the most obviously dramatic.

Yet in spite of critical agreement that Browning is somehow dramatic, there is widespread disagreement as to how much Browning influenced the development of the dramatic monologue form and thus, by implication, much of modern poetry. Critical opinion ranges all the way from the assertion that Browning is in fact the inventor of the dramatic monologue form[1] to the denial that he had anything at all to do with innovations in a form which had existed in all its essential details since A.D. 750. According to a critic holding this latter view, 'Browning took over a ready-made vehicle used by scores of preceding and contemporary poets.'[2]

Much of this critical disagreement is based on what appears to be the central issue in many of these studies: the very definition of the dramatic monologue. A broad definition naturally leads to a wide inclusion of many poems, under the heading 'dramatic monologue'; while a view which presupposes Browning as the inventor of the dramatic monologue is more likely to lead to a definition of the form in stricter terms and with the characteristics of Browning's poems as guidelines. Thus, discussions of Browning's place in the history of the dramatic monologue frequently revolve around attempts to establish a definition of the dramatic monologue in terms of a limited number of certain characteristics.

What makes this attempt such a challenge to so many critics is that characteristics involved in these definitions of the dramatic monologue – for example, 'oral realism' and 'auditor-focus' (Fuson's terms) – are difficult to confine to any one genre. The medium of poetry is words, and words are inextricably linked with speech. Moreover, a poem is not only speech, but *public* speech. Thus a lyric poem, which might by its very nature appear to be the opposite of the dramatic monologue, still may exhibit both 'oral realism' (it is a speech spoken by someone) and 'auditor-focus' (it is a public speech). And a ballad, or other narrative poem, although apparently as counter to the dramatic monologue by its emphasis on the objective facts of a story as the lyric is by its emphasis on narrative subjectivity, might still exhibit dramatic monologue characteristics through the feelings expressed by the narrator. Moreover, narrative poetry, although primarily the reporting of an event, often involves so much direct quotation that what might be called a dramatic element becomes very evident:

> 'Hearken! hearken!' sayd the Sheriffe,
>   'I heare now tydings good,
> For yonder I heare Sir Guy's horne blowe,
>   And he hath slaine Robin Hood.
>
> 'Yonder I heare Sir Guy's horne blowe,
>   Itt blowes soe well in tyde,
> And yonder comes that wight yeman,
>   Cladd in his capull-hyde.
>
> 'Come hyther, come hyther, thou good Sir Guy,
>   Aske what thou wilt of mee.' –

'O I will none of thy gold,' sayd Robin,
    'Nor I will none of thy fee' . . .
        ('Robin Hood and Guy of Gisborne',[3] XLVIII–L)

As Robert Frost has pointed out, every poem is dramatic in the sense that someone is felt to be speaking it.[4] And John Crowe Ransom has added to this linking of all poetry with the dramatic by talking of poetry as being derivative of drama, historically and logically:

> If a poem is not a drama proper, it may be said to be a dramatic monologue. . . . and Browning only literalized and made readier for the platform of the concert hall the thing that had always been the poem's lawful form. ('The Tense of Poetry')[5]

Perhaps, then, in approaching Browning's dramatic method and its relation to modern poetry, it would be more profitable not to argue about Browning's place in the history of the dramatic monologue, but to examine how he used particular dramatic techniques and how the use of these techniques implied a greater freedom in poetic form, a freedom that modern poets have accepted and expanded.

For Browning, dramatic poetry was always connected with what he regarded as an objective approach to the facts. This identification of the objective poet with the dramatic poet is made explicit in his 1852 *Essay on Shelley*. The objective poet, as Browning defines him, represents things external and reproduces them with reference to the common eye. In this sense, the objective poet is a 'fashioner'. He deals with the doings of man, 'the result of which dealing, in its pure form . . . is what we call dramatic poetry' (p. 66).

The subjective poet, in contrast, struggles to embody what God sees, not what man sees. To do this, he 'digs where he stands, – preferring to seek [the primal elements of humanity] in his own soul as the nearest reflex of that absolute Mind' (p. 65). This type of poet, Shelley being an example, Browning called the 'seer' (p. 66).

Using these two as basic types, Browning offered a view of his own position in the history of English poetry, a view in which he saw himself neither as one of many poets writing in an essentially static form, nor as a radical innovator in the sense of inventing a completely revolutionary dramatic approach.

Browning saw the history of poetry not so much as an alternation of styles, but as an alternation of these two basic approaches to

subject-matter: the subjective, and the objective. When the subjective
had gained ascendancy, then the objective would begin to rise, until
it in turn would be taken over by the subjective. However, this
alternation was not within a static context, for each swing of the
pendulum enabled the poet to climb 'one more degree ... in that
mighty ladder' (p. 68). Browning explained the necessity for this
alternation by saying that, for example, objective poetry would begin
to give way to subjective:

> ... when the general eye has, so to speak, absorbed its fill of the
> phenomena around it, whether spiritual or material, and desires
> rather to learn the exacter significance of what it possesses, than to
> receive any augmentation of what is possessed.
>
> (*Essay on Shelley*, p. 68)

At this point the subjective poet will arise, and a new type of poetry
will emerge as a response to the dominance of the old. However, this
alternation between subjective and objective is not a clear-cut one:
after a major poet has explored the subjective approach, there is a
time during which:

> A tribe of successors ... working more or less in the same spirit,
> dwell on his discoveries and reinforce his doctrine; till, at unawares,
> the world is found to be subsisting wholly on the shadow of a
> reality, on sentiments diluted from passions, on the tradition of a
> fact, the convention of a moral, the straw of last year's harvest.
> Then is the imperative call for the appearance of another sort of
> poet, who shall at once replace this intellectual rumination of food
> swallowed long ago, by a supply of the fresh and living swathe;
> getting at new substance by breaking up the assumed wholes into
> parts of independent and unclassed value, careless of the unknown
> laws for recombining them (it will be the business of yet another
> poet to suggest those hereafter), prodigal of objects for men's outer
> and not inner sight, shaping for their uses a new and different
> creation from the last, which it displaces by the right of life over
> death ... (*Essay on Shelley*, p. 68)

Clearly, Browning saw himself as answering this 'imperative call
for ... another sort of poet'. Even in his most Shelleyan poem,
Pauline, he insists on setting himself in opposition to the spirit of
Shelley:

'For I have nought in common with him, shapes
'Which followed him avoid me, and foul forms
'Seek me, which ne'er could fasten on his mind ...'

(212–14)

Yet as an objective or dramatic poet, Browning also saw himself in opposition to the methods used by most other dramatic poets. In his 1835 preface to *Paracelsus*, Browning described his approach as:

an attempt, probably more novel than happy, to reverse the method usually adopted by writers whose aim it is to set forth any phenomenon of the mind or the passions, by the operation of persons and events; and that, instead of having recourse to an external machinery of incidents to create and evolve the crisis I desire to produce, I have ventured to display somewhat minutely the mood itself in its rise and progress, and have suffered the agency by which it is influenced and determined, to be generally discernible in its effects alone, and subordinate throughout, if not altogether excluded: and this for a reason. I have endeavoured to write a poem, not a drama; the canons of the drama are well known, and I cannot but think that, inasmuch as they have immediate regard to stage representation, the peculiar advantages they hold out are really such only so long as the purpose for which they were at first instituted is kept in view. I do not very well understand what is called a Dramatic Poem, wherein all those restrictions only submitted to on account of compensating good in the original scheme are scrupulously retained, as though for some special fitness in themselves – and all new facilities placed at an author's disposal by the vehicle he selects, as pertinaciously rejected. It is certain, however, that a work like mine depends more immediately on the intelligence and sympathy of the reader for its success ...

Within this introduction, Browning makes three essential observations about his own dramatic method; and each of these points has direct relevance to the approach taken by many modern poets. First, in attempting to display a 'mood', Browning is deliberately focusing on what is non-dramatic; if a central aspect of drama is action, then an emphasis on mood without recourse to an 'external machinery of incidents' within the context of a dramatic poem is indeed a reversal of the usual method. Secondly, Browning has a functional attitude towards dramatic conventions; he does not allow these conventions to restrict him, but uses only those which further his purpose. And thirdly, Browning realises that a dramatic poem which exhibits mood rather than action is particularly dependent upon the sympathetic participation of the reader for its success.

All of these aspects of Browning's dramatic poetry can be summarised in his insistence that the dramatic poem is primarily a *poem* rather than a drama. Although this assertion may seem self-evident, it contains an important distinction. What modern poets might have learned from Browning was not so much to do with dramatic devices. These they could have learned directly from drama, as indeed some of them did; or they could have learned them from those earlier writers of dramatic monologues whom critics such as Benjamin Fuson cite as evidence that Browning added nothing essentially new to the dramatic monologue form.[6] The important aspect of Browning's dramatic technique is not in its use of any particular dramatic device, but in its suggestion that dramatic and lyric elements can be synthesised, giving the poet a greater freedom of expression than was possible before in either poetic drama (a drama written to be read rather than performed), or dramatic poetry.

Looked at from this point of view, Browning's dramatic method is seen to be important in precisely those ways in which it is poetic rather than dramatic. Eliot, who was one of the first to develop this synthesis of lyric and dramatic, recognised that although Browning certainly could be considered a dramatic poet, he could not be regarded as a master of the drama. 'And certainly, if any poetry, not of the stage, deserves to be characterised as "dramatic," it is Browning's', said Eliot, observing at the same time that 'It would seem without further examination, from Browning's mastery of the dramatic monologue, and his very moderate achievement in the drama, that the two forms must be essentially different.'[7]

One reason for Browning's 'very moderate achievement in the drama' is that the plays written for the stage – *Strafford* and *The Return of the Druses*, for example – are not particularly suited for staging. The 'action' of *Strafford* consists, for the most part, of long and rather abstract statements of political belief. And in *The Return of the Druses*, the conflict within the soul of Djabal is obscured, rather than dramatically heightened, by the melodramatic nature of the action.

It seems paradoxical, then, that while Browning's plays appear to

be static, his poems seem to be dramatic. Yet this apparent contradiction is clarified when we consider that while Browning was not
particularly interested in the external events – those actions which
comprise the raw material for drama – neither was he primarily
interested in the internal as it is revealed through the products of
man's mind, in the form of ideas. In other words, his interest was
not focused on the dramatic actions of the external world or the
static products of the internal world, but on the dramatic actions of
the internal world. As he said of *Sordello*, 'my stress lay on the
incidents in the development of a soul: little else is worth study'
(1863 dedication to Milsand).

By 1846 Browning had begun to realise that his real interests lay
not in writing plays but in writing 'drama' of an entirely different
nature. His last play, *Luria*, he called 'a pure exercise of *cleverness*'
and a 'reproduction of what was conceived by another faculty'.[8]
And in the same year, soon after finishing *Luria*, he told Elizabeth
Barrett that on the occasion of the Literary Fund dinner he would
'try and speak for about five minutes on the advantages of the Press
over the Stage as a medium of communication of the Drama . . .'[9]

As Browning saw it, the truth of the soul was not revealed but
rather concealed by the outward actions which drama presented. In
a remarkable section in *Paracelsus*, Browning presented what might
be taken as his own way of getting through the 'baffling and per-
verting carnal mesh' to the truth:

> But, friends,
> Truth is within ourselves; it takes no rise
> From outward things, whate'er you may believe.
> There is an inmost centre in us all,
> Where truth abides in fulness; and around,
> Wall upon wall, the gross flesh hems it in,
> This perfect, clear perception – which is truth.
> A baffling and perverting carnal mesh
> Binds it, and makes all error; and to KNOW
> Rather consists in opening out a way
> Whence the imprisoned splendour may escape,
> Than in effecting entry for a light
> Supposed to be without. (I, 725–37)

Thus Browning is more interested in working from the inside out –

'opening out a way' – than from outside in, the approach taken by drama.

At first glimpse, this casting 'external things away' would seem to contradict Browning's own definition of the objective poet as 'one whose endeavour has been to reproduce things external'. But Browning included under this heading both he who reproduces 'phenomena of the scenic universe', and he who reproduces 'the manifested action of the human heart and brain' (*Essay on Shelley*, p. 63). For Browning, focus on internal action not only allows the poet access to truth (to be found 'within'), but also enables him to present this truth with the objectivity of the dramatist.

The dramatist of the 'inmost life' substitutes for the dramatic stage the inner stage of the mind. On this stage, the customary activity is thought, not external action. Of course Browning does utilise an 'external stage' in that the speaker of a dramatic monologue often reveals the details of his physical setting or discusses his own actions in a narrative form. Even so, external details often serve as a sort of image of the internal action. When Bishop Blougram reveals the setting of his monologue to be his home during a time immediately after dinner, he is also revealing his own characteristic approach to truth – a sort of after-dinner playfulness, secondary to the material demands of the body, and the opposite of an intense, impassioned search which disregards the consequences:

> ... don't you know,
> I promised, if you'd watch a dinner out,
> We'd see truth dawn together? – truth that peeps
> Over the glasses' edge when dinner's done,
> And body gets its sop and holds it noise
> And leaves soul free a little. (15–20)

At the end of the dramatic monologue, we have a fairly good idea of how Blougram's mind works. From this, we might be tempted to infer what action he is likely to take when his physical comfort is at stake – that is, if we can believe what Blougram says about himself. Browning's epilogue seems to suggest that perhaps we cannot:

> For Blougram, he believed, say, half he spoke.
> The other portion, as he shaped it thus
> For argumentatory purposes,
> He felt his foe was foolish to dispute. (980–3)

Thus, to know a character's thought is not necessarily to know his actions. Yet within the traditional drama, action has always been of primary importance in the creation of a fictional character. And character has always been at the heart of the drama. As Henry James said, 'What is character but the determination of incident? What is incident but the illustration of character?'[10] And Eliot went even further, saying that because character is created and made real only in an action, the 'dramatic monologue cannot create a character'.[11] From this point of view, the dramatic monologue is essentially non-dramatic in its treatment of character. Arthur Symons expressed this difference when he said, 'Shakspere makes his characters live; Browning makes his characters think.'[12]

Another aspect of the non-dramatic nature of the dramatic is that the monologue itself seems to make little difference to the life of the character. As Robert Langbaum has pointed out, the speaker in a dramatic monologue does not even change his mind. The difficulty which prompts the speaking of the monologue is usually resolved before the monologue begins, or at least long before it ends. Fra Lippo Lippi is released as soon as he mentions the friend with whom he is lodging:

> – he's a certain ... how d'ye call?
> Master – a ... Cosimo of the Medici,
> I' the house that caps the corner. (16–18)

Moreover, as Langbaum says, the dramatic monologue does not present 'the Aristotelian complete action but habitual action', and therefore has no necessary beginning or end.[13] Using these characteristics, Langbaum makes an important distinction between the dramatic monologue and its counterpart in the drama, the soliloquy. The soliloquy is an attempt by an observer to understand himself so that the audience can understand him or some action which he is about to do. The dramatic monologue character, however, is not interested in finding the truth or in 'self-analysis and internal debate', but in trying to impress a certain point of view on the outside world:

> The meaning of the soliloquy is equivalent to what the soliloquist reveals and understands, the poetic statement being as much as he has been able to rationalize, to see in terms of the general perspective. But the meaning of the dramatic monologue is in disequilibrium with what the speaker reveals and understands. We understand the speaker's point of view not through his description

of it but indirectly, through seeing what he sees while judging the limitations and distortions of what he sees. The result is that we understand, if not more, at least something other than the speaker understands . . .[14]

Although both Browning and the Romantics wrote what Langbaum terms 'the poetry of experience', there is an important distinction between Browning's dramatic monologues and the dramatic poems of some of his Romantic predecessors. In Byron's *Manfred*, for example, the main character is shown suffering because he cannot escape the knowledge of who he is and what he has done:

> I have known
> The fulness of humiliation – for
> I sunk before my vain despair, and knelt
> To my own desolation. (II, iv, 39–42)

Yet Manfred is no ordinary mortal, and, as the First Destiny informs the reader: 'His sufferings/Have been of an immortal nature' (53–4). Thus they are to be taken at face value. The reader is not to question what Manfred reveals in his speeches.

Similarly, Tennyson's *Maud: A Monodrama* presents a reflection of a state of mind in which there is little to suggest a different point of view. When the speaker describes the 'hollow behind the little wood' as 'dreadful', it is this way that the reader is directed to see it as well:

> I hate the dreadful hollow behind the little wood,
> Its lips in the field above are dabbled with blood-red heath,
> The red-ribbed ledges drip with a silent horror of blood,
> And Echo there, whatever is asked her, answers 'Death.'
>
> (I–I, 1–4)

In contrast, when Browning's Duke describes his last Duchess, the reader eventually sees the Duchess from a point of view entirely different from that of the Duke. How the reader comes to this double view is at the very heart of the difference between dramatic poems such as *Maud* or *Manfred* and those of Browning. In *Manfred*, the single point of view is created by the correspondence of Manfred's subjective experience with the objective opinion of the other characters. Even if seen as aspects of his own soul, the destinies and spirits confirm Manfred's own inner feelings of suffering and guilt. In

Maud, the speaker may reveal a point of view in one section and then another, slightly varying point of view in the next; but these variations occur at different times and are those of the speaker's feelings rather than those of the reader's changing interpretation.

In 'My Last Duchess', however, through a close attention to the language, the reader receives a double impression. For example, when the Duke attempts to describe the exact nature of the specific flaw which he found in his Duchess, he says:

> She had
> A heart – how shall I say? – too soon made glad,
> Too easily impressed . . .

The hesitation expressed in the phrase '– how shall I say –' reveals the Duke in the process of creating an impression on his auditor, an impression of himself as magnanimous and forgiving to a fault. On the one hand, the hesitation implies that he could have said, 'She had a heart that was fickle indeed, without the slightest trace of judgement or restraint'. This might have sounded somewhat harsh coming from a gallant and charitable gentleman, and, without any further evidence, might have also revealed the extent to which the Duke was jealous. On the other hand, the hesitation and then the finding of the delicate phrasing reveals the Duke in the process of hiding his true self, a self made insanely jealous by a wife who 'liked whate'er/ She looked on' and whose 'looks went everywhere'. The Duke continues this process of building up a desirable image of himself, slipping in an attack only after he has made a concession, and then following the attack with a remark designed to deny its significance:

> She thanked men, – good! but thanked
> Somehow – I know not how – as if she ranked
> My gift of a nine-hundred-years-old name
> With anybody's gift. Who'd stoop to blame
> This sort of trifling?

Because the Duke himself is the speaker of the poem, the image he creates for the auditor is the image presented to the reader as well. The poet does not step in to tell the reader that the Duke's words are not the same as the Duke's thoughts, or that the Duke's real self is not revealed in the impression he is seeking to make. Yet if the reader follows Browning's advice to experience the poem with 'sympathy' and 'intelligence', he does sense a distinction between the impression the character is in the process of creating, and the character beneath the impression. It is as if the character wears a mask. All the reader can see is the mask, and yet he sees it as a mask, and senses the presence of the real character beneath it.

Browning, even in the nineteenth century, was considered a 'psychological' poet. Yet from the point of view of self-analysis, Manfred and the speaker in *Maud* are much more 'psychological' in relation to themselves. In contrast to these, a Browning character is seldom engaged in describing his state of mind or examining its sources. In fact, a Browning character is not so much interested in psychological truth as he is in psychological plausibility; and thus, he is shown not in the process of analysing himself, but of constructing a persona which will be accepted by the auditor.

It is this focus on the process of the character creating a mask, rather than the character revealing himself through his actions, that modern poets have emphasised in their approach to dramatic poetry. Pound entitled the collections of his early poetry *Personæ* (1909 and 1926), an echo of Browning's *Dramatis Personae*. In Pound's view, Browning was the forerunner of this modern approach to the dramatic – 'Browning's Sordello is one of the finest *masks* ever presented'.[15]

For Browning, the examination of human nature was of necessity the examination of masks. In *Fifine*, Browning describes a dream in which Don Juan, looking down upon a fair of men and women, sees not faces, but masks:

And what I gazed upon was a prodigious Fair,
Concourse immense of men and women, crowned or casqued,
Turbanned or tiar'd, wreathed, plumed, hatted or wigged, but
masked –
Always masked, – only, how? No face-shape, beast or bird,
Nay, fish and reptile even, but someone had preferred,
From out its frontispiece, feathered or scaled or curled,
To make the vizard whence himself should view the world,
And where the world believed himself was manifest. (XCV)

The actual creation of the mask involves a skilful manipulation of words and concepts. Browning's characters excel in the art of building up arguments from the least likely of foundations. What sometimes seems like extreme wordiness on Browning's part is often only the measure of the distance a character is travelling from an established point of view to one of his own making. As Don Juan asserts, 'ugliness had withered' when observed from his own point of view. Moreover, says Don Juan, 'I could pick and choose, project my weight':

> Determine to observe, or manage to escape,
> Or make divergency assume another shape
> By shift of point of sight in me the observer: thus
> Corrected, added to, subtracted from, – discuss
> Each variant quality, and brute-beast touch was turned
> Into mankind's safeguard! (CI)

It has sometimes been said that Browning was fascinated by the shadowy side of human nature. But this fascination is not so much with a character's evil deeds or even with the motives for these deeds, but with the ability of the character to create an explanation, a mask, which, by value of its very coherence, makes the ugliness of the deeds 'wither'.

Browning is indeed a 'crafty dissector', as Pound asserts in 'Mesmerism', but he is a dissector of points of view, not of character. For Browning, the objective poet was like a scientist of the imagination, creating minds and then seeing how they would think. The poet's point of view was analytic, or as Browning put it in *Pauline*, the poet was 'bound to trust/All feelings equally, to hear all sides' (597–8).

George Bernard Shaw, charter member of the Browning Society, might have learned something from Browning's method of dissecting points of view. Like Don Juan in *Fifine*, Undershaft in *Major Barbara* seems calculated as a direct challenge to that point of view most likely held by the audience. Through Don Juan, Browning creates plausible arguments supporting what the reader might regard as a heartless philanderer who leaves his wife to run after a gypsy. Similarly, in *Major Barbara* Shaw points out that not only can a man who manufactures bombs be a dramatic hero, but that in reality, he is the only hero possible in the modern world.

Of course, both Shaw and Browning also present the conventional point of view, the common wisdom against which these atypical heroes argue. However, the drama is not primarily that of one idea against another, although at times the sheer mass of argument might make it appear that way. What Browning has done in *Fifine* is not to set the idea of fidelity against the idea of freedom, but the persona Don Juan has created against the picture of him which is reflected

by his wife. This would seem to set Browning at an enormous dis-
advantage in terms of audience sympathy. Browning could expect his
audience to be prejudiced not only against Don Juan's argument, but
also against Don Juan himself, and in favour of the suffering, be-
trayed wife.

Yet to read a poem of 2355 lines told entirely from the point of
view of one character usually requires either sympathy with the
character or an interest in seeing what the character will do. However, Browning's portrayal of a character already familiar to his
audience does not present any new actions – merely new explanations
for the actions. It is significant that Browning's Don Juan elicits
neither sympathy nor interest in his future actions, in contrast, for
example, to the Don Juan of Byron. The reader of Byron's *Don Juan*
is not required to weigh the moral issues, for the hero seems to be
outside the realm of morals altogether. The focus of the poem is on
Don Juan's amorous adventures, not on any moral attitude towards
them. In fact, if moral considerations are mentioned at all, it is only
in order to dismiss them, the implication being that it is foolish to
bother with such things:

> 'Tis a sad thing, I cannot but say,
> And all the fault of that indecent sun,
> Who cannot leave alone our helpless clay,
> But will keep baking, broiling, burning on,
> That howsoever people fast and pray,
> The flesh is frail, and so the soul undone:
> What men call gallantry, and gods adultery,
> Is much more common where the climate's sultry.
>
> (Canto I, LXIII)

Another approach which tends to render the potentially unsym-
pathetic hero acceptable to the reader is that which presents the hero
or speaker in such torments of suffering or madness that no judgement is called forth from the reader. In both Tennyson's *Maud* and
Byron's *Manfred*, the main character has already judged himself. Like
the souls in torment in Dante's *Hell*, these characters elicit sympathy,
even if their deeds would never have received the reader's approval.

Most of Browning's speakers, however, are devoid not only of any
sympathetic madness, but also of suffering. Don Juan is in the best of
health and spirits. The Bishop at St Praxed's Church suffers only
from his own greed. Bishop Blougram, far from suffering pangs of

conscience for his materialism and hypocrisy, is so content with his fine wines and prestige that he denies that any way of life could be better:

> No, friend, you do not beat me: hearken why!
> The common problem, yours, mine, every one's,
> Is – not to fancy what were fair in life
> Provided it could be, – but, finding first
> What may be, then find how to make it fair
> Up to our means: a very different thing! (86–91)

Thus, the readers of *Fifine* and others of Browning's poems are not engaged in the poem through either sympathy with a suffering hero or identification with the speaker's philosophy. Yet, as Browning said, the success of his poem depends more immediately on the 'intelligence and sympathy of the reader' (preface to *Paracelsus*, 1835).

For most nineteenth-century readers, however, a peculiar difficulty was that of finding Browning's own position within the mass of arguments for opposing points of view. Even the most sympathetic of Browning's readers, Elizabeth Barrett, criticised an approach which held the reader at arm's length and hindered what many Victorians felt to be the primary function of poetry – to teach:

> I do not think that, with all that music in you, only your own
> personality should be dumb, nor that having thought so much &
> deeply on life & its ends, you should not teach what you have
> learnt, in the directest & and most impressive way, the mask
> thrown away [off] however moist with the breath. And it is not, I
> believe, by the dramatic medium, that poets teach most
> impressively . . . I have seemed to observe *that!* . . . it is too difficult
> for the common reader to analyze, and to discern between the
> vivid & the earnest. Also he is apt to understand better always,
> when he *sees the lips move.* Now, here is yourself, with your
> wonderful faculty! – it is wondered at & recognised on all sides
> where there are eyes to see – it is called wonderful & admirable!
> Yet, with an inferior power, you might have taken yourself
> closer to the hearts & lives of men, & made yourself dearer, though
> being less great. Therefore I do want you to do this with your
> surpassing power – it will be so easy to you to speak, & so noble,
> when spoken.[16]

Throw the mask away, advised Elizabeth Barrett, for the common reader finds it too difficult to discern between the 'vivid and the earnest'. Elizabeth Barrett was accurate in her observation, even if misguided in her advice. The dramatisation of a character makes vivid what he says, but does not necessarily specify what the poet means to teach as truth. Browning wrote to Elizabeth Barrett that he was attempting to 'speak out' as she did, but that 'it seems bleak melancholy work, this talking to the wind...'[17] Yet Browning continued to write dramatic monologues and, as an objective poet, defended his practice of 'getting at new substance by breaking up the assumed wholes into parts of independent and unclassed value...' (*Essay on Shelley*, p. 68) The reader must approach the poem directly, and focus his attention on the character speaking rather than on the subject of the character's speech. If, for example, the reader hears only the tale the Duke is telling in 'My Last Duchess' rather than observing the Duke's creation of a persona, he comes away with little more than a sordid melodrama, splendidly told. Yet Browning's readers did focus on the tale in many instances, and concluded that if the message were not clearly to be seen in the lines themselves, then perhaps it could be gleaned from reading between the lines, or by forming societies in which to discuss the poems.

This common feeling of the need to read between the lines was one reason for the popularity of the Browning Society. Even Furnivall, its founder, praised Browning's *Essay on Shelley* primarily because in it the poet speaks in his own voice:

> The interest lay in the fact, that Browning's 'utterances' here are *his*, and not those of any one of the 'so many imaginary persons,' behind whom he insists on so often hiding himself, and whose necks I, for one, should continually like to wring, whose bodies I would fain kick out of the way, in order to get face to face with the poet himself, and hear his own voice speaking his own thoughts, man to man, soul to soul.[18]

Ironically, this essay was Browning's most direct attempt to justify his own 'objective' approach. In it he states that knowing the biography of a subjective poet like Shelley is useful because the man himself is so closely interwoven with the poetry. But the biography of an objective poet like Shakespeare, although perhaps interesting in itself, is unnecessary – 'The man passes, the work remains. The work speaks for itself, as we say' (p. 65). Later in his career Browning repeated this assertion:

Outside should suffice for evidence:
And whoso desires to penterate
Deeper, must dive by the spirit-sense –
No optics like yours, at any rate!

'Hoity-toity! A street to explore,
Your house the exception! *"With this same key
Shakespeare unlocked his heart,"* once more!'
Did Shakespeare? If so, the less Shakespeare he!

('House', IX–X)

In Browning's view, to read the work of an objective poet as an expression of the poet's own feelings is to misread it. In a letter to Ruskin, Browning insisted that he should not be identified with his characters:

The last charge I cannot answer, for you may be right in
preferring it, however unwitting I am of the fact. I *may* put
Robert Browning into Pippa and other men and maids. If so,
peccavi: but I don't see myself in them, at all events.[19]

According to Browning, the reader should approach the dramatic monologue on its own terms as an utterance by a fictional character – 'poetry always dramatic in principle, and so many utterances of so many imaginary persons, not mine', as Browning put it in the 1852 'Advertisement' to *Dramatic Lyrics* and again in the 1867 preface to *Pauline*.

Modern poets have echoed this insistence. Frost said he wrote to keep '"the over curious" out of the secret places of his mind'.[20] Pound gave to William Carlos Williams what amounts to a warning to the reader: 'Good Lord! of course you don't have to like the stuff I write... Remember, of course, that some of the stuff is dramatic and in the character of the person named in the title.'[21] Eliot, too, gave instructions to his readers:

... I have distributed my own theories quite indiscriminately
among the speakers; and the reader must not try to identify the
persons in the dialogue with myself or anyone else. They are not
even fictions; they are merely voices ...

(Preface to 'A Dialogue on Poetic Drama')[22]

Thus, what Pound, Eliot and others faced in their task of educating their readers had also been faced by Browning. Like Browning, poets who wrote a new sort of poetry also demanded a new sort of approach from the reader. Pound even went so far as to write an *ABC of Reading*[23] as part of his continuing effort to educate the public.

In spite of his insistence on objectivity, Browning sometimes fulfilled his readers' demand 'to hear his own voice speaking his own thoughts', as Furnivall put it. It is in Browning's attitude towards his contemporaries' expectations of gleaning truth from poetry that an explanation can be found for the somewhat contradictory image he conveys to twentieth-century readers. On the one hand, Browning responded to this expectation, and when he did throw away the mask and speak directly, he often filled his poetry with what Yeats called 'impurities'.[24] On the other hand, Browning saw himself as pursuing truth through an objective method, and in this pursuit, truth-as-ideas was only a means for getting at the truth which emerged as a character created a mask. Thus while Yeats criticised Browning for filling his poetry with impurities, he also recognised that 'thought and speculation were to Browning means of dramatic expression much more than aims in themselves'.[25]

Yeats's words could be applied to his own poetry as well as to Browning's. If readers were to seek in Yeats's poetry only that which might be called the philosophical meaning, they would find an obscure system of semi-private mythology. But when the symbols and characters of this mythology are seen as beautiful and expressive 'masks' of the poet, and the creation of these masks is seen as the end to which thought and speculation are servants, then it is not necessary to 'separate the vivid from the earnest' in order to appreciate the poem:

> The gyres! the gyres! Old Rocky Face, look forth;
> Things thought too long can be no longer thought,
> For beauty dies of beauty, worth of worth,
> And ancient lineaments are blotted out. ('The Gyres')

Those readers who did not see philosophical ideas in Browning's poetry or who did not look for clues to the poet's biography in the characters he created, were still likely to retain a prejudice – the expectation that a dramatic poem exhibit the characteristics of drama. With this expectation, a reader would immediately notice that the speaking voice of one dramatic monologue is almost indistinguishable from that of another. The resulting criticism is that ironically, for all Browning's insistence on the distance between himself and his characters, we hear his voice only too clearly through the thin masks of the characters.

If Browning does not seem to take pains to make one speaking voice differ from another, if he gives complex sentence structures to the speech of the uneducated Pompilia as readily as he does to the Pope, it is because he is not interested in the outward verisimilitude of his characters. On the dramatic stage, different voices, dress and mannerisms are immediately apparent. But on the inner stage of the mind, differences in character are differences in thought processes. As Arthur Symons pointed out, Browning gives us not so much what his characters would probably say, as what they would certainly think.[26] Where a differentiation in speech patterns is made, as in 'Caliban upon Setebos', the variation of sentence structure indicates a variation in self concept. When Caliban omits the personal pronoun 'I', the context is one of personal devaluation in which he sees himself as low in the eyes of Prospero and Setebos as birds and crabs are in his.[27]

Yet even though Browning varied the speech patterns of Caliban, the narrative voice of the poem is still that of the poet. As Eliot pointed out:

> In The Tempest, it is Caliban who speaks; in 'Caliban upon Setebos', it is Browning's voice that we hear, Browning talking aloud through Caliban. It was Browning's greatest disciple, Mr. Ezra Pound, who adopted the term 'persona' to indicate the several historical characters through whom he spoke: and the term is just.[28]

The recognition that the voice of poetry differs from that of drama, that the creation of a mask is a fundamentally different activity from the creation of a character, is a significant aspect of modern dramatic poetry. Eliot makes a triple distinction: the voice of the poet speaking to himself 'or to nobody', the voice of the poet addressing an audience, and the voice of a poet 'when he attempts to create a dramatic character speaking in verse; when he is saying, not what he would say in his own person, but only what he can say within the limits of one imaginary character addressing another imaginary character.'[29] Yet it is not under this last voice that Eliot classifies Browning, but the second voice, that of a poet addressing an audience:

When we listen to a play by Shakespeare, we listen not to
Shakespeare but to his characters; when we read a dramatic
monologue by Browning, we cannot suppose that we are listening
to any other voice than that of Browning himself.
    In the dramatic monologue, then, it is surely the second voice,
the voice of the poet talking to other people, that is dominant. The
mere fact that he is assuming a role, that he is speaking through a
mask, implies the presence of an audience: why should a man put
on fancy dress and a mask only to talk to himself?[30]

The poet talking to other people dons a mask, or, as in Browning's
case, presents a character who is himself creating a persona. The
mask is an artifact; yet, paradoxically, it is also live, for the creator
is within, animating it. Browning's image of this process is of a poet
welding words to hammer out a crude armour, and:

> This obtained
> With some ado, no obstacle remained
> To using it; accordingly he took
> An action with its actors, quite forsook
> Himself to live in each, returned anon
> With the result – a creature, and, by one
> And one, proceeded leisurely to equip
> Its limb in harness of his workmanship.
>
> (Sordello, II, 579–86)

Thus there are two levels on which Browning is involved in the
process of creating masks: the level of the character creating a
persona and the level of the poet creating a mask – the poem itself.
For twentieth-century poets, this preoccupation with masks is
directly related to the modern recognition that every man, not just
the charlatan or the hypocrite, wears a mask. Psychologists emphasise
that the self, assumed to be an indivisible entity, could more realistically be regarded as a system of masks and defences. As C. G. Jung
defined it:

The persona is a complicated system of relations between individual
consciousness and society, fittingly enough a kind of mask,
designed on the one hand to make a definite impression upon
others, and, on the other, to conceal the true nature of the
individual.[31]

Thus, 'All the world's a stage' has been taken literally in that every man, to some extent, plays roles and is an actor on that stage.

Browning's early insight into the nature of the persona resulted in an approach to poetry very different from that which his nineteenth-century readers expected. If each man builds a mask, and the mask is built of words and ideas, then one can hardly expect all of these words and ideas to present straightforward philosophical 'truths'. In *Fifine*, Browning talks about the difference between *hearing* these words and *seeing* the 'truth':

> but, – since on me devolved
> To see, and understand by sight, – the vulgar speech
> Might be dispensed with. 'He who cannot see, must reach
> As best he may the truth of men by help of words
> They please to speak, must fare at will of who affords
> The banquet,' – so I thought. 'Who sees not, hears and so
> Gets to believe; myself it is that, seeing, know,
> And, knowing, can dispense with voice and vanity
> Of speech.' (xcviii)

'Who sees not, hears and so/Gets to believe' – to get to the *truth*, rather than mere *belief*, one has 'To see, and understand by sight'. For Browning, the best poets were those who, seeing, 'Impart the gift of seeing to the rest' (*Sordello*, III, 868). Clearly, Browning's way of imparting the gift of seeing to the rest was to present his characters in such a way that the words they spoke would be both a mask and a means for the reader to see the truth:

> They talked, themselves among,
> Of themselves, to themselves: I saw the mouths at play,
> The gesture that enforced, the eye that strove to say
> The same thing as the voice, and seldom gained its point
> – That this was so, I saw; but all seemed out of joint
> I' the vocal medium 'twixt the world and me. I gained
> Knowledge by notice, not by giving ear, – attained
> To truth by what men seemed, not said: to me one glance
> Was worth whole histories of noisy utterance,
> – At least, to me in dream. (*Fifine*, c)

Given Browning's emphasis on the mask which each man made for himself, it is not surprising to find that he greatly admired good acting. His career as a poet began one night after he had been particularly inspired by Kean's performance of *Richard III*. On that night, 22 October 1832, he determined to write a poem, a novel and an opera.[32] Later, W. M. Rossetti said that Browning had told him that Tommaso Salvini acting *Oedipus* was

> the finest effort of art he had ever beheld; not only the finest in the art of acting, but in any art whatsoever, including painting, music, etc. I do not say that this statement of Browning's was a perfectly reasonable one, but certain it is that he made it to me, and this in a tone of entire conviction.[33]

Browning may have prized 'stage-play, the honest cheating' (*Fifine*, LXXXVII) for the same reason that Don Juan in *Fifine* praises the actors:

> Actors! We also act, but only they inscribe
> Their style and title so, and preface, only they,
> Performance with 'A lie is all we do or say.' (LXXXV)

Then Browning adds: 'Each has a false outside, whereby a truth is forced/To issue from within' (LXXXVI). Oscar Wilde later expanded this appreciation of 'the false outside' by claiming that 'Lying and poetry are arts – arts, as Plato saw, not unconnected with each other...'[34] Wilde then adds:

> In point of fact what is interesting about people in good society ... is the mask that each one of them wears, not the reality that lies behind the mask. .... Where we differ from each other is purely in accidentals: in dress, manner, tone of voice, religious opinions, personal appearance, tricks of habit and the like. The more one analyses people, the more all reasons for analysis disappear. Sooner or later one comes to that dreadful universal thing called human nature.[35]

The appreciation of the mask as interesting in itself was further emphasised by Yeats. In 'The Mask', one speaker refuses to comply with a lover's request to 'Put off that mask', answering that:

> 'It was the mask engaged your mind,
> And after set your heart to beat,
> Not what's behind.'

Man creates masks not only to impress others and to conceal his faults, but also to hide himself from his own eyes. When a face covered by a mask is reflected in a mirror, only the mask is judged. Consequently, as Yeats saw it, creation of masks is the only source of happiness:

> I think that all happiness depends on the energy to assume the mask of some other self: that all joyous or creative life is a rebirth as something not oneself, something which has no memory and is created in a moment and perpetually renewed. We put on a grotesque or solemn painted face to hide us from the terror of judgment . . . one loses the infinite pain of self-realization.[36]

The alternate approach and retreat from 'the infinite pain of self-realization' is seen in much of modern poetry. Where Browning would have created a fictional character in a particular situation, a poet like Robert Lowell deliberately creates a myth, projecting himself as hero and using his own family history as building material:

> 'I won't go with you. I want to stay with Grandpa!'
> That's how I threw cold water
> on my Mother's and Father's
> watery martini pipe dreams at Sunday dinner.
> . . . Fontainebleau, Mattapoisett, Puget Sound . . .
> Nowhere was anywhere after a summer
> at my Grandfather's farm.
> Diamond-pointed, athirst and Norman,
> its alley of poplars
> paraded from Grandmother's rose garden
> to a scarey stand of virgin pine,
> scrub, and paths forever pioneering.
> ('My Last Afternoon with Uncle Devereux Winslow', 1)

> Only teaching on Tuesdays, book-worming
> in pyjamas fresh from the washer each morning,
> I hog a whole house on Boston's
> 'hardly passionate Marlborough Street' . . .

> I was so out of things, I'd never heard
> of the Jehovah's Witnesses.
> 'Are you a C.O.?' I asked a fellow jailbird.
> 'No,' he answered, 'I'm a J. W.'
> (from 'Memories of West Street and Lepke')

In the poetic mask the subjective and objective meet; the personal voice of the poet animates the fictional character, a character who may represent the poet himself. John Berryman's 'Henry' sometimes stands outside the poet, so that his adventures are related from a third person point of view ('Henry reacted like a snake to praise': '287'); sometimes beside the poet so that both Berryman and Henry become characters in the same poem ('The Irish sunshine is lovely but a Belfast man/last night made a pass at my wife: Henry, who had passed out,/was horrified/to hear this news when he woke': '313'); and sometimes the boundary line between the poet and his creation shifts within the poem itself:

> Tears Henry shed for poor old Hemingway
> Hemingway in despair, Hemingway at the end,
> the end of Hemingway,
> tears in a diningroom in Indiana
> and that was years ago, before his marriage say,
> God to him no worse luck send.
>
> Save us from shotguns & fathers' suicides.
> It all depends on who you're the father of
> if you want to kill yourself –
> a bad example, murder of oneself,
> the final death, in a paroxysm, of love
> for which good mercy hides?
>
> A girl at the door: 'A few coppers pray'
> But to return, to return to Hemingway
> that cruel & gifted man.
> Mercy! my father; do not pull the trigger
> or all my life I'll suffer from your anger
> killing what you began. ('235')

What Browning regarded as an essentially objective activity – the creation of dramatis personae – modern poets have used as a means to explore the most subjective aspects of self:

> It is suggested, then, that a dramatic poet cannot create characters of the greatest intensity of life unless his personages, in their reciprocal actions and behaviour in their story, are somehow dramatizing, but in no obvious form, an action or struggle for harmony in the soul of the poet.[37]

Browning saw himself as pursuing truth, a truth to be found through fusing 'my live soul and that inert stuff' (*The Ring and the Book*, I, 469). Pound characterised the modern approach when he described his poetry as a 'search for the real': 'I began this search for the real in a book called *Personæ*, casting off, as it were, complete masks of the self in each poem. I continued in long series of translations, which were but more elaborate masks.[38]

Translation as a creation of masks by the translator seems radically different from translation as an attempt to carry a poem from one language into another with the least possible damage to the meaning. Of course the question of whether any poem can really be translated has often been argued. Shelley's opinion was that translation was 'vanity':

> it were as wise to cast a violet into a crucible that you might
> discover the formal principle of its colour and odour, as seek to
> transfuse from one language to another the creations of a poet. The
> plant must spring again from its seed, or it will bear no flower –
> and this is the burthen of the curse of Babel.
>
> (A *Defence of Poetry*, p. 29)

However, many modern poets have published translations, not because they disagree with the idea that real translation is impossible, but because in the context of twentieth-century relativity, all but the most mathematical of communications are seen to be impossible without some translation taking place. Hence, the 'vanity' of translating poetry is just one of a number of 'vain' exercises performed by man. As Auden says:

> Translation is, in theory, impossible but, in practice, each of us
> translates every day. . . . whenever we speak to each other about
> anything except the most purely impersonal matters, the listener
> has to translate into terms of his own experience what the speaker
> utters in terms of his.[39]

Dryden saw translation to be divided into three categories: metaphrase ('turning an author word by word, and line by line, from one language into another'), paraphrase ('where the author is kept in view by the translator ... but his words are not so strictly followed as his sense'), and imitation ('where the translator [if now he has not lost that name] assumes the liberty not only to vary from the words and sense, but to forsake them both as he sees occasion').[40] It is significant that whereas most nineteenth-century translations were closer to 'paraphrase', in that a poem in another language was taken as the model for an English poem of the same or similar meaning, the tendency of most modern poets is towards either metaphrase or imitation. In other words, modern translations are illustrations of the modern approach to poetry in general: from one point of view, a poem is an object as a painting or a sculpture are objects; from another point of view, a poem is a mask, a dramatic persona created by the poet. Depending on which point of view is stressed, a translation will approach either metaphrase – the attempt to create an object as close to the original as possible – or imitation – the attempt to 'make something foreign, or something remote in time, live with our own life...'[41] Of further significance is the fact that in keeping with his approach towards his own poetry, Browning experimented with both metaphrase and imitation, and in these experiments exhibits characteristics found in more extreme forms in modern translations.

The new approach to translation was recognised by Ford Madox Ford who, in praising Pound, said: 'For it is not literal translation that is needed for this purpose. The valuable rendering may be full of verbal mis-translations or even of misunderstandings of meanings...[42]

The 'mis-translations' in *Homage to Sextus Propertius*, for example, have been compared by some critics to 'schoolboys' howlers' or to 'the sophomore's technique of dealing with an unprepared passage'.[43] For example, in Section XII, as J. P. Sullivan points out, "'*tale facis carmen docta testudine quale/Cynthius impositis temperat articulis*' (literally: you produce such a poem as the Cynthian god produces, with his fingers on his artistic lyre) becomes in Pound

> Like a trained and performing tortoise,
> I would make verse in your fashion, if she should command it."[44]

And, in Pound's translation of *The Seafarer*, 'eorþan rices' appears as 'earthen riches', rather than as 'kingdoms of the earth'.[45]

While this 'mis-translation' may appear the result of a kind of whimsical impulse, it also can be seen as the logical outcome of approaching a text with an emphasis on style and on the associations suggested by sound and rhythm rather than on a strict following of literal meaning. If each word is an object in itself, then each word must be translated on the basis of its physical properties as well as its meaning. On this basis, 'earthen riches' might be seen to render 'eorþan rices' more accurately than 'kingdoms of the earth', in that 'earthen riches' re-creates or approximates the shape and rhythm of the original, while 'kingdoms of the earth' merely conveys the sense.

That this new approach makes a difference in translation becomes immediately apparent when one of the most extreme of modern translations, Celia and Louis Zukofsky's *Catullus*, is compared with versions of earlier translators. The opening of Byron's translation of 'LI', although characteristically 'Byronic' in rhythm and tone, conveys a fairly literal 'prose' sense of the original:

> Equal to Jove that youth must be –
> Greater than Jove he seems to me –
> Who, free from Jealousy's alarms,
> Securely views thy matchless charms.[46]

The Zukofsky translation, in contrast, exhibits Pound's technique of translating the sound of the word in the original language, as if what is being conveyed is the *physical* aspect of the original. In the 'Translators' Preface' this principle is made explicit: 'This translation of Catullus follows the sound, rhythm, and syntax of his Latin – tries, as is said, to breathe the "literal" meaning in him.'[47] Consequently, the Latin *'Ille mi par esse'* becomes 'He'll hie me, par *is* he?'; and *'te/spectat et audit'* is translated to read 'in-/spect it and audit':

> He'll hie me, par *is* he? the God divide her,
> He'll hie, see fastest, superior deity,
> quiz – sitting adverse identity – mate, in-
>   spect it and audit – ...

The Zukofsky version even has a 'stage direction' in the middle of the poem – '[voice hoarse in a throat]'. A glance at the Zukofsky Latin text reveals '[*vocis in ore*]' where most other versions simply indicate an ellipsis.

While Browning certainly did not go to these lengths, his translations indicate that he was less interested in educating his reader, that is, in getting the subject-matter across, than in presenting to his reader a faithful copy of the original object. Like the Zukofsky translation of Catullus, Browning's translation of *Agamemnon* often exhibits a very contorted appearance. Even Pound admitted that:

> ... it is still undisputable that I have read Browning off and on for seventeen years with no small pleasure and admiration, and am one of the few people who know anything about his *Sordello*, and

have never read his *Agamemnon*, have not even now when it falls into a special study been able to get through his *Agamemnon*.⁴⁸

Yet in lines such as the following (spoken by 'Klutaimnestra'), for all their twisted syntax, there is a powerful sense of something entirely different, not only from the English language, but also from western European experience:

> I stand where I have struck, things once accomplished:
> And so have done, – and this deny I shall not, –
> As that his fate was nor to fly nor ward off.
> A wrap-round with no outlet, as for fishes,
> I fence about him – the rich woe of the garment:
> I strike him twice, and in a double 'Ah-me!'
> He let his limbs go – *there!* And to him, fallen,
> The third blow add I, giving – of Below-ground
> Zeus, guardian of the dead – the votive favour.
> Thus in the mind of him he rages, falling,
> And blowing forth a brisk blood-spatter, strikes me
> With the dark drop of slaughterous dew – rejoicing
> No less than, at the god-given dewy-comfort,
> The sown-stuff in its birth-throes from the calyx. (1406–19)

As Edward Lucie-Smith has pointed out, Browning's translation of *Agamemnon*, like Zukofsky's Catullus, has a curious literal quality about it.⁴⁹ This literalness is not of sense, but of word. That is, what the reader experiences is not the literal meaning of the original in its totality, a meaning perhaps most clearly conveyed in a prose summary; the experience is rather that of understanding word by word. In his introduction to *Agamemnon*, Browning said that he required a translator 'to be literal at every cost save that of absolute violence to our language'. He then went on to describe his work as succeeding if it gave 'a mere strict bald version of thing by thing, or at least word pregnant with thing . . .'

Browning's translation of *Agamemnon* was dedicated to Carlyle, who said that although he was highly honoured, for his soul's salvation he couldn't make out the meaning.⁵⁰ It seems evident, as Lucie-Smith asserts, that in this translation 'English is laid on the altar of Greek . . .'⁵¹ A classical scholar of the time praised the translation as being 'faithfully and rigidly true to its prototype' in atmosphere, phrase, 'even in naïveté'.⁵²

Browning's experiment with metaphrase in the translation of *Agamemnon* has an interesting parallel in his approach to translation as imitation. When Pound called his translations 'but more elaborate masks', he was referring to the sense in which he used the original poem as raw material for a poem of his own. The plot, characters, ideas, general outline of the poem – all were there in the original. Pound then stepped into the setting and animated the character with his own spirit.

Robert Lowell is another of the modern poets whose translations are masks of the self. In his introduction to *Imitations*, Lowell confesses to being 'reckless with literal meaning' in order to write 'live English'. Strict metrical translators are 'taxidermists, not poets, and their poems are likely to be stuffed birds'.[53] And translation into free or irregular verse 'commonly turns out a sprawl of language, neither faithful nor distinguished, now on stilts, now low, as Dryden would say'.[54] Unlike these literal translations, Lowell's *Imitations*, as he said, is 'partly self-sufficient and separate from its sources, and should be first read as a sequence, one voice running through many personalities, contrasts and repetitions.'[55] This one voice heard in poems from Homer to Pasternak is of course the voice of Lowell himself.

Although Browning never published a series of translations as masks of the self or even a complete translation as imitation, the idea of using a historical character as raw material for the making of a new persona is clearly seen in his poetry. It is in Pound's poetry that the step from using a historical character as speaker of the dramatic monologue to speaking through the mask of another poet's poem takes place:

> Gradually in Pound's work the emphasis shifts from the re-creation of character to the significance of the re-creation, and his own projective energy undergoes a similar shift from the point of view of the persona to the point of view implied by the augmentation of the persona. Not the old speaker but his modern significance, is what the reader must ultimately see.[56]

This approach to translation, or to writing poetry (depending on whether one looks at 'earthen riches', for example, as being more Pound than *The Seafarer*), is implied in Browning's translation of an excerpt from Molière's *Don Juan* which appears as an introductory quotation to *Fifine*. In one sense, Browning has prefigured Pound in that *Fifine* itself is a poem whose speaker is a character taken from

another writer's work. In this case, Browning presents the reader
with a quotation from Molière and then offers a translation which,
while very close to the original, deviates from it just enough to
further Browning's presentation of his own Don Juan.

The passage Browning picked out was one in which Don Juan is
confronted by his latest wife, Donna Elvira, whom he has just
deserted. Browning translates:

Donna Elvira: Don Juan, might you please to help one give a guess,
                Hold up a candle, clear this fine mysteriousness?
Don Juan: Madam, if needs I must declare the truth, – in short...
Donna Elvira: Fie, for a man of mode, accustomed at the court
                To such a style of thing, how awkwardly my lord
                Attempts defence! You move compassion, that's the
                                                            word –
                Dumb-foundered and chap-fallen! Why don't you
                    arm your brow
                With noble impudence? Why don't you swear and
                                                            vow
                No sort of change is come to any sentiment
                You ever had for me? Affection holds the bent,
                You love me now as erst, with passion that makes
                                                            pale
                All ardor else: nor aught in nature can avail
                To separate us two, save what, in stopping breath,
                May peradventure stop devotion likewise – death!

In his translation, Browning manages through a number of ways to
convey much more emphasis to Donna Elvira's voice than might be
seen in the original. In translating from prose to verse, Browning
adds 'hold up a candle', an addition which slows the tempo of the
passage, changing a straightforward request to an image which can
be visualised. In Don Juan's reply Browning indicates a dramatic
pause through the addition of characteristic punctuation. Another
example of the emphasis Browning has given to the passage is seen in
his translation of 'J'ai pitié de vous voir la confusion que vous avez'
as 'You move compassion, that's the word – /Dumb-foundered and
chap-fallen!' Again, in the original, 'rien n'est capable de vous
détacher de moi que la mort' follows in a smooth flow from the rest of
the sentence; whereas in Browning's translation, not only is the
word 'death' placed at the end of the sentence, set off by a dash and

followed by an exclamation point, but the sentence to which it forms the period leads up to this one word with a series of modifying phrases which occupy two lines. The rhyme with 'breath' adds further emphasis.

The emphatic challenge which Donna Elvira gives to Don Juan in Browning's translation is answered during the course of *Fifine*. Browning's Don Juan does not merely engage in amorous adventures, forgetting one woman as he goes to the next, but uses these adventures as the basis for a long series of arguments concerning the search for the infinite in the finite – a search curiously like Browning's own. Yet, as Browning makes clear towards the end of the poem, although Don Juan had the right goal, he utilised the wrong methods:

> His problem posed aright
> Was – 'From the given point evolve the infinite!'
> Not – 'Spend thyself in space, endeavouring to joint
> Together, and so make infinite, point and point:
> Fix into one Elvire a Fair-ful of Fifines!' (CXXIX)

Like *Fifine*, *Balaustion's Adventure* can be considered as a mask which Browning has created, beginning with material of another poet. As Robert Langbaum says: 'We probably ought to understand the poem as we understand Ezra Pound's translations – as a creative appropriation of ancient material, a way of giving an ancient poet a historical consciousness he himself could not have had.'[57] Moreover, through Balaustion, Browning also defends his own method of writing. A 'brisk little somebody,/Critic and whippersnapper' cries:

> 'The girl departs from truth!
> Pretends she saw what was not to be seen,
> Making the mask of the actor move, forsooth! . . .
>
> As she had seen each naked fleshly face,
> And not the merely-painted mask it wore!
>
> (308–10, 315–16)

Browning answers:

> Well, is the explanation difficult?
> What's poetry except a power that makes?
> And, speaking to one sense, inspires the rest,
> Pressing them all into its service; so
> That who sees painting, seems to hear as well

The speech that's proper for the painted mouth;
And who hears music, feels his solitude
Peopled at once – for how count heart-beats plain
Unless a company, with hearts which beat,
Come close to the musician, seen or no?
And who receives true verse at eye or ear,
Takes in (with verse) time, place, and person too,
So, links each sense on to its sister-sense,
Grace-like: and what if but one sense of three
Front you at once? The sidelong pair conceive
Thro' faintest touch of finest finger-tips, –
Hear, see and feel, in faith's simplicity,
Alike, what one was sole recipient of:
Who hears the poem, therefore, sees the play. (317–35)

Like Balaustion, Browning disagreed with critics who attempted to limit the poet to reporting only 'the truth' of what can be seen. For this reason, in Browning's hands the dramatic monologue is indeed fundamentally different from the drama; and because of his attitude towards 'all those restrictions' of the 'dramatic poem', Browning's dramatic monologues are also very different from many of those of his contemporaries. For example, Matthew Arnold's *Empedocles on Etna*, which Browning admired, was called 'A Dramatic Poem' and was organised to include the traditional dramatic unity of time and place. Although the presence of many songs and long speeches might make this dramatic poem unacceptable as drama, there is nothing within it which would be impossible to represent on an actual stage. Although Browning often includes lines which contain implicit stage directions, most of his poems, when examined from the point of view of actual staging, would be almost impossible for an audience to follow.

In writing dramatic poetry, Browning used only those elements of drama and poetry which would allow him more freedom. For example, in a dramatic poem like *Pippa Passes*, Browning does not hesitate to introduce his own voice as a poet into the poem. This appearance of the poet in his own creation is not really possible in the drama. If the dramatist were to make himself appear in the play, he could only appear as one of the characters. Even if he appeared as 'the author' or 'the dramatist', he would appear within the confines of the play. To overcome this limitation, some dramatists have used a chorus as the voice of higher authority. However, people on the stage, even those designated as a chorus, tend to take on the nature of characters through association with the dramatic context. Working with this tendency, some ancient dramatists made the chorus 'townspeople' or other characters. Eliot also used this device in *Murder in the Cathedral*.

Browning took advantage of the freedom of a poet to enter his poem. In *Sordello*, for example, Browning made frequent personal appearances, apologising early in the poem for what he felt was the necessity to do so. The running title summarises this apology as 'Why the poet himself addresses his audience':

> Appears
> Verona ... Never, – I should warn you first, –
> Of my own choice had this, if not the worst
> Yet not the best expedient, served to tell
> A story I could body forth so well
> By making speak, myself kept out of view,
> The very man as he was wont to do,
> And leaving you to say the rest for him. (I, 10–17)

But, as he goes on to say, although he should 'delight in watching first to last' Sordello's progress, 'as you watch it, not a whit/More in the secret than yourselves,' (22–4), a poem such as *Sordello* might be an unprecedented experience for the reader, and as such, might require a guide in the form of the author himself:

> But it seems
> Your setters-forth of unexampled themes,
> Makers of quite new men, producing them,
> Would best chalk broadly on each vesture's hem
> The wearer's quality; or take their stand,
> Motley on back and pointing-pole in hand
> Beside him. So, for once I face ye, friends ... (I, 25–31)

The appearance of the poet in the midst of his own creations lends a peculiarly reflective quality to *Sordello*, especially since Browning refers to *Sordello* the poem in the midst of the poem itself. There are two different levels of reality involved here: that of the created reality of the characters, and that of the unmasked author. This produces a duality of effect similar to that experienced when an actor on a screen talks with an animated cartoon character whom he has just been shown in the act of drawing.

Other ways in which Browning utilises the devices of poetry in a dramatic context include his frequent use of rhyme and punctuation to give emphasis to the action. Of course rhyme has always been used for emphasis – but if used on the stage, it usually either operates on a subconscious level or becomes so noticeable as to interrupt the illusion of reality. As for punctuation, on the stage, it is conveyed only through the voice of the actor; in a poem, subtle uses of punctuation can be apparent to the eye even if unnoticed by the ear. For example, one of the things which makes 'Porphyria's Lover' a strangely eerie poem is the calm tone in which the madman tells of his murder. Here, unlike many of Browning's other poems, the text does not carry sprinklings of dashes and exclamation marks (there is one dash and only two exclamation marks). Rather than emphasise words through stressing them, Browning has chosen to emphasise the significant pauses – and for this he has made deliberate and careful use of the colon:

> The rain set early in to-night,
> The sullen wind was soon awake,
> It tore the elm-tops down for spite,
> And did its worst to vex the lake:
> I listened with heart fit to break.

In this, as well as in the following example, the pause indicated at the colon is followed by a second line which not only rhymes with the first, but also ends with a distinct pause. Yet, as Browning indicates with his punctuation, the two pauses are different; for the pause indicated by the colon 'looks forward', whereas that indicated by the full stop signifies completion:

> But passion sometimes would prevail,
> Nor could to-night's gay feast restrain
> A sudden thought of one so pale
> For love of her, and all in vain:
> So, she was come through wind and rain.

This deliberate pattern of rhythm, rhyme and double pauses leaves the reader formally unprepared for the breaking of the pattern which follows – just as he is psychologically unprepared for Porphyria's murder. The ponderous brooding is interrupted not by indications of dramatic violence, but by only a slight shift in the pattern: a slight pause in the middle of the line rather than at the end, followed by several lines rather than one, and Porphyria has been strangled:

> That moment she was mine, mine, fair,
> Perfectly pure and good: I found
> A thing to do, and all her hair
> In one long yellow string I wound
> Three times her little throat around,
> And strangled her.

Although 'Porphyria's Lover' could be enjoyed if recited by an actor on a stage, these subtleties of form and punctuation would be missed entirely or would be apparent only on the level of the subconscious. Like most modern poetry, Browning's poems, even those considered to be 'dramatic', are designed to be read with conscious attention paid to the formal poetic devices, an attention which could not be given to a play on a stage. In reading, the eye retains a visual picture of the words themselves, and there is 'time' to pause and reflect, for the pace, unlike that of drama and music, is largely determined by the reader. In this respect, although poetry is an art 'in time', it partakes of the nature of a 'static' art like painting, in that the reader has the object before him and therefore can linger at one point or look twice at another.

Perhaps the clearest example of Browning's use of poetic devices within a dramatic context can be seen in *Pippa Passes*. For the most part, the reader's attention is drawn to the dramatic effects, as when Ottima, saying she hates her murdered husband, provokes a response in Sebald which reveals the action which has accompanied her words:

> Ottima.   I would go back and hold
> His two dead hands, and say, 'I hate you worse,
> 'Luca, than ...'
> Sebald.   Off, off – take your hands off mine,
> 'T is the hot evening – off! oh, morning is it?

(I, 110–13)

Browning also takes care to give individual traits to the minor characters such as the students and the girls, even though many of these characters are not even named. On the stage, of course, minor characters assume individuality through differences in dress, voice and mannerisms. That Browning has chosen to indicate differences in personality is indicative of his attention to characters, an attention which is essentially dramatic.

Yet Browning's attention to the dramatic aspects of *Pippa Passes* did not include a strict observation of dramatic conventions. Although he called *Pippa* 'a drama', Browning did not hesitate to take liberties which would be impossible in conventional stage drama. For example, immediately before the scene in which the students talk with each other, Browning gives the reader a small paragraph to inform him that during this time, 'Pippa is passing from the hill-side to Orcana' (1). Moreover, Browning gives the reader certain background information with a directness impossible on the stage. Descriptions of a scene in a stage play are conveyed to the audience through the stage setting, programme notes, or the conversation of the characters ('But look, the morn in russet mantle clad/Walks o'er the dew of yon high eastward hill'). However, Browning's scene descriptions are written to be read; and thus the description of Pippa as 'from the Silk-mills', a description which would not be apparent to an audience, can be directly conveyed to a reader ('Introduction').

Shakespeare's description of the 'morn in russet mantle clad', an effect difficult to produce on the stage in the absence of modern lighting, was of necessity spoken by a character in the drama. In *Pippa Passes*, however, Browning saw no need to place himself under the restrictions of stage drama. Thus, the initial description of a sunrise is lyrical and hyperbolic, even though the only character 'on stage', Pippa from the silk-mills, could not really have made such a speech. Yet with only a space between lines to mark a break in the verse, the lyrical description becomes a speech in the first person in which Pippa uses this imagery of day boiling over night's brim:

> But forth one wavelet, then another, curled,
> Till the whole sunrise, not to be suppressed,
> Rose, reddened, and its seething breast
> Flickering in bounds, grew gold, then overflowed the world.
>
> Oh, Day, if I squander a wavelet of thee,
> A mite of my twelve hours' treasure ... ('Introduction', 9–14)

The link in the imagery indicates that the initial lines are also Pippa's, that they exist in her mind even though as a character she could not have formed the thoughts into such speech as Browning has given her. Here Browning has taken the poet's liberty of presenting the essence or inner aspect of a character directly to the reader in a language not restricted by the necessity of speaking through the character.

In addition to freeing himself from the restrictions of dramatic realism, Browning also used whatever poetic devices could most heighten the effect he wished to produce. For example, the particular effect of a sunbeam reflected from a basin of water is not only an effect difficult to reproduce on the stage, but is also described in such a way that rhythm and rhyme are emphasised in a typically *poetic* as opposed to *dramatic* way:

> One splash of water ruins you asleep,
> And up, up, fleet your brilliant bits
> Wheeling and counterwheeling,
> Reeling, broken beyond healing:
> Now grow together on the ceiling!
>
> ('Introduction', 77–81)

This combination of dramatic and lyric provided the primary foundation of the method of many modern poets. Pound's description of the 'dramatic lyric . . . the sort of thing I do' could be seen as an elaboration of Browning's original description of *Dramatic Lyrics* – 'often Lyric in expression, always Dramatic in principle . . .':

To me the short so-called dramatic lyric – at any rate the sort of thing I do – is the poetic part of a drama the rest of which (to me the prose part) is left to the reader's imagination or implied or set in a short note. I catch the character I happen to be interested in at the moment he interests me, usually a moment of song, self-analysis, or sudden understanding or revelation. And the rest of the play would bore me and presumably the reader. I paint my man as I *conceive* him. Et voilà tout![58]

For Browning as well as for modern poets, the combination of the objectivity of the drama and the subjectivity of the lyric resulted in a new approach to poetry. No longer either a singer of intimate songs, or a shadowy figure moving puppets on a stage, the poet is the creator of masks, which serve both as objects of analysis and as mouthpieces for the poet himself. The poet is thus a sort of scientist

of 'the inmost real', and the delight with which he watches the crowd
of his masked characters must be, as Browning puts it:

> Akin to that which crowns the chemist when he winds
> Thread up and up, till clue be fairly clutched, – unbinds
> The composite, ties fast the simple to its mate,
> And, tracing each effect back to its cause, elate,
> Constructs in fancy, from the fewest primitives,
> The complex and complete, all diverse life, that lives
> Not only in beast, bird, fish, reptile, insect, but
> The very plants and earths and ores. Just so I glut
> My hunger both to be and know the thing I am,
> By contrast with the thing I am not; so, through sham
> And outside, I arrive at inmost real, probe
> And prove how the nude form obtained the chequered robe.
>
> (Fifine, CIII)

5
The Musical Analogy

Pound and the Imagists insisted that the poem is an object in the same sense that a painting or a sculpture are objects. Yet, in addition to this comparison, there was another made by Pound, Eliot, W. C. Williams and other modern poets: the analogy of poetry with music. Pound made these two analogies explicit when he said:

> There have always been two sorts of poetry which are, for me at least, the most 'poetic'; they are firstly, the sort of poetry which seems to be music just forcing itself into articulate speech, and secondly, that sort of poetry which seems as if sculpture or painting were just forced or forcing itself into words.[1]

In 'Vorticism' Pound identified the poetry in which music 'seems as if it were just bursting into speech' as 'lyric', and the poetry in which painting or sculpture seems as if it were '"just coming over into speech"' as 'Imagisme'.[2] However, it is perhaps best not to take this separate classification too rigidly, for Pound emphasised throughout his career that the concrete image was important, and that all poets should study music: 'Poets who are not interested in music are, or become, bad poets. I would almost say that poets should never be too long out of touch with musicians. Poets who will not study music are defective.'[3]

The relation between music and poetry has been explored not only by Pound, but also by many modern critics, especially those concerned with Eliot's poetry. John Press,[4] I. A. Richards,[5] F. R. Leavis,[6] Herbert Howarth,[7] Genesius Jones,[8] H. S. Gross[9] and others have discussed Eliot's poems in relation to music – Jones saying, for example, that the *Four Quartets* is structurally related to Bartók's *Sixth String Quartet*, and Howarth asserting that the relation is not to Bartók, but to Beethoven's *Quartet in A minor*, op. 132.[10]

Other critics, however, have protested against any close analogy of poetry to music. In *Theory of Literature*, René Wellek and Austin Warren argue that 'musicality' in verse is really very different from 'melody' in music; that literary imitations of musical structures like the sonata can be better understood by using explanations based on familiar literary devices; that 'With such romantic poets as Tieck and, later, Verlaine, the attempts to achieve musical effects are largely attempts to suppress the meaning structure of verse, to avoid logical constructions, to stress connotations rather than denotations'; and that poetry suggesting definite musical sounds often uses devices 'not much beyond ordinary onomatopoeia' – Poe's 'Bells' being an example.[11]

For Poe and many nineteenth-century poets, a 'musical' poem was one which exhibited a certain flowing smoothness of rhythm and sound:

> And the Raven, never flitting, still is sitting, still is sitting
> On the pallid bust of Pallas just above my chamber door;
> And his eyes have all the seeming of a demon's that is dreaming,
> And the lamplight o'er him streaming throws his shadow on the
> floor;
> And my soul from out that shadow that lies floating on the floor
> Shall be lifted – nevermore! ('The Raven')

The one-word refrain – 'nevermore' – was chosen primarily on the basis of its sound. Poe reasoned that the close of each stanza, 'to have force, must be sonorous and susceptible of protracted emphasis':

> ... and these considerations inevitably led me to the long *o* as the most sonorous vowel, in connection with *r* as the most producible consonant.
>
> The sound of the *refrain* being thus determined, it became necessary to select a word embodying this sound ...[12]

Although not stressing sound before sense to this extent, Tennyson, also, was very conscious of what might be called the musical quality of his verse. In this, he saw himself as different from his fellow poet, Browning:

> Browning ... never greatly cares about the glory of words or beauty of form: he has told me that the world must take him as it finds him. ... He has a mighty intellect, but sometimes I cannot read him. He seldom attempts the marriage of sense with sound, although he shows a spontaneous felicity in the adaptation of words to ideas and feelings. I wish I had written his two lines:
> 'The little more and how much it is,
> The little less and what worlds away.'
> He has plenty of music in him, but he cannot get it out.[13]

And Carlyle made a similar observation, although in characteristically blunter fashion: 'Alfred knows how to jingle, but Browning does not.'[14]

For twentieth-century poets, however, the analogy of music to poetry is based on far different grounds from an ability to 'jingle', or a care for 'the glory of words'. What is likely to be considered musical about modern poetry is not its sound but its shape; not the frequency of alliteration and harmonious vowel sounds, but the use of structures uniquely fitted to express highly complex states of feeling. Not music's beauty, but music's power, is what modern poets seek.

Poetry was to take on this power through two specific approaches. First, 'as regarding rhythm: to compose in the sequence of the musical phrase, not in sequence of a metronome.'[15] Modern poets began to shape their lines around the rhythm of the speaking voice rather than following any predetermined poetic form. Pound advised poets to

Let the beginning of the next line catch the rise of the rhythm wave, unless you want a definite longish pause.
    In short, behave as a musician, a good musician, when dealing with that phase of your art which has exact parallels in music. The same laws govern, and you are bound by no others.[16]

The second approach of poetry to music involved the conscious attempt to express that which was abstract through a particular arrangement of concrete terms. Pound's 'Vorticism' opened with the statement that:

'It is no more ridiculous that a person should receive or convey an emotion by means of an arrangement of shapes, or planes, or colours, than that they should receive or convey such emotion by an arrangement of musical notes.'
    I suppose this proposition is self-evident. Whistler said as much, some years ago, and Pater proclaimed that 'All arts approach the conditions of music.'[17]

Eliot, speaking of Pound's emphasis on the importance of music for the poet, pointed out that

Such a relation between poetry and music is very different from what is called the 'music' of Shelley, or Swinburne, a music often nearer to rhetoric (or the art of the orator) than to the instrument. For poetry to approach the condition of music (Pound quotes approvingly the dictum of Pater) it is not necessary that poetry should be destitute of meaning. Instead of slightly veiled and resonant abstractions, like:

> Time with a gift of tears,
> Grief with a glass that ran –

of Swinburne, or the mossiness of Mallarmé, Pound's verse is always definite and concrete, because he has always a definite emotion behind it.[18]

So far was Pound's notion of the relation of music and poetry different from that of the nineteenth century, that when he desired to 'resurrect the art of the lyric' ('words to be sung'), he chose as a model Browning – 'And with a few exceptions (a few in Browning) there is scarcely anything since the time of Waller and Campion. And a mere imitation of them won't do.'[19]

It is significant that Pound should cite Browning in connection with the 'music of verse', for the primary nineteenth-century examples of the conscious influence of music on verse are found in the French poets. Baudelaire and Mallarmé were drawn to the music of Wagner, Mallarmé partially because of Wagner's use of music 'to suggest an object or a state without naming it'.[20] And of all nineteenth-century poetry, that of the French Symbolists exhibits the most pervasive use of structures of syntax and techniques of association so characteristic of much modern poetry. 'Against this serious action', as Pound referred to the French literature of the nineteenth century, 'England can offer only Robert Browning. He has no French or European parallel.'[21]

In addition to writing the lyrics which Pound admired, Browning would not have fallen under Pound's category of those 'defective' poets who refused to study music. Browning's interest and training in music is well documented; at one point Browning even thought that music might be 'his Métier.'[22] Even as a poet, Browning considered music to be the supreme art. When Paracelsus asks Aprile to 'Tell me what thou wouldst be', Aprile says that first he 'would carve in stone, or cast in brass,/The forms of earth' (II, 421–2). Then, later, 'I would contrive and paint/Woods, valleys, rocks and plains, dells, sands and wastes' (II, 450–1). Thirdly,

> I would throw down the pencil as the chisel,
> And I would speak . . .
>
> And this in language as the need should be,
> Now poured at once forth in a burning flow,
> Now piled up in a grand array of words.
>
> (II, 464–5, 472–4)

But after the carving, the painting and the speaking had ended, the last and highest artistic activity would be to 'supply all chasms with music':

> This done, to perfect and consummate all,
> Even as a luminous haze links star to star,
> I would supply all chasms with music, breathing
> Mysterious motions of the soul, no way
> To be defined save in strange melodies. (II, 475–9)

From *Pauline* to the poems written in the last years of his life, Browning praised music not so much for its beauty as for its power to express the indefinable movements of feeling. 'Thought hankers after speech', said Browning, 'while no speech may evince/Feeling like music . . .' (*Fifine*, XC):

> Up with thy fine free force, oh Music, that canst thrid,
> Electrically win a passage through the lid
> Of earthly sepulchre, our words may push against,
> Hardly transpierce as thou! Not dissipate, thou deign'st,
> So much as tricksily elude what words attempt
> To heave away, i' the mass, and let the soul, exempt
> From all that vapoury obstruction, view, instead
> Of glimmer underneath, a glory overhead. (*Fifine*, LXI)

What Browning admires here is the very freedom of music. Like electricity, music can pass through the barrier of solid matter. Words, however, are laden with matter, for wherever they are used, they carry with them certain fixed meanings. When Zukofsky called a poem 'a context associated with "musical" shape', he emphasised 'musical with quotation marks since it is not of notes as music, but of words more variable than variables, and used outside as well as within the context with communicative reference.'[23] It is this necessary association of words with meanings which leads Stephen Spender, for one, to criticise a term such as 'absolute poetry' used in conjunction with a musical analogy. Reviewing Clark Emery's *The World of Dylan Thomas*, Spender said:

> Describing this poem ['Altarwise by owl-light'] as 'absolute poetry' he [Emery] remarks that 'No one expects a Bach fugue to describe anything or to be anything but what it is,' which, with all respect, seems to me to be fashionable cant. . . . Words are words and not notes in music. Language as a medium, even when used within the insulated context of the most hermetic poem, retains meanings evocative of the meaning of language outside the poem itself.[24]

While agreeing with Spender's rejection of too close an identification of words with notes in music, one can still see a sense in which 'Altarwise by owl-light' is radically different from any nineteenth-century poem. The meaning which emerges from Thomas's particular use of words is not the sort of meaning which one can even begin to restate in other terms. The sound and movement of the words seem to contribute as much to the 'meaning' as the words themselves; and in this sense an analogy to music might be the most appropriate way of describing the peculiar effect of the poem. This approach to poetry Eliot contrasted to that taken by a poet such as Kipling:

> For Kipling the poem is something which is intended to *act* – and for the most part his poems are intended to elicit the same response from all readers, and only the response which they can make in common. For other poets – at least, for some other poets – the poem may begin to shape itself in fragments of musical rhythm, and its structure will first appear in terms of something analogous to musical form; and such poets find it expedient to occupy their conscious mind with the craftsman's problems, leaving the deeper meaning to emerge from a lower level. It is a question then of what one chooses to be conscious of, and of how much the meaning, in a poem, is conveyed direct to the intelligence and how much is conveyed indirectly by the musical impression upon the sensibility – always remembering that the use of the word 'musical' and of musical analogies, in discussing poetry, has its dangers if we do not constantly check its limitations: for the music of verse is inseparable from the meanings and associations of words. ('Rudyard Kipling')[25]

If the poet's conscious mind is concerned primarily with 'the craftsman's problems', the sort of meaning which emerges from a lower level is obviously not one of conscious logical arguments or ideas; rather, it is a meaning conveyed through associations, and the interactions between images and between sounds – a meaning which is felt, more than understood. The poem is built of words and images, objects from the realm of things to be experienced sensuously. Yet the order into which the words and images are placed, the structural net which binds these 'objects' together is not in itself 'objective', but very much connected with the inner workings of the poet's mind, with that lower level from which meaning emerges. For modern poetry, said Zukofsky, 'Emotion is the organizer of poetic form. The image is at the basis of poetic form.'[26] And F. R. Leavis, speaking of Eliot's *The Waste Land*, pointed out further implications of this new approach to poetic form:

> . . . the unity of *The Waste Land* is no more 'metaphysical' than it is narrative or dramatic, and to try to elucidate it metaphysically reveals complete misunderstanding. The unity the poem aims at is that of an inclusive consciousness: the organization it achieves as a work of art is . . . an organization that may, by analogy, be called musical. It exhibits no progression.[27]

Pound's *Cantos* also reflect this lack of obvious narrative or logical progression. The meaning emerges from the work as a whole rather than being conveyed directly from poet to reader as the poem proceeds. When Pound began his *Cantos*, he was very much aware of what Browning had done before him – 'Hang it all, there can be but one *Sordello!*' (from an early draft of Canto I). *Sordello*, like Pound's *Cantos* and *The Waste Land*, is organised not through any logical progression of ideas or narrative sequence of events, but as a network of related images, recurring themes, and the juxtaposition of past, present and future. The difficulty this created for the nineteenth-century reader was noted by Elizabeth Barrett:

> I think that the principle of association is too subtly in movement throughout it – so that *while* you are going straight forward you go at the same time round & round, until the progress involved in the motion is lost sight of by the lookers on. Or did I tell you that before?[28]

The principle of association evident throughout *Sordello* was the result of an attempt to overcome that difficulty language has in clothing 'perceptions whole' (II, 589). The lack of straightforward progression in the story is reflected in the frequent absence of regular grammatical progression in the lines. The reader must skip back and forth in the sentence, holding individual words in suspension until he is able to relate one word to another and create a meaningful pattern from the pieces. The following is a relatively simple example of a syntactical structure common in *Sordello*:

> Nor turned he till Ferrara's din
> (Say, the monotonous speech from a man's lip
> Who lets some first and eager purpose slip
> In a new fancy's birth – the speech keeps on
> Though elsewhere its informing soul be gone)
> – Aroused him, surely offered succour. (VI, 16–21)

Here the subject of the dependent clause – 'Ferrara's din' – is separated from its main verb – 'Aroused' – by four lines of parenthetical comparison. If the reader has turned his full attention to these parenthetical lines, he has probably forgotten the subject by the time he reaches the verb. Understanding the passage would then require that he go back to the subject in order to fit it to the verb – 'Till Ferrara's din ... Aroused him'; and finally, that he re-read the parenthetical comparison in order to connect it to the elements of the main clause surrounding it.

Through employing antitheses and repetition, as well as other linking devices, Browning continually forces one element to partake of others, thus not merely pointing out the interrelatedness of one idea to another, but causing the reader to experience this interrelatedness in finding his way through the density of structure. It is this very density of interrelated structures which is one of the main barriers to the reading of *Sordello*; for if everything is connected with everything else, not in sense but through the grammatical structures and the imagery, the reader is required to piece together an extremely complex pattern from a large number of lines.

For example, the words 'The real way seemed made up of all the ways' in itself presents no problem in reading. But this initial statement Browning carries through twenty-one lines, gathering concepts and phrases in every line, so that by the end of the sentence, if the reader has managed to hold all the structural pieces together in his mind, he has not merely witnessed a description of Sordello's moods, but has actually read through 'Mood after mood of the one mind in him':

> The real way seemed made up of all the ways –
> Mood after mood of the one mind in him;
> Tokens of the existence, bright or dim,
> Of a transcendent all-embracing sense
> Demanding only outward influence,
> A soul, in Palma's phrase, above his soul,
> Power to uplift his power, – such moon's control
> Over such sea-depths, – and their mass had swept
> Onward from the beginning and still kept
> Its course: but years and years the sky above
> Held none, and so, untasked of any love,
> His sensitiveness idled, now amort,
> Alive now, and, to sullenness or sport
> Given wholly up, disposed itself anew
> At every passing instigation, grew
> And dwindled at caprice, in foam-showers spilt,
> Wedge-like insisting, quivered now a gilt
> Shield in the sunshine, now a blinding race
> Of whitest ripples o'er the reef – found place
> For much display; not gathered up and, hurled
> Right from its heart, encompassing the world. (VI, 36–56)

The density of structure is a static density – like a web, the syntax suspends a number of elements, and the reader must experience these elements not one by one, but all together.

In modern poetry, also, the principle of association is closely related to the syntactical structure. However, unlike *Sordello*, where the inner or emotional organisation is carried by the syntax, many modern poems exhibit a straightforward syntax of ordinary speech – but within this structure, the words and images which are brought together are not in any sense 'ordinary'. And again, the meaning emerges only through the association of these elements, not through any logical progression from one to another:

> You, Doctor Martin, walk
>   from breakfast to madness. Late August,
> I speed through the antiseptic tunnel
>   where the moving dead still talk

of pushing their bones against the thrust
of cure. And I am queen of this summer hotel
or the laughing bee on a stalk

of death. (Anne Sexton, 'You, Doctor Martin')

When this principle of association is carried somewhat further, one can understand how a term such as 'absolute poetry' might originate:

Altarwise by owl-light in the half-way house
The gentleman lay graveward with his furies;
Abaddon in the hangnail cracked from Adam,
And, from his fork, a dog among the fairies,
The atlas-eater with a jaw for news,
Bit out the mandrake with tomorrow's scream.

('Altarwise by owl-light')

Within this straightforward syntactical structure, most of the nouns are concrete: dog, fork, fairies. But when the words are brought together, and even when only two words are linked, the ostensibly 'objective' syntax and grammar begin to take on a highly 'subjective' cast. One can imagine 'atlas' and one can imagine 'eater', but 'atlas-eater', even though composed of concrete elements, becomes a very abstract image.

The meaning of such a poem is primarily felt rather than understood on a logical level; or, in Eliot's terms, the meaning emerges from 'a lower level'. In this emergence of meaning, syntax plays a large part. For example, in 'Altarwise by owl-light', merely by substituting other nouns and adjectives, one can compose a perfectly meaningful sentence – 'meaningful' in the ordinary sense of the term:

Afterwards, by moonlight in the large, old house,
The gentleman lay wrestling with his sorrows.

The point of this exercise would be merely to illustrate how syntax operates on a 'lower level' to create meaning, an operation which is highly formal and abstract. Using this tendency of syntax to carry meaning, computers have been programmed to generate verse:

The clean
wall attacks the clean
brain. Brightly the grave
jar rides my
dream . . .[29]

The most familiar example of the creation of meaning through the exploitation of familiar forms and sounds is found in *Through the Looking-Glass*:

> 'Twas brillig, and the slithy toves
> Did gyre and gimble in the wabe:
> All mimsy were the borogoves,
> And the mome raths outgrabe. ('Jabberwocky')

Without going to the lengths of this parody, modern poets have frequently exploited familiar syntactical constructions in the association of words from many different contexts. The wrenching of words from their normal contexts – a device common to poetry of all ages – has been especially emphasised in modern poetry. For example, in E. E. Cummings's 'my father moved through dooms of love', within one line, an adjective ('same') becomes a noun ('sames'), and three verbs become the objects of prepositions ('of am through haves of give'). The words, all of them very 'ordinary', assume an unexpected power when given a new syntactical context:

> my father moved through dooms of love
> through sames of am through haves of give,
> singing each morning out of each night
> my father moved through depths of height...

The most striking anticipation of this twentieth-century characteristic is to be found in the poetry of Hopkins. In 'Carrion Comfort', for example, the adjective 'rude' is placed in a verbal position and thus carries the force of a verb within the syntactical structure:

> But ah, but O thou terrible, why wouldst thou rude on me
> Thy wring-world right foot rock?

While Browning's poetry does not display this characteristic as consistently as does that of Hopkins, it is certainly present throughout much of the earlier poet's work:

> But human promise, oh, how short of shine!
> How topple down the piles of hope we rear!
>
> (*The Ring and the Book*, I, 295–6)

Modern poets have used syntax not only as a means to associate disparate elements, but also as a formal poetic device in itself. Many of Eliot's poems are composed of units arranged in parallel syntactical order:

Who walked between the violet and the violet
Who walked between
The various ranks of varied green ...

('Ash Wednesday', IV)

Paint me a cavernous waste shore
    Cast in the unstilled Cyclades,
Paint me the bold anfractuous rocks
    Faced by the snarled and yelping seas.

('Sweeney Erect')

After the torchlight red on sweaty faces
After the frosty silence in the gardens
After the agony in stony places ...

(The Waste Land, V, 22-4)

As Hopkins provided the clearest example in the nineteenth century of the moving of parts of speech from their usual contexts, so
Whitman is perhaps the forerunner to this modern emphasis on
syntactically parallel structures.[30]

Not heaving from my ribb'd breast only,
Not in sighs at night in rage dissatisfied with myself,
Not in those long-drawn, ill-supprest sighs,
Not in many an oath and promise broken ...

('Not Heaving from my Ribb'd Breast Only')

Within the analogy of music and poetry, it is syntax which
modern poets have exploited as one of the major devices to appropriate for language the power of music. Within a syntactical structure
lies a pattern of meaning, not so much understood as felt – a pattern
abstract and flexible enough to carry within it the most disparate
of elements. It is this pattern of meaning, rather than the pattern of
sound, which becomes the music in poetry; or as H. S. Gross has put
it:

Syntax, the order of words as they arrange themselves into
patterns of meaning, is the analogue to harmony in music. Like
harmony, syntax generates tension and relaxation, the feelings of
expectation and fulfillment which make up the dynamics of poetic
life.[31]

Yet the pattern of sound in the structure of syntax cannot be ignored. What Eliot called the 'auditory imagination' might partially account for the sense that the rhythm and the sound of words is also somehow a part of the felt meaning:

> ... the 'auditory imagination' is the feeling for syllable and rhythm, penetrating far below the conscious levels of thought and feeling, invigorating every word; sinking to the most primitive and forgotten, returning to the origin and bringing something back, seeking the beginning and the end. It works through meanings, certainly, or not without meanings in the ordinary sense, and fuses the old and obliterated and the trite, the current, and the new and surprising, the most ancient and the most civilised mentality. ('Matthew Arnold')[32]

Although the auditory imagination works through meanings, Eliot himself said 'that a poem, or a passage of a poem, may tend to realise itself first as a particular rhythm before it reaches expression in words, and that this rhythm may bring to birth the idea and the image...'[33]

For all his roughness of texture, Browning, too, was aware of the power of rhythm to create a sort of hypnotic movement of sound. Indeed, several of Browning's poems seem to exist primarily for the sake of the rhythmical effect:

> As I ride, as I ride,
> With a full heart for my guide,
> So its tide rocks my side,
> As I ride, as I ride ...
> ('Through the Metidja to Abd-El-Kadr', 1)

> Where the quiet-coloured end of evening smiles
> Miles and miles
> On the solitary pastures where our sheep
> Half-asleep
> Tinkle homeward thro' the twilight, stray or stop
> As they crop ... ('Love Among the Ruins', 1)

The hypnotic aspect of 'Love Among the Ruins' was noticed by D. H. Lawrence who presented Birkin in *Women in Love* as riding in a train, reciting the first verse 'like a man condemned to death'.[34]

It might be argued that this sort of hypnotic repetition of syntactical structures is just the sort of 'musical' effect which twentieth-century poets wished to avoid, and that in fact, the best examples of this kind of writing are to be found in a nineteenth-century poet – Tennyson:

> The woods decay, the woods decay and fall,
> The vapours weep their burthen to the ground,
> Man comes and tills the field and lies beneath,
> And after many a summer dies the swan.
>
> ('Tithonus', 1–4)

With the opening of 'Tithonus' Tennyson sets an appropriate scene for the story to follow. The decay of the natural world reflects the mood of Tithonus, and the rhythm of the verse further helps to convey this mood to the reader.

Yet between nineteenth- and twentieth-century poetry there is a significant difference in the use of parallel syntax, a difference which can be seen when the opening of 'Tithonus' is compared with that of 'Ash Wednesday':

> Because I do not hope to turn again
> Because I do not hope
> Because I do not hope to turn . . . (I)

Perhaps the most immediately noticeable difference is that in Eliot, the parallel construction is emphasised; not only is the syntactical structure repeated, but the same word occupies the same place in each line. However much the syllables and rhythm operate below the level of conscious thought and feeling, they are apparent to the reader on a conscious level as well, so that the reader recognises this pattern wherever it occurs in the poem – 'Because I do not hope to know again', 'Because I know I shall not know', 'Because I know that time is always time', 'Because I do not hope to turn again' (I). This awareness of repeated patterns becomes a conscious experience of the formal sonal elements of the verse – the reader feels the structural bones beneath the flesh, much as the audience of a folk-ballad performance might.

This calling of attention to parallel syntactical structures is a characteristic found in much modern poetry. Form is made a focus of experience for the reader as well as the poet. Where, for example, in 'Sea Surface Full of Clouds', Wallace Stevens uses the same structure again and again, the variations become extremely important:

    I. In that November off Tehuantepec,
        The slopping of the sea grew still one night
        And in the morning summer hued the deck

        And made one think of rosy chocolate
        And gilt umbrellas...

    II. In that November off Tehuantepec
        The slopping of the sea grew still one night.
        At breakfast jelly yellow streaked the deck

        And made one think of chop-house chocolate
        And sham umbrellas...

    III. In that November off Tehuantepec,
        The slopping of the sea grew still one night
        And a pale silver patterned on the deck

        And made one think of porcelain chocolate
        And pied umbrellas...

    IV. In that November off Tehuantepec
        The night-long slopping of the sea grew still.
        A mallow morning dozed upon the deck

        And made one think of musky chocolate
        And frail umbrellas...

    V. In that November off Tehuantepec
        Night stilled the slopping of the sea. The day
        Came, bowing and voluble, upon the deck,

        Good clown.... One thought of Chinese chocolate
        And large umbrellas...

The sea appears different from morning to morning because there is a sensitive intelligence to see the difference in sameness, and to create analogies to express this difference. In this way, the poet becomes like the singer in 'The Idea of Order at Key West':

It was her voice that made
The sky acutest at its vanishing.
She measured to the hour its solitude.
She was the single artificer of the world
In which she sang. And when she sang, the sea,
Whatever self it had, became the self
That was her song, for she was the maker.

In many modern poems, as in 'Sea Surface Full of Clouds', not
only are the syntactical parallels emphasised, but also certain images
are repeated and developed within the course of the poem. Imagery
does not only paint a background picture or help to create an atmosphere, but is in itself part of the structural skeleton of the poem.

Modern poets writing in this way have influenced modern critics
to look much more closely at poetic structure than their nineteenth-
century predecessors did. Conversely, it could be argued that the
very nature of the twentieth century has induced both artists and
critics to analyse a poem from the point of view of its structure
rather than its philosophy. This new critical approach was in part
developed by critics who were themselves poets – Eliot and John
Crowe Ransom being obvious examples. The questions put to a
modern poem are not so much 'what can we learn from it?' and 'is it
beautiful and harmonious?' but 'how is it constructed?' and 'how
does it produce its effects?' For purposes of analysis, the poem is seen
as a self-contained world with its own systems of organisation and
internal dynamics.

Using this close critical approach, modern critics have re-examined
Shakespeare and Donne and discovered complex structures of syntax
and imagery – the result has been a new appreciation for these poets
in the twentieth century. However, nineteenth-century poets such
as Tennyson and Browning have not received as much close critical
attention, possibly because their long poems require a more extended
analysis than the sonnets of Shakespeare and Donne and the characteristically shorter poems of the modern poets. Yet when a close
analysis is made of Browning's poems, for example, patterns of
imagery begin to reveal a structural significance. As Park Honan has
pointed out, Browning often uses imagery as a way of creating
character.[35] The drama of Caliban is largely shown through the
interweaving of numerous animal images. In thinking about Setebos,
Caliban does not reason with abstract terms, but uses the material

of his physical existence – life as embodied in living creatures rather than ideas. Moreover, Caliban's images often reflect his own sense of powerlessness, for most of them are of crawling things or insects – bees, spiders, moles, tortoises, leeches, worms, ants, grubs, maggots, crabs, flies, beetles, crickets, serpents. These images develop the initial picture of Caliban, sprawling on his belly in the mire and looking from his cave out to sea.

In Browning's poetry, syntax is not used as the vehicle of meaning to the extent that it is in Dylan Thomas's poetry, nor is parallel syntax as important a formal device as it is in Eliot. Yet Browning's own concern with form, and with newness of form – a concern extended by modern poets – is reflected in his poetry. *Sordello*, with its complex syntactical structures and its interwoven patterns of repeated imagery and colours, is one such laboratory of formal devices. Another is *Pippa Passes*, written near the time of *Sordello*, but entirely different in its use of language and poetic form.

In *Pippa Passes*, a series of apparently unrelated incidents and the alternation of various poetic styles from prose to blank verse to irregular rhyming stanzas, are held together by the appearance in each section of the wandering Pippa, singing a song. In addition to this tying together on a spatial plane, there is also a temporal connection upheld by the underlying imagery of the passing of a day, from morning through noon and evening, into the night. The Introduction to the four sections sets up the underlying structure in the same way that an overture to an opera introduces the arias and choruses to follow – and in this Browning could be said to have fulfilled something of his desire to write an opera.[36]

The four scenes of the drama introduced in the 'overture', Pippa's song to the day, are linked to the movements of the day itself – morning, noon, evening, night. Pippa challenges the day to rain on 'Asolo's Four Happiest Ones': if morning rained on Ottima, Sebald would only press her closer; if the mid-day were gloomy, Jules and Phene would still have sunshine within; if the eve were misty, Luigi and his mother would be content, and would be received by the 'cheerful town'; and if the night were stormy, the Monsignor's peace would not be disturbed, for his thoughts would ward off thunder, and the angels would guard him (42–68). The irony of Pippa's term 'Asolo's Four Happiest Ones', is revealed to the reader scene by scene; and a further irony is evident in that Pippa's own day has a profound influence on each of the 'happy ones' she passes.

A closer examination of the Introduction reveals the surprising
variety of structural devices used in this 'drama'. The first word –
'Day!' – stands on a line by itself. This abrupt opening is followed
by a remarkable image, extended over the next twelve lines, of the day
as liquid boiling over the brim of the night. The image of the boiling
sun is then carried over into Pippa's speech to the day, the division
between the description and Pippa's speech being indicated by
a slight shift in rhythm from predominantly iambic to anapaestic:

> Oh, Day, if I squander a wavelet of thee,
> A mite of my twelve hours' treasure,
> The least of thy gazes or glances,
> (Be they grants thou art bound to or gifts above measure)
> One of thy choices or one of thy chances,
> (Be they tasks God imposed thee or freaks at thy pleasure)
> – My Day, if I squander such labour or leisure,
> Then shame fall on Asolo, mischief on me!
>
> ('Introduction', 13–20)

The tightness of construction in Pippa's opening speech is characteristic of Browning's conscious attention to elements of syntax. The
first and last lines form the central idea: 'Oh, Day, if I squander a
wavelet of thee ... Then shame fall on Asolo, mischief on me!' This
linking of first and last lines is further emphasised by the rhyme
pattern. In effect, the middle lines are parenthetical, an expansion of
the central idea which creates a density of texture in the verse.
Within these parenthetical lines are yet further associations of form
and meaning. The lines explicitly enclosed within parentheses are
linked through parallel syntactical construction and rhyme ('measure' – 'pleasure'). Furthermore, the language in these eight lines
develops the initial image of the day as liquid gold. Pippa says she
must not 'squander' a 'mite' of her 'twelve hours' treasure', whether
the glances of the day are 'grants' or 'gifts'. She must spend her
liquid gold wisely or, as she warns herself, 'shame fall on Asolo,
mischief on me!' That shame would have fallen on Asolo and mischief on herself is, as Browning shows, exactly what would have
happened if Pippa had not spent her treasure wisely.

In the Introduction, then, is outlined the double pattern of the
action and theme. The action is Pippa's movement through the day,
her influence on four types of lovers: the worldly lovers, the romantic
lovers, the parent and child, and the man who loves God. Interwoven

through this action is the theme – the importance of the lesser in
relation to the larger. Pippa's mite of her twelve hours' treasure is
like the widow's mite which Jesus considered to be more precious
than the money of all those who gave of their riches. The day 'God
lends to leaven/What were all earth else' (39–40) becomes in turn
the yeast which leavens the hours of others, as Pippa goes through
Asolo singing. In the first song, which Pippa sings to herself, the
theme of the importance of the small is made explicit: 'Say not "a
small event!" Why "small"?' (196). And in the second song, the
theme is implicit in the sequence of the imagery:

> The year's at the spring
> And day's at the morn;
> Morning's at seven;
> The hill-side's dew-pearled;
> The lark's on the wing;
> The snail's on the thorn:
> God's in his heaven –
> All's right with the world! (I, 221–8)

As Archibald Hill points out, the metrical structure of the song is
'remarkably rigid'.[37] The first three lines present the year, the day
and the morning at their best – spring, morn, seven. The sequence
here is from large to small. The fifth to seventh lines present three
'creatures' each in their 'best places' – and here the sequence is
from smaller to largest. The final line then acts as a summary – 'All's
right with the world!'[38]

In a sense, Browning later provided his own interpretation of
these lines, one which does not contradict that presented by Hill:

> We find great things are made of little things,
> And little things go lessening till at last
> Comes God behind them.
>
>   ('Mr Sludge, "the Medium,"' 112–14)

As Hill said, his analysis 'rests on one of the most basic assumptions in linguistics, that it is form which gives meaning and not
meaning which gives form.'[39]

This is not to say that the ideal is not a perfect harmony of form
and meaning; but that modern thought, as a corrective to what was
perceived to be an undue emphasis on meaning in nineteenth-century
studies, has stressed the close examination of formal structures. In

modern lyric poetry, as in Browning's poetry, the prose directness of everyday speech is carried within highly formal, even if unconventional, verse structures.

Browning claimed for himself the freedom to combine poetic and dramatic elements. Yet within this freedom there is a tight poetic form which bears the close scrutiny normally paid to a modern lyric. Pippa's song is not a song to be sung (for it is in a drama to be read); nor is it a 'verse' which could be read aloud on a stage with any dramatic success; rather, it is a formal device which by its very structure bears in miniature the meaning which comes through the drama as a whole.

The combination of the prose directness of everyday speech with the poetic intensity of formal verse-structures is evident throughout *Pippa Passes*. For example, when Luigi speaks to his mother, the change of mood as Luigi's description of practical details of the assassination becomes a vision of heroic sacrifice, is mirrored by the change in syntax:

> Take the great gate, and walk (not saunter) on
> Thro' guards and guards – I have rehearsed it all
> Inside the turret here a hundred times . . .
>
> Walk in – straight up to him; you have no knife:
> Be prompt, how should he scream? Then, out with you!
> Italy, Italy, my Italy!
> You're free, you're free! Oh mother, I could dream
> They got about me – Andrea from his exile,
> Pier from his dungeon, Gualtier from his grave!
>
> (III, 110–12, 118–23)

The straightforward language of the opening is suddenly interrupted by 'Italy, Italy, my Italy!' and 'You're free, you're free!' These exclamations are followed by the colloquial 'O mother, I could dream / They got about me –'; and then the passage ends with the very formal listing, in parallel construction, of the three earlier patriots:

> Andrea from his exile
> Pier from his dungeon
> Gualtier from his grave!

The parallel structure exhibits a progression as well – exile, dungeon, grave – which perhaps carries a hint of Luigi's fate.

Elizabeth Barrett called the conception of *Pippa Passes* 'most exquisite & altogether original – and the contrast in the working out of the plan, singularly expressive of various faculty.'[40] The variety of form in *Pippa Passes* can be seen in Browning's abrupt transitions from one sort of lyric poetry to another, or to prose, and from one tone to another. For example, Ottima's 'Not to me – to him, O God, be merciful!' is followed by a short stage direction and then the first student's:

> Attention! My own post is beneath this window, but the pomegranate clump yonder will hide three or four of you with a little squeezing, and Schramm and his pipe must lie flat in the balcony. (I, 283–7)

Again, after Jules' closing words in Part II, there is only a brief pause while 'Pippa is passing from Orcana to the Turret' and then Bluphocks' prose appears:

> JULES.   And you are ever by me while I gaze
> – Are in my arms as now – as now – as now!
> Some unsuspected isle in the far seas!
> Some unsuspected isle in far-off seas!
>
> *Talk by the way, while* PIPPA *is passing from Orcana to the Turret.*
> *Two or three of the Austrian Police loitering with* BLUPHOCKS, *an*
> *English vagabond, just in view of the Turret.*
>
> BLUPHOCKS. So, that is your Pippa, the little girl who passed us singing? Well, your Bishop's Intendant's money shall be honestly earned: – now, don't make me that sour face because I bring the Bishop's name into the business; we know he can have nothing to do with such horrors: we know that he is a saint and all that a bishop should be, who is a great man beside. *Oh were but every worm a maggot, Every fly a grig, Every bough a Christmas faggot, Every tune a jig!* (II, 324–37)

In modern poetry, even where separate characters are not formally introduced, this rapid transition from one narrative tone to another is often accompanied by an implied transition from one voice to another. For example, in Yeats's 'Words for Music Perhaps' the italicised lines indicate the speech of another voice or point of view:

> Bring me to the blasted oak
> That I, midnight upon the stroke,
> (*All find safety in the tomb.*)

> May call down curses on his head
> Because of my dear Jack that's dead.
> Coxcomb was the least he said:
> *The solid man and the coxcomb.*
>
> (I, 'Crazy Jane and the Bishop')

Eliot, too, uses the counterpointing of one voice with another. In Eliot's own recorded reading of *The Waste Land*, this changing of voices becomes very obvious indeed. The change is one not just of point of view, but of speech patterns as well. The difference between this approach to the use of various voices in the same poem and that of Tennyson's *The Two Voices*, for example, is that in *The Waste Land*, the shift in point of view often occurs without transition, whereas in *The Two Voices*, the speech of one voice is formally separated from that of the other. The reader of *The Waste Land* is given no introduction to the speaker, nor can he expect to hear from the speaker again during the course of the poem. In *The Two Voices*, however, the shift from voice to voice is clearly indicated, and the voices differ not so much in style as they do in philosophy:

> The still voice laughed. 'I talk,' said he,
> 'Not with thy dreams. Suffice it thee
> Thy pain is a reality.'
>
> 'But thou,' said I, 'hast missed thy mark,
> Who sought'st to wreck my mortal ark,
> By making all the horizon dark.'
>
> (*The Two Voices*, 385–90)

> The hot water at ten.
> And if it rains, a closed car at four.
> And we shall play a game of chess,
> Pressing lidless eyes and waiting for a knock upon the door.
>
> When Lil's husband got demobbed, I said –
> I didn't mince my words, I said to her myself,
> HURRY UP PLEASE ITS TIME
> Now Albert's coming back, make yourself a bit smart.
>
> (*The Waste Land*, II, 135–42)

As Eliot saw it, a long poem requires either the introduction of 'a more impersonal point of view' or a splitting of the poem into 'various personalities' ('Blake').⁴¹ Browning's most extended use of various points of view is found in *The Ring and the Book*. However, in *The Ring and the Book*, although the speaker in each monologue may appear to address several different audiences during the course of his speech, there is only one speaker in each monologue, and the monologues are placed side by side, rather than being woven together. In this respect, Browning's series of dramatic monologues is not, like Eliot's, a kind of *collage*,⁴² for the voices are formally separated from each other.

Yet Browning did experiment with a collage of points of view in one of his poems – *Sordello*. For Eliot, the splitting up of the one voice into many is a way to sustain intensity over a large number of lines. One reason for the density of structure in *Sordello* is that, like Eliot, Browning maintains intensity through introducing various personalities as well as a more impersonal point of view. In *Sordello*, these personalities are all aspects of the Poet: the Poet as Sordello, the Poet as subject of Sordello's thought, and the Poet as Browning creating *Sordello*. Sometimes Browning seems to participate in the action through Sordello, sometimes he looks down from an omnipotent height and discourses objectively, and sometimes he steps into the action as the author himself:

> I muse this on a ruined palace-step
> At Venice: why should I break off, nor sit
> Longer upon my step, exhaust the fit
> England gave birth to? (III, 676–9)

Whereas Eliot's changes of voice are often made evident through indentation, a spacing between lines, italics or even quotation marks, Browning's change of voice is usually heralded only by what Michael Mason has called 'signal-words':

> An obscure passage like 2.659–689, for example, can only be
> disentangled by sensing the alternating voices of 'Poet' and 'Man';
> the reader must be alert to the persuasive colourings in such
> signal-words as 'forsooth', 'no time', 'astounding' – a skill that is
> in fact the initiation to a reading of most of Browning's poetry.⁴³

In this collage of points of view, the lines of association faintly traced by the poet must be drawn and experienced by the reader. Similarly, in *Sordello* and in much modern poetry, the images also form a pattern of meaning suggested through association. As men-

tioned in Chapter 1, this modern practice in poetry has a counterpart
in the use of montage in filming. First, images are abstracted from
the scene as a whole. Then these images are presented in a spatial or
temporal sequence. Their significance is created by the audience
which makes connections between one image and the next. In this
way, the film director does not merely record the scene. Yet neither
does he comment directly on the scene, or tell the viewer how to
judge the action. He focuses on details, and by highlighting these
details and putting them into a sequence, he suggests to the viewer
a certain pattern of meaning.

In *Sordello*, Browning uses this technique of presenting a series of
images in sharp detail. The characteristically striking presentation of
isolated images is partly due to his practice of suppressing the 'hues
that softening blend':

> 'I take the task
> 'And marshal you Life's elemental masque,
> 'Show Men, on evil or on good lay stress,
> 'This light, this shade make prominent, suppress
> 'All ordinary hues that softening blend
> 'Such natures with the level.' (v, 583-8)

In *Sordello*, as well as in many modern films and poems, what
causes difficulty in comprehension is not the images themselves, but
the lack of any explicit connection between them – or rather, the
dependence on the reader to feel the emergence of a 'deeper meaning'
from a 'lower level', to create a pattern of meaning not necessarily of
a logical or narrative order. One of the reasons for the narrow appeal
of modern poetry, according to Graham Hough, is just this 'deliberate
cultivation of modes of organization that are utterly at variance with
those of ordinary discourse.'[44]

In Robert Langbaum's view, modern poets are direct descendants of
the Romantics in that they, too, see the poem as a 'quasi-natural
organism':

> The organic theory also breaks down the distinction between the
> poet and his material, because the material is what the poet puts
> forth; and between the poet and the reader, because to apprehend
> the poem the reader must put himself in the poet's place – he must
> make the poem an out-growth of his own mind as well.[45]

While this is an important connection between modern poets and their predecessors, there are significant distinctions as well. In Romantic poetry, the relation of the poet to the narrator is usually made clear; and the structure of the poem itself exhibits a narrative or emotional progression. But in modern poetry, the reader cannot simply 'put himself in the poet's place', because it is not always clear exactly where the poet stands behind his narrative mask; and the structure of the poem is often based on connections the reader himself must make, so the meaning of the poem is seldom made explicit. The experience which the reader shares with the poet is not the 'emotion recollected in tranquillity' of Wordsworth, but the emotion which creates the underlying formal structure of the poem. Zukofsky speaks of writing which is 'the detail, not mirage, of seeing, of thinking with the things as they exist, and of directing them along a line of melody.'[46]

In modern poetry, then, there is an emphasis on the combination of elements – inner and outer, subjective and objective, musical and dramatic. The images of the poems are factual, objective, 'things as they exist'. However, the connection between these images is associative; the poet directs these things as they exist along a 'line of melody', but the ultimate connections must be made in the mind of the reader. And finally, these objective images within a musical structure are conveyed in language of ordinary speech, a dramatic rather than 'poetic' language. This combination of elements in modern poetry is thus able to come closer to expressing what Eliot felt was 'beyond the nameable, classifiable emotions and motives of our conscious life when directed towards action – the part of life which prose drama is wholly adequate to express – ...'[47] In dramatic poetry, 'at its moments of greatest intensity', said Eliot, '... we touch the border of those feelings which only music can express.'[48] What Eliot felt was within the power of dramatic poetry to express, modern poets have taken for lyric poetry as well. Eliot's analysis of the opening of *Hamlet* reveals what he called 'a kind of musical design ... which reinforces and is one with the dramatic movement'.[49]

In Browning's poetry, also, there can be seen the attempt to combine the dramatic with the musical. The series of pamphlets which included *Pippa Passes* Browning entitled 'Bells and Pomegranates', explaining that this title was to indicate 'an endeavour towards something like an alternation, or mixture, of music with discoursing, sound with sense, poetry with thought...'[50] However different Browning's modes of organisation sometimes appear from those of twentieth-century poets, his aim, like theirs, was to appropriate for poetry the power of music, to combine 'feeling with knowledge', the outer concrete with the inner abstract. Yet though Browning felt 'There is no truer truth obtainable/By Man than comes of music' ('Charles Avison', VI), he also realised that music, like poetry, could never fully capture life's flowing movement of time and matter:

> To match and mate
> Feeling with knowledge, – make as manifest
> Soul's work as Mind's work, turbulence as rest,
> Hates, loves, joys, woes, hopes, fears, that rise and sink
> Ceaselessly, passion's transient flit and wink,
> A ripple's tinting or a spume-sheet's spread
> Whitening the wave, – to strike all this life dead,
> Run mercury into a mould like lead,
> And henceforth have the plain result to show –
> How we Feel, hard and fast as what we Know –
> This were the prize and is the puzzle! . . .
>
> Could Music rescue thus from Soul's profound,
> Give feeling immortality by sound,
> Then were she queenliest of Arts! Alas –
> As well expect the rainbow not to pass!
> ('Charles Avison', VII and VIII)

6

The Prose–Poetry Borderline

Traditionally, the borderline between poetry and prose was very clear: poetry was 'verse', and prose was not. In modern literature, however, this distinction has become blurred. A passage in a novel may exhibit patterns of rhythm, alliteration and other characteristics usually associated with verse:

> Bronze by gold heard the hoofirons, steelyringing
> Imperthnthn thnthnthn.
> Chips, picking chips off rocky thumbnail, chips.
> Horrid! And gold flushed more.
> A husky fifenote blew.
> Blew. Blue bloom is on the
> Gold pinnacled hair. (Joyce, *Ulysses*)[1]

And a poem may contain sections which not only read as if they were paragraphs of expository prose, but are printed in paragraph form:

> P. S. That I'm back here at 21 Pine Street causes me to add that that mystery as to who forged the 'Cress' on that money order and also took one of Brown's checks (though his was *not* cashed, and therefore replaced later) never did get cleared up. And the janitor who was here at the time, is dead now. I don't think it was he took any of the money. (Williams, *Paterson*, III)[2]

This interweaving of poetry into prose and prose into poetry is a significant aspect of modern literature. Modern prose writers borrow certain devices traditionally associated with poetry, and poets exploit characteristics usually found in prose. Moreover, both modern poets and modern novelists share certain common concerns: that the novel, like the poem, should be considered an art-object and be judged on its form and treatment of subject-matter rather than on the subject-matter itself; that the approach to the subject should be seen as a particular point of view, one identified with its author not directly, but through a mask or persona; and that the language of art should be, not an artificial language, but the common language, invested with power through the free use of modes of organisation based on association rather than on a narrative or logical order. What makes Browning important to modern literature is that he, too, shared these concerns; and consequently, his poetry exhibits not only many of those aspects of prose so characteristic of modern poetry, but also many of the particular poetic techniques which have been used by modern novelists.

At the turn of the century, many modern poets felt that the poetic tradition which they had inherited from the nineteenth century was incapable of expressing the realities of the twentieth century. As Eliot pointed out, the language which was important to modern poets was not the verse of writers like Swinburne, but 'that which is struggling to digest and express new objects, new groups of objects, new feelings, new aspects, as, for instance, the prose of Mr. James Joyce or the earlier Conrad.'[3] And Pound, in considering what role poetry should assume, wondered, should he 'sulk and leave the word to novelists?'[4]

Even though he did not, he continued to emphasise the study of prose for modern poets. 'Flaubert's *Trois Contes*, especially "Coeur Simple," contain all that anyone knows *about* writing', he said.[5] And as if to emphasise this point, he added: 'And English poetry???? Ugh. Perhaps one shouldn't read it at all.'[6] Yet in the same letter in which he advised a writer to '... kick out every sentence that isn't as Jane Austen would have written it in prose', he also suggested a reading of *Sordello* – 'To limber your muscles ...'[7]

This reference to *Sordello* in the same context as Jane Austen might at first seem surprising. Certainly the contorted syntax and density of structure in *Sordello* are in striking contrast to Jane Austen's clear, crisp prose. But in setting out his 'réformé' for poetry, Pound frequently emphasised the study not only of Flaubert ('mot juste, présentation ou constatation'), but also that of Browning ('dénué des paroles superflues').[8] A novelist and a poet are mentioned not as representatives of separate crafts, but together, as makers of a language from which modern poets could learn. And when Pound insisted on the importance of the language of prose writers for modern poets, he included Browning in his list of writers to study – as if Browning himself were a writer of 'prose'. 'The only English poet that matters twopence is Browning', said Ford in a conversation with Pound, adding that the emotions Browning's work gave him were those of reading prose. Pound agreed.[9]

Pound and Ford were not the first to recognise in Browning 'a prose effect' or to mention him in the context of prose writers. Hopkins, for example, criticised Browning's description of the market place at Florence as 'a pointless photograph of still life, such as I remember in Balzac...'[10] And later, Wilde, who appreciated Browning as a writer of 'fiction', remarked that Browning used poetry 'as a medium for writing in prose'.[11]

Yet if modern poets were not the first to recognise Browning's 'prose effect', they were certainly among the first to praise it. For Pound and others, what Browning had to teach was similar to what prose had to teach. And what prose had to teach poetry, above all else, was directness of language and clarity of mental image.

When Eliot called Browning the only poet of the late nineteenth century 'to devise a way of speech that might be useful to others', he gave two examples of what Browning had to teach: the use of 'non-poetic material' and the reassertion of 'the relation of poetry to speech'.[12] Perhaps Browning's love of the novels of Balzac had something to do with his use of subject-matter which most other nineteenth-century poets left for contemporary novelists to explore. The poetic tradition in English deals for the most part with 'elevated' subject-matter in language more formal than everyday speech; so that when Robert Lowell, for example, attempted to create poetry from the raw material of his life, he concluded by feeling that 'the best style for poetry was none of the many poetic styles in English, but something like the prose of Chekhov or Flaubert.'[13] As Virginia Woolf said, 'prose is so humble that it can go anywhere; no place is too low, too sordid, or too mean for it to enter.'[14]

Prose implied the use of a certain straightforward objectivity which Pound and others felt might serve as an antidote to sentimentality, to sloppiness of expression and to the use of trite 'poetic' phrases. Browning foreshadowed Pound's insistence on straightforward presentation. In a tone and spirit which even sounds Poundian to modern ears, Browning criticised Swinburne's verses as 'florid impotence':

> – the *minimum* of thought and idea in the *maximum* of words and phraseology. Nothing said and done with, left to stand alone and trust for its effect in its own worth. What a way of writing is that wherein, wanting to say that 'a man is sad,' you express it as, 'he looketh like to one, as one might say, who hath a sadness and is sad indeed, so that beholders think "How sad is he!"'[15]

Pound admitted that it was impossible to 'kick out every sentence that isn't as Jane Austen would have written it in prose'. But, he added, 'when you *do* get a limpid line in perfectly straight normal order, isn't it worth any other ten?'[16]

What Pound was stressing here and what he praised in Daniel and others was not prose for the sake of prose, but 'straight normal order' in which the clarity of the mental image, not poetic 'ornamentation', was paramount. Writing of Laurent Tailhade, Pound said:

> I think this sort of clear presentation is of the noblest tradition of our craft. It is surely the scourge of fools. It is what may be called the 'prose tradition' of poetry, and by this I mean that it is a practice of speech common to good prose and good verse alike.... It means constatation of fact. It presents. It does not comment.... It is not a criticism of life. I mean it does not deal in opinion. It washes its hands of theories. It does not attempt to justify anybody's ways to anybody or anything else.[17]

Pound recommended reading *Sordello* at the same time that he recommended writing as Jane Austen would have in prose because in *Sordello* he saw the qualities of prose which he felt were also characteristics of the best poetry. Speaking of *Sordello*, Pound said:

> It will be seen that the author is telling you something, not merely making a noise, he does not gum up the sound. The 'beauty' is not applied ornament, but makes the mental image more definite. The author is not hunting about for large high-sounding words, there is a very great variety in the rhyme but the reader runs on unaware.... the reader must read it as prose, pausing for the sense and not hammering the line-terminations.[18]

Modern poetry, by its very form, often leads the reader to 'perform' or read the lines with the stress on the prose rhythm rather than on the formal metrical pattern. The regular preordained length of the line has given way, in many cases, to stanzas used more like verse paragraphs – as units of thought.

And yet, poetic tightness of structure remains. However complex and formally rigid the verse structure is, the skeleton lies buried beneath the prose surface of the verse, under that ideal 'limpid line in perfectly straight normal order'. For Browning, as for Pound, the best poetry was the most direct embodiment of a mental image – in

Browning's words, a 'strict bald version of thing by thing'.[19] But more attention was paid to the rough surface of his verse ('more blank than verse' and 'of a prosaic texture', as one critic put it)[20] than to the structural skeleton – the incredible tightness of form in *Pippa Passes*, for example, hidden by the common diction and dramatic context. But twentieth-century poets found in Browning's use of prosaic texture and formal poetic skeleton a model for their own verse. Robert Lowell said:

> The couplet I've used is very much like the couplet Browning uses in 'My Last Duchess,' in *Sordello*, run-on with its rhymes buried. I've always, when I've used it, tried to give the impression that I had as much freedom in choosing the rhyme word as I had in any of the other words. Yet they were almost all true rhymes, and maybe half the time there'd be a pause after the rhyme. I wanted something as fluid as prose; you wouldn't notice the form, yet looking back you'd find that great obstacles had been climbed.[21]

'Something as fluid as prose', a form which would emphasise the clarity of the mental image without superfluous ornamentation, poetry with a prose directness – all characteristic of modern poetry and all most clearly seen in Browning. William Rossetti claimed that Browning's poems were first written as prose and that when he turned the prose into verse, he was striving 'after the greatest amount of condensation possible; thus, if an exclamation will suggest his meaning, he substitutes this for a whole sentence.'[22]

Rossetti's description of Browning's poetry points out one of the most obvious characteristics of modern poetry as well – that while the verse structure may be as 'fluid as prose', the density of mental imagery creates an over-all effect which is not fluid. In a poem like *Sordello*, not only are superfluous poetic ornamentations banished, but so also are the syntactical patterns of most prose, where one idea follows another in orderly linear progression, each idea rests in its own modifying phrase, and the entire sentence carries the reader forward to the next. Browning, on the other hand, loads each syntactical unit with a great density of meaning. Modifying phrases, for example, may be used in such a way that they refer both to that which has preceded and to that which follows:

> His sensitiveness idled, now amort,
> Alive now, and, to sullenness or sport

> Given wholly up, disposed itself anew
> At every passing instigation, grew
> And dwindled at caprice ... (VI, 47–51)

Technically, the phrase 'At every passing instigation' modifies the phrase immediately preceding it; but because it is positioned between 'disposed itself anew' and 'grew/And dwindled at caprice', and because it is on the same line as the beginning of the phrase which follows it, its modifying function spreads to both phrases. Upon reaching 'At every passing instigation', the reader must look both backward and forward in the lines, at least to the extent that the significance of the phrase spreads in all directions.

The result of this method of extreme condensation is that Browning's poetry, while not studded with superfluous poetic ornamentation, also does not exhibit the clarity characteristic of Jane Austen or Chekhov. Ruskin complained to Browning that:

> ... your Ellipses are quite Unconscionable: before one can get through ten lines, one has to patch you up in twenty places, wrong or right, and if one hasn't much stuff of one's own to spare to patch with! You are worse than the worst Alpine Glacier I ever crossed. Bright, & deep enough truly, but so full of Clefts that half the journey has to be done with ladder & hatchet.[23]

Browning's reply indicated that far from being 'unconscionable', his use of elliptical construction was in fact designed to carry what ordinary construction could not:

> I know that I don't make out my conception by my language; all poetry being a putting the infinite within the finite. You would have me paint it all plain out, which can't be; but by various artifices I try to make shift with touches and bits of outlines which succeed if they bear the conception from me to you. You ought, I think, to keep pace with the thought tripping from ledge to ledge of my 'glaciers,' as you call them; not stand poking your alpenstock into the holes, and demonstrating that no foot could have stood there; – suppose it sprang over there? In prose you may criticise so – because that is the absolute representation of portions of truth, what chronicling is to history – but in asking for more ultimates you must accept less mediates, nor expect that a Druid stone-circle will be traced for you with as few breaks to the eye as

the North Crescent and South Crescent that go together so cleverly in many a suburb.²⁴

It is significant that the distinction Browning makes between poetry and prose is not one based on beauty, subject-matter, or even formal verse structures – but one which stresses the difference between the *suggestion* of 'ultimates' (poetry) and the *representation* of portions of truth (prose). Prose is language which supplies all the 'mediates', piles fact upon fact in logical progression; poetry is that which in reflecting the ultimates depends for its meaningful connections on the mind of the reader – 'indeed were my scenes stars it must be his co-operating fancy which, supplying all chasms, shall connect the scattered lights into one constellation – a Lyre or a Crown.'²⁵ Prose is utilitarian and complete – the 'suburbs'; poetry is suggestive, and completed only in the mind of the beholder – the 'Druid stone-circle'.

It is this distinction between poetry and prose, one based on function rather than the external characteristics of form, that has become important to modern writers. Zukofsky described Pound's *Cantos* as approaching 'a state of music wherein the ideas present themselves sensuously and intelligently and are of no predatory intention.'²⁶ While the doctrine of 'art for art's sake' was a mis-taken' one, said Eliot, it did contain 'this true impulse behind it, that it is a recognition of the error of the poet's trying to do other people's work.'²⁷

The verse of modern poetry is, therefore, closer to the prose of modern novels than either is to the prose which contains ideas of 'predatory intention' or the verse which attempts to do the work of philosopher or priest. With this distinction in mind, the relation between the characteristics of Browning's poetry which modern poets have developed and the coming together of prose and poetry in twentieth-century literature becomes clearer. For example, in Browning's poetry, as well as in much modern poetry, the object of perception is seen to be relative to the point of view from which it is perceived. No object or subject-matter is fixed; nor is one subject necessarily more appropriate than another. Poetic subject-matter is that which is used poetically, whether the subject be the love of a fair maiden, or skunks swilling sour cream from a garbage pail (Lowell's 'Skunk Hour'). Moreover, as W. H. Auden points out, the characteristic hero in modern poetry 'is neither the "Great Man" nor

the romantic rebel, both doers of extraordinary deeds, but the man or
woman in any walk of life who, despite all the impersonal pressures
of modern society, manages to acquire and preserve a face of his own'
('The Poet and the City').[28] Such a hero, when he did appear in
nineteenth-century literature, was more likely to be found in novels
than in poetry.

Browning's use of common speech which was not *merely* common
speech is particularly important to the modern distinction between
prose and poetry. Pound insisted on a 'simplicity and directness of
utterance' but one which was 'different from the simplicity and
directness of daily speech'.[29] In the modern world, said Eliot, 'anything that can be said as well in prose can be said better in prose.'[30]

As Eliot saw it, the simple distinction between prose and poetry
was inadequate; what was needed was the double one between poetry
and verse on the one hand, and 'good prose' and 'bad prose' on the
other.[31] But for early readers of free verse, the most obvious characteristic of the new poetry was that if printed in paragraph form
rather than as a series of lines, free verse would be no different from
literary prose. To this criticism, Amy Lowell replied that yes, not
only was there no essential difference, but that the lack of difference
might be a significant advantage:

> Typography is not relevant to the discussion. Whether a thing is
> written as prose or as verse is immaterial. But if we would see the
> advantage which Meredith's imagination enjoyed in the freer
> forms of expression, we need only compare these lyrical passages
> from his prose works with his own metrical poetry.[32]

Another advantage of this new *vers libre* was pointed out by Eliot:
'Rhyme removed, the poet is at once held up to the standards of
prose. Rhyme removed, much ethereal music leaps up from the word,
music which has hitherto chirped unnoticed in the expanse of
prose.'[33]

For modern poets, the criticism that *vers libre* was really only prose
printed as poetry was irrelevant, a matter of 'typography'. Eliot
went even further – his response to criticisms of *vers libre* was to
argue that it simply did not exist:

> And as for *vers libre*, we conclude that it is not defined by absence
> of pattern or absence of rhyme, for other verse is without these;
> that it is not defined by non-existence of metre, since even the

worst verse can be scanned; and we conclude that the division
between Conservative Verse and *vers libre* does not exist, for
there is only good verse, bad verse, and chaos.[34]

In speaking of Pound's poetry, Eliot again made the point that there
are not two kinds of verse, the strict and the free, but only 'a
mastery which comes of being so well trained that form is an instinct
and can be adapted to the particular purpose in hand.'[35] Pound
himself then took up this approach, quoting Eliot as saying '"No
vers is *libre* for the man who wants to do a good job."'[36]

Yet there was something to the 'freedom' implied in '*vers libre*'.
Lawrence called free verse 'direct utterance from the instant, whole
man'.[37] In other words, organic form grew in response to the utterance itself; the mental image was not stretched or shrunk to fit the
poetic form. In this, Lawrence is one with the spirit of Browning,
who gently teased the poetry confined to 'proper' forms:

> I praise these poets: they leave margin-space;
> Each stanza seems to gather skirts around,
> And primly, trimly, keep the foot's confine,
> Modest and maidlike ... (*The Inn Album*, I, 4–7)

On the relatively few occasions when Browning himself used such
'maidlike' stanzas, in contrast to his usual elliptical 'proselike' lines,
he was clearly aware of the stretching which he was engaging in to
accommodate it. When he sent the following stanza to Felix Mos-
cheles, Browning said: '... I advise that you take the last four lines:
I put in the preceding, for symmetry's sake'.[38]

> Dear, the pang is brief;
>   Do thy part,
> Have thy pleasure. How perplext
>   Grows belief!
> Well, this cold clay clod
>   Was man's heart.
> Crumble it – and what comes next?
>   Is it God? ('In a Year')[39]

As is obvious in the stanza itself, the abstract and rather formal
language of the first four lines ('thy pang', 'thy part', 'thy pleasure')
creates a very different effect from the vigorous, informal, and
concrete nature of the closing lines ('Well, this cold clay clod ...
Crumble it').

Clearly the *vers libre* designed to do away with lines put in for symmetry's sake was more than a matter of typography, the printing of prose as verse. If prose rhythms proved necessary to the 'most direct utterance' of the 'whole man', then *vers libre* implied the freedom to use these rhythms.

Later, poets began to exploit typography to make explicit the interaction between prose forms and verse forms. Among the poems of Lowell's *Life Studies* is a long section in prose. Another of the sections, written in verse, was originally written in prose.[40] In *Paterson* sections of prose are found throughout the poem, a practice which Williams declared

> is *not* an antipoetic device ... It *is* that prose and verse are both *writing*, both a matter of the words and an interrelation between words. ... I want to say that prose and verse are to me the same thing, that verse (as in Chaucer's tales) belongs *with* prose, as the poet belongs with 'Mine host' ... [41]

'Verse belongs with prose' is an assertion which could lie behind much modern prose as well as poetry. In shaping the novel, the prose writer handles words with a care and attention similar to that exhibited by poets. Consequently, modern novelists, like modern poets, have concentrated on presenting the word as closely to the object as possible. As in the case of Hemingway and Pound, prose writers learned from poets what those poets had learned from earlier prose writers. Hemingway acknowledged Pound as 'the man I liked and trusted the most as a critic then, the man who believed in the *mot juste* – the one and only correct word to use – the man who taught me to distrust adjectives.'[42] And earlier, Hardy had said 'For my own part I think – though all writers may not agree with me – that the shortest way to good prose is by the route of good verse', and that 'the best poetry is the best prose'.[43] Hardy himself wrote both verse and prose and on one occasion, 'dissolved' some of his poems into the prose of one of his novels, *Desperate Remedies*.[44]

Thus, if modern poets have appropriated the best aspects of prose for their purposes, modern prose writers have certainly incorporated poetic elements into their writing. For example, the interior monologue so characteristic of the modern novel is closely related to the dramatic monologue form. In Browning's monologues, the only information the reader receives is reflected from the narrator's limited perception. In the novels of Henry James, the awareness of the relativity of point of view becomes a central aspect of the structure. The dramatic monologue technique is elaborated and refined to convey a story which stretches out over years and hundreds of pages. James was able to see a potential novel in Browning's *The Ring and the Book*.[45] But one might speculate that Browning, given the chance, would have discovered the dramatic monologues inherent in James's novels.

In Browning's poetry, as in James's prose, the focus of interest is not so much on the actions and thoughts of a character, but on how these actions are seen by an observer, and then how the original character reacts to his own observation of the observer's reaction to him. In *Paracelsus*, Browning reveals the thought of Festus not by having Festus speak, but by having Paracelsus report what Festus is probably about to say – 'I can say/Beforehand all this evening's conference!' (I, 163–4) – and then describe his own possible reactions to Festus's probable speech:

> first,
> Or he declares, or I, the leading points . . .
>
> Next, each of us allows
> Faith should be acted on as best we may;
> Accordingly, I venture to submit
> My plan, in lack of better, for pursuing
> The path which God's will seems to authorize.
> Well, he discerns much good in it, avows
> This motive worthy, that hope plausible,
> A danger here to be avoided, there
> An oversight to be repaired: in fine
> Our two minds go together – all the good
> Approved by him, I gladly recognize,
> All he counts bad, I thankfully discard,
> And nought forbids my looking up at last
> For some stray comfort in his cautious brow.
>
> (I, 165–6, 169–82)

Thirty lines later, a third character turns to Festus, who has remained silent all this time, and asks, 'is it so?'

Even in a poem written in dramatic form, such as *In a Balcony*, Browning's characters are more involved in interpreting each other's thoughts and feelings than in acting or speaking directly. Constance tells Norbert what he feels and what he thinks the Queen must feel;

and then explains that the Queen does not feel the way he thinks she feels, and that therefore he must change his own feelings. The entire drama revolves on a mistake in perception – Constance supposes that the Queen has no tenderness 'left to wake', and that, therefore, Norbert's proposal to the Queen will be taken merely as a gesture of loyalty.

With emphasis on *how* something is perceived rather than on the factual details of the object of perception, the state of mind of the observer assumes a greater significance than the external action. Thus, James may show a character engrossed in beholding the same situation, but gradually coming to perceive it in a different light. Or Faulkner may choose one point in time and then reveal the variety of different characters' experiences of that time. A similar approach to this modern method was made by Browning in *The Ring and the Book* in which the same set of facts is examined from twelve different points of view. James said that in *The Ring and the Book*, Browning had applied his 'favourite system':

> that of looking at his subject from the point of view of a curiosity
> almost sublime in its freedom, yet almost homely in its method,
> and of smuggling as many more points of view together into that
> one as the fancy might take him to smuggle, on a scale on which
> even he had never before applied it . . .[46]

In modern novels, as well as in modern poetry, the omniscient, omnipresent author has largely given way to the use of masks or personae through which a deliberately individualistic point of view is developed. The modern novel is not so much a slice of life as the camera might record it, but a glimpse into the interior life of a fictional creation. And yet, this fictional creation, through revealing the internal order of the mind, is seen to come nearer to the truth than an account which realistically reports a reality of events. In Browning's terms, history comes closer to 'ultimates' than a chronicle of facts would. In Yeats's words: 'Because these imaginary people are created out of the deepest instinct of man, to be his measure and his norm, whatever I can imagine those mouths speaking may be the nearest I can go to truth.'[47]

Yeats here was speaking of myth – that final expression of patterns imprinted on the psychological consciousness of a race. As Browning saw it, beneath the everyday actions of a common man an archetypal pattern may be seen, illuminating even the most mundane of details.

For example, in *Pauline*, *Balaustion's Adventure*, 'Francis Furini' and others of his poems, the myth of Perseus and Andromeda provides both theme and a structure for action;[48] and in *The Ring and the Book*, it is the myth behind the external action which helps to transform a sordid Roman murder-case into a poem of wider significance. '*The Ring and the Book* is an important poem, because it moves in the right direction', said Langbaum:

> It moves away from myth as overt subject matter; yet it goes so far as to bring back the mythical pattern – not the particular events and characters of the Andromeda story, but the pattern – as inherent in the very structure of the mind, in what we would nowadays call the unconscious.[49]

'The next stage forward from *The Ring and the Book* is Joyce's *Ulysses*', said Lucie-Smith. 'Here, too, we find the epic at grips with the trivial, and Bloom and Molly seem to me the literary offspring of Guido and Pompilia.'[50]

When both poets and prose writers become concerned with life as experienced rather than life as seen, or with what might be called internal reality rather than those external details which are agreed upon as reality by common consent, it is perhaps predictable that prose and poetry should come closer together in technique. In her diary, Virginia Woolf wrote:

> I mean to eliminate all waste, deadness, superfluity: to give the moment whole; whatever it includes. . . . Waste, deadness, come from the inclusion of things that don't belong to the moment; this appalling narrative business of the realist: getting on from lunch to dinner: it is false, unreal, merely conventional. Why admit anything to literature that is not poetry – by which I mean saturated?[51]

Basically what Virginia Woolf wished to eliminate were the 'prose' connections between the poetic moments, the chronicle of external facts from the history of significant experience. Thus, in her writing, as in the writing of many modern poets, a new type of organisation develops, one based not on a narrative progression of events, but one which rests on the interaction of images and themes, and on the pattern of association which the mind perceives.

As Virginia Woolf recognised, a novel organised around significant moments, one which reflects the events of the inner world, must also reflect the peculiar nature of time in that world. A feeling which in the outer world is measured as taking only a minute, may, in the inner world, seem to last for hours or days. What literature must do then, according to Virginia Woolf, is to capture these moments, to expand in space what is significant in time. The significant moment may, from the outside, seem very insignificant indeed. For Proust, a moment of reflection, which begins when he tastes the crumb of madeleine soaked in tea, spreads in wider and wider circles of associations which, expressed in words, takes hundreds of pages of print.

In Browning's poetry, it is these inner moments which are explored, not the moments in which outer actions occur. The life story of *Sordello* is told through occasional flashbacks rather than in any narrative sequence; and most of the poem is occupied not with the external history of *Sordello* but with the 'states/Of his soul's essence' (VI, 459–60). In 'By the Fire-side' the narrator sits by his wife in the evening, and that one moment expands to embrace the entire poem, the past and the future, and even the memory of another such moment: 'Oh moment, one and infinite!' (XXXVII)

The importance of the 'infinite moment' in Browning's poetry has been recognised by critics – W. O. Raymond, for example, uses this phrase as the title of his book of essays on Browning.[52] In modern poetry, also, the significance of the moment is readily discernible, often, as in Eliot's *Four Quartets*, comprising a major theme. It is true, as Langbaum says, that

> Browning sketches out what has come to be the dominant
> twentieth-century theory about poetry – that it makes its effect
> through the association in the reader's mind of disparate elements,
> and that this process of association leads to the recognition, in
> what has been presented successively, of static pattern.[53]

The infinite moment brings together the near and the far in space, the past and the present in time. Thus, in *The Waste Land*, 'Elizabeth and Leicester' (III, 279) are juxtaposed with 'Trams and dusty trees' (III, 292), and the affair of the typist is perceived by Tiresias ('I who have sat by Thebes': III, 245). Just as the perceiving mind connects all times and places, so, too, does it bring together various languages and cultures. In modern poetry, direct quotations from other literary contexts is a way of bringing the contexts themselves into the poem. 'Hieronymo's mad againe./Datta. Dayadhvam. Damyata.'

And in modern prose, a novel like *Ulysses* illustrates the lengths to which a fabric of associations patterned on myth can be stretched. *Ulysses* contains hundreds of different styles, rhythms, points of view and grammatical constructions. Like Browning before him, Joyce claimed the freedom to escape definitions, to weave the language of everyday speech into abstract and highly complex patterns, to join the texture of romance with that of parody, to fill the external form of the epic with an internal atmosphere varying from the sublime to the lowly. The novel of the future will be written in prose, said Virginia Woolf, 'but in prose which has many of the characteristics of poetry. It will have something of the exaltation of poetry, but much of the ordinariness of prose. It will be dramatic, and yet not a play. It will be read, not acted.'[54]

The use of poetic devices within the novel, and the willingness of poets to include prose rhythms and forms in their verse resulted in part from the approaches to art which both modern poets and modern novelists have in common. The novel, like the poem, is seen as an object of art, a construction which exists independently, not merely as a vehicle for philosophical thought or social criticism. Virginia Woolf wrote an essay on 'Craftsmanship' in which she commented that 'there is something incongruous, unfitting, about the term "craftsmanship" when applied to words.'[55] Yet Pound and other poets did talk of craft in connection with words; and of words as if they were solid matter and not primarily carriers of messages (as in ordinary prose) or sounds to fill out a line (as in formal verse). If words are seen as solid matter, then the difference between prose and poetry is fundamentally one of material or substance rather than over-all form – 'prose and poetry are to literature as composition and color are to painting, or as light and shadow to the day ...'[56] Just as the painter uses both colour and composition, so the poet uses the resources of both verse and prose. 'The truth is', said William Carlos Williams, 'that there's an *identity* between prose and verse, not an antithesis. It all rests on the same time base, the same measure. Prose, as Pound has always pointed out, came after verse, not before it ...'[57]

'The same time base, the same measure' which verse and prose have in common is the music of human speech. For modern poets, the rigid forms of conversational poetic structures and the artificiality of heightened poetic diction distort this music just as surely as the mundane reporting of mere prose ignores it. Now 'the measure, that is to say, the count, having got rid of the words, which held it down, is returned to the *music*', said William Carlos Williams. 'Now, with

music in our ears the words need only be taught to keep as distinguished an order, as chosen a character, as regular, according to the
music, as in the best of prose.'[58]

Conversely, the best of modern prose reveals the heightened attention to language characteristic of poetry. 'What poet sets pen to
paper without first hearing a tune in his head?' asked Virginia
Woolf. 'And the prose-writer, though he makes believe to walk
soberly, in obedience to the voice of reason, excites us by perpetual
changes of rhythm following the emotions with which he deals.'[59]

Poetry lends significance to the common occurrences of everyday
life just as the myth revealed behind the action illumines the
commonplace. Eliot was in favour of poetic drama not because it
would lend dignity to the theatre, but because it would lend meaning
to the life lived outside the theatre:

> ... the audience should find, at the moment of awareness that it is
> hearing poetry, that it is saying to itself: 'I could talk in poetry
> too!' Then we should not be transported into an artificial world; on
> the contrary, our own sordid, dreary, daily world would be
> suddenly illuminated and transfigured.[60]

Such a poetry, close enough to prose to carry the weight of everyday reality, would, in Browning's words, 'Impart the gift of seeing to
the rest' (Sordello, III, 868). The difficulty of this task, as he realised,
is not only that the 'rest' of the world is blind to the scenes they pass
every day, but that the poetry created to make them see, in itself
tends to dwindle down to the 'commonplace old facts' of the prose
world:

> You see how poetry turns prose.
> Announcing wonder-work, I dwindle at the close
> Down to mere commonplace old facts which everybody knows.
> So dreaming disappoints! The fresh and strange at first,
> Soon wears to trite and tame, nor warrants the outburst
> Of heart with which we hail those heights, at very brink
> Of heaven, whereto one least of lifts would lead, we think,
> But wherefrom quick decline conducts our step, we find,
> To homely earth, old facts familiar left behind. (Fifine, CXXVI)

The difference between prose and poetry which Browning emphasises here is not in terms of external form, but based on a distinction
between what is 'fresh and strange' and what is 'trite and tame'. The

freedom of the artist is the freedom *for* expression rather than merely the freedom *from* certain rules. In helping others to see, the poet uses whatever means are necessary – whether these include prose or any other breaking of what is usually considered the poetic norm. Like many modern poets after him, Browning was often criticised for the rules he broke rather than for what he had created in breaking these rules.

Swinburne, in speaking of *Sordello*, compared Browning's treatment of 'the Queen's innocent English' with the agonising execution of a family during the St Bartholomew slaughter:

> Count the conjunctions torn out by the roots, the verbs impaled, the nouns crucified, the antecedents broken on the wheel, the relatives cut off by the neck or sawn through the middle, the entire sentences blundering, screaming, plunging, snorting, like harpooned whales or smashed locomotives, through whole horrible paragraphs of mutilation and confusion . . . [61]

By the 1870s this kind of criticism was so common that Browning inserted a whimsical rejoinder in the beginning of *The Inn Album*:

> That bard's a Browning; he neglects the form:
> But ah, the sense, ye gods, the weighty sense! (I, 17–18)

In *Pacchiarotto*, Browning again countered his critics' charge of formlessness:

> Was it 'grammar' wherein you would 'coach' me –
> You, – pacing in even that paddock
> Of language allotted you *ad hoc*,
> With a clog at your fetlocks, – you – scorners
> Of me free of all its four corners? (XXVIII)

Like Browning, modern poets see form as growing from the needs of the individual poem rather than as an external standard which governs their verse. What Swinburne considered to be the slaughter of 'the Queen's innocent English', writers such as Wyndham Lewis have declared as a way of escaping from the prose prison of commonplace language:

> I sabotage the sentence! With me is the naked word.
> I spike the verb – all parts of speech are pushed over on their backs.
> I am master of all that is half uttered and imperfectly heard.

Return with me where I am crying out with the gorilla and the
                              bird. (*One Way Song*, VIII)[62]

One reason so many different types of writers seem to stem from
Browning is that he, more than any other writer of Victorian
England, insisted on the freedom to use whatever means were best, to
break rules, if necessary, in order to 'impart the gift of seeing to the
rest'.

'Yes, Browning was great', said Wilde. 'And as what will he be
remembered? As a poet? Ah, not as a poet! He will be remembered
as a writer of fiction, as the most supreme writer of fiction, it may be,
that we have ever had.'[63]

Looking back at Robert Browning in the light of the significant
changes which have occurred in modern poetry, one can appreciate
the foresight and enthusiasm with which he followed his own ideas
of what poetry should be. Insisting that the poem speak for itself, in
its own language, he refused to 'turn my work into what the many
might, – instead of what the few must, – like.'[64] For his subject-
matter he chose images from the life around him, preferring, like
Eliot, to transfigure the 'sordid, dreary, daily world'. His language
was that of contemporary speech, its dramatic elements heightened
by a careful attention to the use of punctuation. Before the influence
of Freud, he explored the creation of masks to conceal and impress;
and before the influence of modern science, he was aware of the
relativity of 'facts' to the point of view through which they were
seen. Yet even while using everyday language and subject-matter,
he still insisted on the freedom to shape his poems into whatever
pattern he felt could best capture the 'perceptions whole...the
simultaneous and the sole' (*Sordello*, 589, 594), even if this freedom
resulted in the inclusion of different styles or voices, or the condensation through ellipsis into a texture so dense as to be obscure.
'...my art intends/'New structure from the ancient' (*Sordello*, V,
642–3). At the same time, he realised that

                              As with hates
And loves and fears and hopes, so with what emulates
The same, expresses hates, loves, fears and hopes in Art:
The forms, the themes – no one without its counterpart
Ages ago ... (*Fifine*, XCII)

Yet within this backward and forward motion of poetic styles, Browning felt there was also a forward motion in time. The poetry which followed his would involve the climbing of one more degree 'in that mighty ladder, of which, however cloud-involved and undefined may glimmer the topmost step, the world dares no longer doubt that its gradations ascend' (*Essay on Shelley*, p. 68).

The examination of Browning's relation to modern poetry does not reveal him to be a modern poet, nor does it suggest that modern poets are *Sordello*-style Victorians. Rather, this study is made in the hope that by looking at Browning from a twentieth-century viewpoint, and by looking at modern poetry through a significant figure in the nineteenth-century background, the developments of both modern poets and of Browning will be more deeply appreciated. For, as Browning said,

> don't suppose the new was able to efface
> The old without a struggle, a pang! (*Fifine*, XCII)

Notes

Short titles

Browning and Wedgwood *Letters*
    Robert Browning and Julia Wedgwood: A Broken Friendship as Revealed in their Letters, ed. Richard Curle. London, 1937.
Dearest Isa
    Dearest Isa: Robert Browning's Letters to Isabella Blagden, ed. Edward C. McAleer. Austin, 1951.
DeVane
    DeVane, William Clyde. *A Browning Handbook*. New York, 1935.
Learned Lady
    Learned Lady: Letters from Robert Browning to Mrs. Thomas Fitzgerald 1876–1889, ed. Edward C. McAleer. Cambridge, Mass., 1966.
Letters
    Letters of Robert Browning Collected by Thomas J. Wise, ed. Thurman L. Hood. New Haven, 1933.
New Letters
    New Letters of Robert Browning, ed. William C. DeVane and Kenneth L. Knickerbocker. London, 1951.
RB and EBB Letters
    The Letters of Robert Browning and Elizabeth Barrett Barrett 1845–1846, ed. Elvan Kintner. 2 vols. Cambridge, Mass., 1969.
Browning's 1835 preface to *Paracelsus* and the running titles for *Sordello* are taken from *Browning: Poetical Works*, ed. Ian Jack. London, 1970.

Introduction

1   William C. DeVane discusses this point in 'Robert Browning', *The Victorian Poets: A Guide to Research*, ed. Frederic E. Faverty (Cambridge, Mass., 1956) p. 58.
2   *Browning and the Modern Novel*, St John's College Cambridge Lecture, 1961–2 (Hull, 1962) p. 4.
3   Letter to René Taupin, May 1928; in *The Letters of Ezra Pound 1907–1941*, ed. D. D. Paige (London, 1951) p. 294.
4   Preface to *Literary Essays of Ezra Pound* (London, 1954) p. xi.
5   Chapter headings in A. Allen Brockington's *Browning and the Twentieth Century: A Study of Robert Browning's Influence and Reputation* (London, 1932). The other full-length study of Browning's influence, Dallas Kenmare's *Browning and Modern Thought* (London, 1939), considers Browning as a poet of 'humanity', 'love', 'art and nature', and 'Christianity'.
6   See, for example, Edward Lucie-Smith's introduction to *A Choice of Browning's Verse* (London, 1967); Harvey S. Gross, *Sound and Form in Modern Poetry* (Ann Arbor, 1964); Roy E. Gridley, 'Browning among the Modern Poets', *Browning* (London, 1972); Robert Langbaum, *The Poetry of Experience* (London, 1957) and *The Modern Spirit* (London, 1970); and Hugh Kenner, *The Pound Era* (Berkeley, 1971).

7 *Pacific Spectator*, 8, no. 3, pp. 218–28; reprinted in *Browning's Mind and Art*, ed. Clarence Tracy (London, 1968) pp. 184–97.
8 T. S. Eliot, quoted by Francis O. Matthiessen, *The Achievement of T. S. Eliot: An Essay on the Nature of Poetry*, 3rd ed. (London and New York, 1958) p. 90.
9 'The Critic as Artist', *The Works of Oscar Wilde* (London, 1963) p. 859.
10 Robert Frost as quoted by Stanley Burnshaw (ed.), *The Poem Itself* (New York, 1967) p. xi.
11 'Tradition and the Individual Talent', (1919), *Selected Essays*, 3rd ed. (London, 1951) p. 14.

Chapter 1

1 C. K. Stead in *The New Poetic* (London, 1964) uses 1909 to 1916 as the years during which were generated the 'new techniques of poetry, together with new critical ideas' (p. 15). I have used 1908 to 1920 simply because those were the years Pound was residing in London as the centre of the Imagist movement and other poetic activities.
2 The various dates suggested for the beginning of the 'modern movement' as well as the definition of modernism itself are discussed at length in many critical works. See, for example, John Press, 'Imagism and the New Poetry', *A Map of Modern English Verse* (Oxford, 1969) pp. 30–52. Monroe K. Spears in *Dionysus and the City: Modernism in Twentieth-Century Poetry* (New York, 1970) discusses many of the critical works concerning the modern movement, notably those by Frank Kermode, Edmund Wilson, Northrop Frye, Donald Davie and H. M. McLuhan.
3 *After Strange Gods* (London, 1934) p. 42.
4 Letter to Robert McAlmon, 23 Feb 1944; in *The Selected Letters of William Carlos Williams*, ed. John C. Thirlwall (New York, 1957) p. 220.
5 Letter to Sarah Perkins Cope, 22 Apr 1934; in *Letters of Ezra Pound*, ed. Paige, p. 342.
6 Letter to Laurence Binyon, 22 Apr 1938; in *Letters*, p. 403.
7 See, for example, 'How to Read', *Literary Essays of Ezra Pound*, p. 33.
8 For a detailed discussion of this influence, see Myles Slatin in 'Mesmerism: a Study of Ezra Pound's Use of the Poetry of Robert Browning' (Dissertation, Yale University, 1957).
9 Arthur Symons, 'Is Browning Dramatic?', *The Browning Society's Papers*, 1885–6, 2 (1885) 1.
10 'A Retrospect', *Literary Essays of Ezra Pound*, p. 10.
11 K. K. Ruthven, *A Guide to Ezra Pound's Personæ (1926)* (Los Angeles, 1969) p. 128.
12 Letter to Elizabeth Barrett, 14 June 1845; in *RB and EBB Letters*, I, p. 95.
13 'A Retrospect', p. 6.
14 *The Autobiography of William Carlos Williams* (New York, 1951) p. 264.
15 'Swinburne as Poet', *The Sacred Wood: Essays on Poetry and Criticism*, 3rd ed. (London, 1932) p. 149.
16 *Projective Verse* (New York, 1959) p. 7.
17 Letter to Iris Barry, 27 July 1916; in *Letters*, p. 142.
18 'D. H. Lawrence', *The Dyer's Hand* (London, 1963) p. 287.
19 'The Relations between Poetry and Painting', *The Necessary Angel: Essays on Reality and the Imagination* (London, 1960) p. 160.
20 Monroe K. Spears, *Dionysus and the City: Modernism in Twentieth-Century Poetry* (New York, 1970) p. 151.

21 'Vorticism', *Fortnightly Review* 96 (1914) 461.
22 *The Necessary Angel: Essays on Reality and the Imagination* (London, 1960) pp. 159–76.
23 Spears, *Dionysus and the City*, p. 151.
24 Ed. Edith Heal (Boston, 1958) p. 29.
25 Quoted by J. M. Brinnin, *William Carlos Williams* (Minneapolis, 1963) p. 14.
26 Quoted by Elizabeth Sewell, *The Structure of Poetry* (London, 1951) pp. 174–5; originally in *Pièces sur l'Art*.
27 Quoted by Philip Drew, *The Poetry of Browning: A Critical Introduction* (London, 1970) p. 210. Drew also points out how frequently and 'almost obsessively' Browning draws the parallel between painting and poetry (p. 64).
28 'There's printing a book of "Selections from R. B." (SCULPTOR and poet) which is to popularize my old things': letter to the Storys, 19 Mar 1862; in Henry James, *William Wetmore Story and his Friends: From Letters, Diaries and Recollections* (London, 1903) II, p. 117.
29 Letter to Isabella Blagden, [7 Jan 1859]; in *Dearest Isa*, p. 23.
30 Letter to the Storys, 21 Jan 1862; in James, *William Wetmore Story*, II, p. 113.
31 Letter to Isabella Blagden, 19 June 1867; in *Dearest Isa*, p. 269.
32 Letter of 11 Mar 1845; in *RB and EBB Letters*, I, p. 39.
33 Warner Barnes, in the preface to his *Catalogue of the Browning Collection, the University of Texas* (Austin, 1966), says that 'judging by the Broughton census of letters Browning wrote more often to Natorp in the years 1884, 1885, and 1887 than to any other person. However, there is no more than a single sentence written in any work about their relationship.' (pp. 7–8)
34 Letter of 13 Jan 1845; in *RB and EBB Letters*, I, pp. 6–7.
35 Letter to Julia Wedgwood, 31 Dec 1864; in *Browning and Wedgwood Letters*, p. 123.
36 Letter to Elizabeth Barrett, 27 Feb 1846; in *RB and EBB Letters*, I, p. 500.
37 These three colours are also used in *The Ring and the Book* in association with the main characters: red for Caponsacchi (courage), black for Guido (villainy) and white for Pompilia (innocence); see Park Honan, *Browning's Characters: A Study in Poetic Technique* (New Haven, 1961) p. 194; however, in the case of *The Ring and the Book*, it seems that Browning has used colours more as emblems than as pigments.
38 *Autobiography*, p. 380.
39 'Vorticism', p. 464.
40 'Vorticism', p. 466.
41 'A Retrospect', *Literary Essays of Ezra Pound*, p. 3.
42 'A Retrospect', p. 3.
43 3rd ed. (London, 1913).
44 Prefatory note to *Georgian Poetry, 1920–1922* (London, 1922) n.p.
45 Ibid.
46 'Vorticism', p. 463.
47 'Vorticism', p. 469.
48 DeVane, p. 204.
49 *The New Poetic*, p. 126.
50 An *'Objectivists' Anthology* (Le Beausset, Var, France, 1932) p. 18.
51 K. L. Goodwin, *The Influence of Ezra Pound* (London, 1966) p. 169.
52 See *ABC of Reading* (London, 1951) p. 22. See also Ruthven, *Guide to Ezra Pound's Personæ*, pp. 15–16 for a discussion of the influences of Fenollosa's

notes on Pound's movement from thinking of the image as static to regarding the image as a vortex.
53 Wylie Sypher, *Rococo to Cubism in Art and Literature* (New York, 1960) p. 283.
54 *Film Form*, trans. and ed. Jay Leyda (1949; repr. Cleveland, 1957) pp. 28–44.
55 Letter to Isabella Blagden, 19 Nov 1863; in *Dearest Isa*, p. 180.
56 P. 15.
57 Ruthven, *Guide to Ezra Pound's Personæ*, p. 2.
58 'How to Read', *Literary Essays*, p. 17.
59 'The Study of Poetry', *Essays in Criticism, Second Series*, ed. S. R. Littlewood (London, 1938) p. 2.
60 *Modern Poetry: A Personal Essay* (London, 1938) p. 197.
61 'Writing', *The Dyer's Hand*, p. 27.
62 *Autobiographies* (London, 1955) p. 167.
63 'William Blake', *Selected Essays*, 3rd ed. (London, 1951) p. 319.
64 Letter to Harriet Monroe, Jan 1915; in *Letters*, p. 91.
65 Letter to Catherine Carswell [11 Jan 1916]; in *The Collected Letters of D. H. Lawrence*, ed. Harry T. Moore (London, 1962) I, p. 413.
66 Review of *Personae of Ezra Pound*, *Times Literary Supplement* (20 May 1909) 191, col. 3.
67 Unpublished lecture; quoted by Matthiessen, *The Achievement of T. S. Eliot*, 3rd ed., p. 90.
68 Edward Dowden, 'Mr Browning's *Sordello*: First Paper', *Fraser's Magazine* (Oct 1867) 518–30.
69 Preface to Eliot's translation of St-J. Perse, *Anabasis* (London, 1930) p. 8.
70 Browning in conversation with Harriet Martineau, *Autobiography of Harriet Martineau* (London, 1877) III, p. 207.
71 Letter to Mrs Fitzgerald, 17 Mar 1883; in *Learned Lady*, p. 157.
72 As quoted by the *Philadelphia Evening Bulletin* (20 Feb 1928); in Thomas H. Jackson, *The Early Poetry of Ezra Pound* (Cambridge, Mass., 1968) p. 173.
73 *Poetry*, 10 (June 1917) 113. This opening was later modified and transferred to the beginning of Canto II.
74 'Conclusion', *The Use of Poetry and the Use of Criticism* (London, 1933) p. 150.
75 Letter of 2 Dec 1855; in David J. DeLaura (ed.), 'Ruskin and the Brownings: Twenty-five Unpublished Letters', *Bulletin of the John Rylands Library*, 54 (spring 1972) 326.
76 Quoted by Thomas R. Lounsbury, *The Early Literary Career of Robert Browning* (New York, 1911) p. 76.
77 'The Editor's Easy Chair ', *Harper's Magazine* (Aug 1856) 428.
78 Quoted by William Sharp, *Life of Robert Browning* (London, 1890) p. 110.
79 From an unsigned review, *Spectator* (14 Mar 1840) p. 257.
80 Letter to Robert Browning, 21 July 1845; in *RB and EBB Letters*, I, p. 131.
81 ' ... the sins of his verse are premeditated, wilful, and incurable': from an unsigned review of *Sordello* in *The Atlas: A General Newspaper and Journal of Literature* (28 Mar 1840).
82 Quoted by Drew, *The Poetry of Browning*, p. 72.
83 Dedication of *Sordello* to Milsand (1863).
84 Letter of 25 May 1886; in *Letters*, p. 248.
85 Letter to Thomas Westwood, Apr 1845; in *The Letters of Elizabeth Barrett Browning*, ed. Frederic G. Kenyon (London, 1897) I, p. 255.
86 Letter of 10 Dec 1855; in W. G. Collingwood, *The Life and Work of John Ruskin* (London, 1893) I, p. 201.

87 Letter of 7 Mar 1846; in *RB and EBB Letters*, I, p. 523.
88 'A Lecture on Modern Poetry', reprinted in Michael Roberts, *T. E. Hulme* (London, 1938) pp. 260–1.
89 Latin preface to *Pauline* taken from '*Hen. Corn. Agrippa, De. Occult. Philosoph. in Præfat*'; trans. Frederick A. Pottle, *Shelley and Browning: A Myth and Some Facts* (Chicago, 1923) p. 40.
90 Letter to Euphrasia Fanny Haworth, May 1840; in *New Letters*, pp. 18–19.
91 Letter of 10 Dec 1855; in Collingwood, *Life and Work of John Ruskin*, I, p. 200.
92 *The Three Voices of Poetry* (London, 1953) pp. 23–4.
93 Quoted by Myles Slatin, 'Mesmerism', p. 111.
94 *Poetry*, 10 (June 1917) 117.

Chapter 2

1 Letter to Ruskin, 10 Dec 1855; in Collingwood, *Life and Work of John Ruskin*, I, p. 200.
2 From an unsigned review of *Sordello* in *Dublin Review*, 8 (May 1840) 551–3; in Boyd Litzinger and D. Smalley, *Browning: The Critical Heritage* (London, 1970) p. 64.
3 Richard Hengist Horne, 'Robert Browning's Poems', *Church of England Quarterly* (Oct 1842) 464–83; in Litzinger and Smalley, *Browning: The Critical Heritage*, pp. 68–9.
4 Letter to Elizabeth Barrett, 31 Jan 1846; in *RB and EBB Letters*, I, p. 428.
5 From an unsigned review, 1 Jan 1876; in Litzinger and Smalley, *Browning: The Critical Heritage*, p. 414.
6 From an unsigned review in the *Spectator* (10 May 1873) 606–7; in Litzinger and Smalley, *Browning: The Critical Heritage*, p. 378.
7 Clifford Bax, compiler, *The Poetry of the Brownings* (London, 1947), p. 10.
8 Letter to Julia Wedgwood, 19 Nov 1868; in *Browning and Wedgwood Letters*, p. 158.
9 Letter to Isa Blagden, 30 Nov 1859; in *Dearest Isa*, pp. 48—9.
10 Letter to Mrs Brotherton; printed in Hallam Tennyson, *Tennyson and His Friends* (London, 1911) pp. 51–2.
11 'The Art of Poetry', III, *Paris Review*, 7, no. 25 (1961) 92.
12 Letter of 21 Oct 1908; in *Letters of Ezra Pound*, ed. Paige, pp. 37–8.
13 *World within World* (London, 1964) p. 95.
14 'Matthew Arnold', *The Use of Poetry and the Use of Criticism: Studies in the Relation of Criticism to Poetry in England* (London, 1933) p. 106.
15 'Vorticism', *Fortnightly Review*, 96 (1914) 464.
16 Bram Dijkstra, *The Hieroglyphics of a New Speech: Cubism, Stieglitz, and the Early Poetry of William Carlos Williams* (Princeton, N.J., 1969) p. xiii.
17 13 Jan 1845; in *RB and EBB Letters*, I, p. 7.
18 Letter to Isa Blagden, 19 Aug 1871; in *Dearest Isa*, p. 365.
19 Browning is praising Vernon Lee's *Baldwin: being Dialogues on Views and Aspirations*, in a letter to its author, 13 May 1886; in *New Letters*, p. 328.
20 Letter of 10 Dec 1855; in Collingwood, *Life and Work of John Ruskin*, I, p. 200.
21 Letter to Edward Dowden, 5 Mar 1866; in *Letters*, p. 92.
22 Letter to Elizabeth Barrett, 6 Feb 1846; in *RB and EBB Letters*, I, p. 439.
23 Letter to Julia Wedgwood, 2 Sep 1864; in *Browning and Wedgwood Letters*, p. 75.

24 Ibid., pp. 75–7.
25 Werner Heisenberg, *The Physical Principles of the Quantum Theory* (Chicago, 1930) p. 3.
26 'The Noble Rider and the Sound of Words', *The Necessary Angel* (London, 1960) p. 25.
27 Letter to Julia Wedgwood [22 Feb 1869]; in *Browning and Wedgwood Letters*, p. 188.
28 John Sparrow, *Sense and Poetry* (London, 1934) pp. xiv–xv.
29 Ibid., p. xv.
30 Ibid., p. xvii.
31 *Three Voices of Poetry*, p. 18.
32 Preface to *Transit of Venus: Poems by Harry Crosby* (Paris, 1931) p. vii.
33 See M. H. Abrams, *The Mirror and the Lamp: Romantic Theory and the Critical Tradition* (New York, 1958).
34 *An 'Objectivists' Anthology*, p. 21.
35 Explanatory note to the first edition, Nov 1891; in vol. 1 of the Mellstock Edition of *The Works of Thomas Hardy* (London, 1919).
36 Florence Hardy, *The Early Life of Thomas Hardy, 1840–1891* (London, 1928) pp. 150–1.
37 Letter to Isa Blagden, 19 Jan 1870; in *Dearest Isa*, p. 328.
38 'In Memoriam' (expanded version of the introduction for the Nelson Classics' edition of *Poems of Tennyson*), *Essays Ancient and Modern* (London, 1936) p. 179.
39 Pound, 'Vorticism', p. 464.
40 'Hamlet', *Selected Essays*, 3rd ed. (London, 1951) p. 145.
41 *World Within World*, p. 95.
42 Ibid., pp. 94–5.
43 'Conclusion', *The Use of Poetry*, p. 151.
44 Letter to Mrs Fitzgerald, 17 Mar 1883; in *Learned Lady*, p. 157.
45 Glenn Hughes, *Imagism and the Imagists: A Study in Modern Poetry* (London, 1931) p. vii.
46 Preface to *Poems*, 1853 ed.; in *The Poetical Works of Matthew Arnold*, ed. C. G. Tinker and H. F. Lowry (London, 1950) p. xx.
47 'From Poe to Valéry', *To Criticize the Critic and Other Writings* (London, 1965) p. 39.

Chapter 3

1 *The Music of Poetry* (Glasgow, 1942) p. 16.
2 'A General Introduction for my Work', *Essays and Introductions* (London, 1961) p. 521.
3 Reprinted in *Selected Poems and Prefaces*, ed. Jack Stillinger (Boston, 1965) p. 446.
4 *Tennyson and His Friends*, ed. Tennyson, p. 264.
5 'Wordsworth', *Essays in Criticism*, ed. Littlewood, p. 92.
6 'Milton', *Proceedings of the British Academy*, 33 (1947) 18.
7 F. O. Matthiessen, *The Achievement of T. S. Eliot*, p. 74.
8 K. K. Ruthven, *Guide to Ezra Pound's Personae*, p. 19.
9 *Thus to Revisit: Some Reminiscences* (New York, 1921) p. 131.
10 See Joseph E. Duncan, 'John Donne and Robert Browning', *The Revival of Metaphysical Poetry: The History of a Style, 1800 to the Present* (Minneapolis, 1959) pp. 50–68.

11   Alexander B. Grosart (ed.), *The Complete Poems of John Donne, D.D.* (London, 1872).

12   *Dante Gabriel Rossetti, His Family Letters: With a Memoir* (London, 1895) I, p. 191.

13   Letter to R. W. Dixon, 12 Oct 1881; in *The Correspondence of Gerard Manley Hopkins and Richard Watson Dixon*, ed. Claude C. Abbott (London, 1935) p. 74.

14   Letter to Kay Boyle [1932]; in *Selected Letters of William Carlos Williams*, ed. Thirlwall, p. 134.

15   Ibid., p. 136.

16   'A Retrospect', *Literary Essays of Ezra Pound*, p. 6.

17   Letter to Edward Marsh, postmarked 19 Nov 1913; in *The Collected Letters of D. H. Lawrence*, ed. Harry T. Moore (London, 1962) I, p. 242.

18   *Poetry and Drama* (Cambridge, Mass., 1951) p. 32.

19   Ibid., p. 27.

20   'Reflections on *Vers Libre*', *New Statesman* (3 Mar 1917); reprinted in *To Criticize the Critic*, p. 185.

21   *The Bow and the Lyre: The Art of Robert Browning* (Ann Arbor, 1964) p. 141.

22   *Some Reminiscences of William Michael Rossetti* (London, 1906) I, p. 237.

23   *Modern Poets on Modern Poetry*, ed. James Scully (London, 1970) p. 70.

24   Introductory quotation in Rosalind S. Miller, *Gertrude Stein: Form and Intelligibility* (New York, 1949).

25   *Autobiography of William Carlos Williams*, p. 265.

26   W. H. Gardner, introduction to *Poems and Prose of Gerard Manley Hopkins* (Baltimore, 1953) p. xx.

27   *The Dyer's Hand*, p. 84.

28   'A Retrospect', p. 5.

29   See K. L. Goodwin's discussion of this point in *The Influence of Ezra Pound* (London, 1966) pp. 158–9.

30   'A Retrospect', p. 12.

Chapter 4

1   Hiram Corson in *An Introduction to the Study of Robert Browning's Poetry* (Boston, 1896) p. v, refers to 'the poet's favorite art-form, the dramatic, or, rather, psychologic, monologue, which is quite original with himself...'

2   Benjamin Willis Fuson, 'Browning and his English Predecessors in the Dramatic Monolog', *State University of Iowa Humanistic Studies*, 8 (July 1942) 9.

3   *The Oxford Book of Ballads*, ed. Arthur Quiller-Couch (Oxford, 1910) p. 583.

4   Philip Wheelwright, *Metaphor and Reality* (Bloomington, Ind., 1964) p. 55.

5   *The World's Body* (London, 1938) pp. 254–5.

6   'Browning and his English Predecessors in the Dramatic Monolog'.

7   *Three Voices of Poetry*, p. 12.

8   Letter to Elizabeth Barrett, 22 Mar 1846; in *RB and EBB Letters*, I, p. 551.

9   Letter of 13 May 1846; in *RB and EBB Letters*, II, p. 701.

10   'The Art of Fiction', *Partial Portraits* (London and New York, 1888); reprinted in *The Art of Fiction and Other Essays* (New York, 1948) p. 13.

11   Eliot, *Three Voices of Poetry*, p. 14.

12   'Is Browning Dramatic?' p. 6.

13   *The Poetry of Experience: The Dramatic Monologue in Modern Literary Tradition* (London, 1957) p. 157.

14 *Poetry of Experience*, p. 146.
15 'Vorticism', *Fortnightly Review*, 96 (1914) 465.
16 Letter to Browning, 25 May 1846; in *RB and EBB Letters*, II, p. 732.
17 Letter of 13 Jan 1845; in *RB and EBB Letters*, I, p. 7.
18 William S. Peterson, *Interrogating the Oracle: A History of the London Browning Society* (Athens, Ohio, 1969) p. 32.
19 10 Dec 1855, in Collingwood, *Life and Work of John Ruskin*, I, p. 201.
20 James Scully (ed.), *Modern Poets on Modern Poetry* (London, 1970) p. 48.
21 21 Oct 1908, *Letters of Ezra Pound*, ed. Paige, p. 36.
22 'A Dialogue on Poetic Drama', printed with John Dryden, *Of Dramatick Poesie* (1668) (London, 1928) p. x.
23 (London, 1951).
24 *Autobiographies*, p. 167.
25 'Browning', *Letters to the New Island*, ed. Horace Reynolds (Cambridge, Mass., 1934) p. 97; originally in *The Boston Pilot* (22 Feb 1890).
26 'Is Browning Dramatic?', p. 11.
27 See E. K. Brown, 'The First Person in "Caliban upon Setebos"', *Modern Language Notes*, 66 (1951) 392–5 for a brief discussion of the relationship of variations in tense and the tension between Caliban's fear and impudence.
28 *Three Voices of Poetry*, pp. 13–14.
29 Ibid., p. 4.
30 Ibid., pp. 14–15.
31 *Two Essays on Analytical Psychology*, vol. VII of *Collected Works*, trans. R. F. C. Hull (London, 1953) p. 190.
32 DeVane, p. 11.
33 *Some Reminiscences of William Michael Rossetti*, I, p. 189.
34 'The Decay of Lying', *The Works of Oscar Wilde* (London, 1963) p. 827.
35 Ibid., p. 829.
36 Quoted by A. R. Jones, 'Robert Browning and the Dramatic Monologue: The Impersonal Art', *Critical Quarterly*, 9 (winter 1967) 313.
37 T. S. Eliot, 'John Ford', *Selected Essays*, 3rd ed. (London, 1951) p. 196.
38 'Vorticism', pp. 463–4.
39 Answer to questionnaire on 'The State of Translation', *Delos*, 2 (1968) 29.
40 'Preface' to *Ovid's Epistles*; in *Of Dramatic Poesy and Other Critical Essays*, ed. G .Watson (London and New York, 1962) I, p. 268.
41 T. S. Eliot, 'Baudelaire in our Time', *Essays Ancient and Modern* (London, 1936) p. 69.
42 *The March of Literature: From Confucius to Modern Times* (London, 1939) p. 50.
43 Quoted by J. P. Sullivan, *Ezra Pound and Sextus Propertius: A Study in Creative Translation* (London, 1965) p. 101.
44 Ibid.
45 Hugh Kenner makes this point in his introduction to *Ezra Pound: Translations*, enlarged ed. (London, 1963) p. 11.
46 *The Poems of Catullus* [translated by various hands], ed. William A. Aiken (New York, 1950).
47 *Catullus: (Gai Valeri Catulli Veronensis Liber)* (London, 1969).
4S 'Translators of Greek', *Make It New* (London, 1934) p. 150.
49 Introduction to *A Choice of Browning's Verse* (London, 1967) p. 23.
50 Quoted by DeVane, p. 373.
51 *A Choice of Browning's Verse*, p. 23.
52 Frederick A. Paley, *Athenæum* (27 Oct 1877); reprinted in Litzinger and Smalley, *Browning: The Critical Heritage*, p. 434.

NOTES 187

53 (London, 1962) p. xi.
54 Ibid., pp. xi–xii.
55 Ibid., p. xi.
56 Wright, The Poet in the Poem (Berkeley, 1960) p. 136.
57 The Modern Spirit (London, 1970) p. 96.
58 Letter to William Carlos Williams, 21 Oct 1908; in Letters of Ezra Pound, ed. Paige, p. 36.

Chapter 5

1 'The Later Yeats', review of W. B. Yeats, Responsibilities; Literary Essays, ed. T. S. Eliot (London, 1954) p. 380; originally in Poetry, 4, no. 2 (May 1914).
2 Fortnightly Review, 96 (1914) 461–2.
3 'Vers Libre and Arnold Dolmetsch', a review of Arnold Dolmetsch, The Interpretation of the Music of the XVIIth and XVIIIth Centuries, in Literary Essays, p. 437.
4 A Map of Modern English Verse (London, 1969) pp. 77–8; Press also cites Richards, Leavis, Jones and Howarth, mentioned above.
5 Principles of Literary Criticism, 2nd ed. (London, 1926) pp. 293–4.
6 New Bearings in English Poetry (London, 1934) p. 103.
7 Notes on Some Figures Behind T. S. Eliot (London, 1965) pp. 278–83.
8 Approach to the Purpose (London, 1964) p. 263.
9 'T. S. Eliot and the Music of Poetry', Sound and Form in Modern Poetry (Ann Arbor, 1964) pp. 169–214.
10 Cited by Press, Map of Modern English Verse, p. 78, and Howarth, Notes on Some Figures, p. 279.
11 3rd ed. (London, 1963) pp. 126–7.
12 'The Philosophy of Composition', The Centenary Poe: Tales, Poems, Criticisms, Marginalia and Eureka by Edgar Allen Poe, ed. Montagu Slater (London, 1949) pp. 494–5.
13 Hallam Tennyson, Alfred Lord Tennyson: A Memoir (London, 1897) II, 285.
14 William Rossetti, Præraphaelite Diaries and Letters (London, 1900) p. 304.
15 'A Retrospect', Literary Essays, p. 3; reprinted (with alterations) from 'Imagisme', Poetry, 1 (1913).
16 'A Retrospect', p. 6.
17 'Vorticism', p. 461.
18 'Ezra Pound: His Metric and Poetry', To Criticize the Critic, p. 170.
19 Letter to Margaret C. Anderson, 1918; in Letters of Ezra Pound, ed. Paige, p. 187.
20 Albert Goldman and Evert Sprinchorn, introduction to Wagner on Music and Drama: A Compendium of Richard Wagner's Prose Works, trans. H. Aston Ellis (New York, 1964) p. 31.
21 'How to Read', p. 33; originally in three instalments in the New York Herald Tribune Books (13–17 Jan 1929).
22 R. W. S. Mendl, 'Robert Browning, the Poet-Musician', Music and Letters 42 (April 1961) 143.
23 An 'Objectivists' Anthology, p. 16.
24 'Shades of Milk Wood', Observer Review (6 June 1971).
25 On Poetry and Poets (London, 1957) p. 238.
26 An 'Objectivists' Anthology, p. 18; see also Chapter 1.
27 New Bearings in English Poetry, p. 103.
28 Letter to Robert Browning, 21 Dec 1845; in RB and EBB Letters, I, p. 342.

29 Unpublished material; computer program devised by William Alexander (University of Texas, 1968).
30 See S. Musgrove, T. S. Eliot and Walt Whitman (Wellington, New Zealand, 1952) pp. 24–5; see also H. S. Gross, Sound and Form in Modern Poetry, p. 85.
31 Sound and Form in Modern Poetry, p. 170.
32 The Use of Poetry and the Use of Criticism, pp. 118–19.
33 The Music of Poetry, p. 28.
34 (London, 1921) p. 62.
35 Browning's Characters: A Study in Poetic Technique (New Haven, 1961) pp. 166–206.
36 DeVane, p. 11.
37 'Pippa's Song', University of Texas Studies in English, 35 (1956) 51.
38 Summary of Hill's analysis.
39 'Pippa's Song', p. 56.
40 Letter to Robert Browning, 17 Feb 1845; in RB and EBB Letters, I, p. 24.
41 The Sacred Wood: Essays on Poetry and Criticism, 2nd ed. (London, 1928) p. 156.
42 This term is used in relation to The Waste Land by Robert Langbaum in The Poetry of Experience, p. 77
43 'The Importance of Sordello', The Major Victorian Poets: Reconsiderations, ed. Isobel Armstrong (London, 1969) p. 136.
44 Image and Experience: Studies in a Literary Revolution (London, 1960) p. 26.
45 The Poetry of Experience, p. 233.
46 An 'Objectivists' Anthology, Appendix, p. 204; reprinted from Poetry (Feb 1931).
47 Poetry and Drama (Cambridge, Mass., 1951) p. 42.
48 Ibid., p. 43.
49 Ibid., p. 19.
50 Preface to Bells and Pomegranates, no. 8 (1846); in DeVane, p. 84.

Chapter 6

1 (New York, 1934) p. 252.
2 (New York, 1963) p. 112.
3 'Swinburne as Poet', The Sacred Wood: Essays on Poetry and Criticism, 2nd ed. (London, 1928) p. 150.
4 From an early version of Canto I, 'Three Cantos – I', Poetry, 10 (June 1917) 118.
5 Letter to Iris Barry, 27 July 1916; in Letters, p. 140.
6 Ibid.
7 Letter to Laurence Binyon, 22 Apr 1938; in Letters, p. 403.
8 Letter to René Taupin, May 1928; in Letters, p. 294.
9 '. . . he did not knock me down, so that I dare say he was substantially in agreement with myself . . .'; in Thus to Revisit: Some Reminiscences (New York, 1921) p. 131.
10 Letter to R. W. Dixon, 12 Oct 1881; in The Correspondence of Gerard Manley Hopkins and Richard Watson Dixon, ed. Claude C. Abbott (London, 1935) p. 74.
11 'The Critic as Artist', The Works of Oscar Wilde (London, 1963) p. 860.
12 Unpublished lecture; as quoted by Matthiessen, The Achievement of T. S. Eliot, p. 74.

13 Quoted by Philip Cooper, *The Autobiographical Myth of Robert Lowell* (Chapel Hill, 1970) p. 6.

14 'The Narrow Bridge of Art', *Granite and Rainbow* (London, 1958) p. 20; originally in *Herald Tribune* (14 Aug 1927).

15 Letter to Isa Blagden, 22 Mar 1870; in *Dearest Isa*, pp. 332–3.

16 Letter to Laurence Binyon, 22 Apr 1938; in *Letters*, p. 403.

17 Quoted by Graham Hough, *Image and Experience: Studies in a Literary Revolution* (London, 1960) p. 13.

18 *ABC of Reading* (London, 1951) p. 191.

19 Introduction to translation of *The Agamemnon of Aeschylus*.

20 George Saintsbury, *A History of English Prosody from the Twelfth Century to the Present Day* (London, 1910) III, p. 299.

21 'The Art of Poetry', III, *Paris Review*, 7, no. 25 (1961) 66.

22 Journal entry for 26 Mar 1850; in *Præraphaelite Diaries and Letters*, pp. 262–3.

23 Letter to Browning, 2 Dec 1855; in 'Ruskin and the Brownings: Twenty-five Unpublished Letters', ed. DeLaura, pp. 326–7.

24 Letter to Ruskin, 10 Dec 1855; in Collingwood, *Life and Work of John Ruskin*, I, p. 200.

25 Preface to *Paracelsus* (1835).

26 *An 'Objectivists' Anthology*, p. 24.

27 *The Use of Poetry and The Use of Criticism*, p. 152.

28 *The Dyer's Hand*, p. 84.

29 'I Gather the Limbs of Osiris – XI', *New Age*, X (15 Feb 1912) 370.

30 Matthiessen, *The Achievement of T. S. Eliot*, p. 40.

31 Introduction to translation of St-J. Perse, *Anabasis*, p. 9.

32 Quoted in Glenn Hughes, *Imagism and the Imagists: A Study in Modern Poetry* (London, 1931) p. 66.

33 'Reflections on Vers Libre', *New Statesman* (3 March 1917); reprinted in *To Criticize the Critic*, pp. 188–9.

34 Ibid., p. 189.

35 'Ezra Pound: His Metric and Poetry' (1917), *To Criticize the Critic*, p. 172.

36 'T. S. Eliot' (1917), *Literary Essays of Ezra Pound*, p. 421.

37 From introduction to *New Poems* (1918); reprinted in John Press, *Map of Modern English Verse*, p. 98.

38 Letter of 6 Apr 1867; in *New Letters*, p. 178.

39 The text here is taken from the letter cited above and differs slightly from that in the standard edition.

40 'Last Afternoon with Uncle Devereux Winslow'; see 'Robert Lowell in Conversation with A. Alvarez', *The Modern Poet: Essays from the Review*, ed. Ian Hamilton (London, 1968) p. 189.

41 Letter to Parker Tyler, 10 Mar 1948; in *Selected Letters of William Carlos Williams*, ed. Thirlwall, p. 263.

42 *A Moveable Feast* (London, 1964) p. 116; see also K. L. Goodwin, *The Influence of Ezra Pound* (London, 1966) p. 43.

43 'A Plea for Pure English', *Thomas Hardy's Personal Writings: Prefaces, Literary Opinions, Reminiscences*, ed. Harold Orel (Lawrence, 1966) p. 147; originally from a speech in *The Times* (4 June 1912).

44 1912 addition to the preface of *Desperate Remedies*; reprinted in *Personal Writings*, p. 4.

45 'The Novel in *The Ring and the Book*', *Notes on Novelists* (London, 1914) pp. 306–26.

46 *Notes on Novelists*, p. 309.

47 *The Autobiography of William Butler Yeats* (New York, 1953) pp. 101–2.
48 See William C. DeVane, 'The Virgin and the Dragon', *Yale Review*, 37 (Sep 1947) 33–46.
49 *The Modern Spirit: Essays on the Continuity of Nineteenth- and Twentieth-Century Literature* (London, 1970) p. 84.
50 Introduction to *A Choice of Browning's Verse* (London, 1967) p. 24.
51 *A Writer's Diary* (London, 1953) p. 139.
52 *The Infinite Moment and Other Essays in Robert Browning*, 2nd ed. (Toronto, 1965).
53 *The Modern Spirit*, p. 87.
54 'The Narrow Bridge of Art', p. 18.
55 *Collected Essays* (London, 1966) II, p. 245.
56 John Gould Fletcher, quoted by Hughes, *Imagism and the Imagists*, pp. 80–1; originally in preface to Fletcher's *Goblins and Pagodas* (Boston, 1916).
57 Letter to Horace Gregory [1948]; in *Selected Letters*, p. 265.
58 Letter to Richard Eberhart, 23 May 1954; in *Selected Letters*, p. 326.
59 'Walter Sickert', *Collected Essays*, II, p. 242.
60 *Poetry and Drama*, p. 32.
61 'The Chaotic School', unpublished essay, *c.* 1863–4, *Browning: The Critical Heritage*, ed. Litzinger and Smalley, pp. 215–16; reprinted from *New Writings by Swinburne*, ed. Cecil Y. Lang (New York, 1964) pp. 40–60.
62 Quoted by John Press, *The Chequer'd Shade: Reflections on Obscurity in Poetry* (London, 1958) p. 7.
63 'The Critic as Artist', *Works*, p. 860.
64 Dedication of *Sordello* to Milsand (1863).

Selected Bibliography

Abrams, Meyer Howard. *The Mirror and the Lamp: Romantic Theory and the Critical Tradition.* New York, 1958.

Allen, Walter, ed. *Writers on Writing.* London, 1948.

Anon. Review of *Personae of Ezra Pound. Times Literary Supplement.* 20 May 1909, p. 191, col. 3.

Armstrong, Isobel, ed. *The Major Victorian Poets: Reconsiderations.* London, 1969.

Arnold, Matthew. *Essays in Criticism: Second Series,* ed. S. R. Littlewood. London, 1938.

Arnold, Matthew. *The Poetical Works of Matthew Arnold,* ed. C. B. Tinker and H. F. Lowry. London, 1950.

Auden, W. H. *City without Walls and Other Poems.* London, 1969.

Auden, W. H. *The Collected Poetry of W. H. Auden.* New York, 1945.

Auden, W. H. *The Dyer's Hand and Other Essays.* London, 1963.

Auden, W. H. Answer to questionnaire on 'The State of Translation', *Delos,* 2 (1968) 29–30.

Baker, Joseph E. *The Reinterpretation of Victorian Literature.* London, 1950.

Barfield, Owen. *Poetic Diction: A Study in Meaning.* 2nd ed. New York, 1952.

Barnes, Warner. *Catalogue of the Browning Collection, The University of Texas.* Austin, 1966.

Bax, Clifford, compiler. *The Poetry of the Brownings: An Anthology.* London, 1947.

Berry, Francis. *Poetry and the Physical Voice.* London, 1962.

Berry, Francis. *Poet's Grammar: Person, Time and Mood in Poetry.* London, 1958.

Berryman, John. *His Toy, His Dream, His Rest: 308 Dream Songs.* London, 1969.

Brockington, A. Allen. *Browning and the Twentieth Century: A Study of Robert Browning's Influence and Reputation.* London, 1932.

Brooke, Stopford A. *The Poetry of Robert Browning.* London, 1911.

Brooks, Cleanth. *Modern Poetry and the Tradition.* Chapel Hill, 1939.

Brooks, Cleanth. *The Well Wrought Urn: Studies in the Structure of Poetry.* London, 1960.

Broughton, Leslie N. *A Concordance to the Poems of Browning.* 2 vols. New York, 1924.

Broughton, Leslie N., C. S. Northup, Robert Pearsall. *Robert Browning: A Bibliography, 1830–1950.* Ithaca, N.Y., 1953.

Brown, E. K. 'The First Person in "Caliban Upon Setebos"', *Modern Language Notes,* 66 (1951) 392–5.

Browning, Elizabeth Barrett. *The Complete Poetical Works of Elizabeth Barrett Browning.* Cambridge Edition. New York, 1900.

Browning, Elizabeth Barrett. *The Letters of Elizabeth Barrett Browning,* ed. Frederic G. Kenyon. 2 vols. London, 1897.

Browning, Robert. *Browning's Essay on Chatterton,* ed. Donald Smalley. Cambridge, Mass., 1948.

Browning, Robert. *A Choice of Browning's Verse,* Introduction by Edward Lucie-Smith. London, 1967.

Browning, Robert. *Dearest Isa: Robert Browning's Letters to Isabella Blagden,* ed. Edward C. McAleer. Austin, 1951.

Browning, Robert. 'An Essay on Percy Bysshe Shelley', *Peacock's Four Ages of Poetry, Shelley's Defence of Poetry, Browning's Essay on Shelley,* ed. H. F. B. Brett-Smith. *The Percy Reprints, no. 3.* Oxford, 1921.

Browning, Robert. *Learned Lady: Letters from Robert Browning to Mrs. Thomas Fitzgerald, 1876–1889,* ed. Edward C. McAleer. Cambridge, Mass., 1966.

Browning, Robert. *Letters of Robert Browning Collected by Thomas J. Wise,* ed. Thurman L. Hood. New Haven, 1933.

Browning, Robert. *New Letters of Robert Browning,* ed. William C. DeVane and Kenneth L. Knickerbocker. London, 1951.

Browning, Robert. *Sordello.* London, 1840.

Browning, Robert. *The Works of Robert Browning,* ed. F. G. Kenyon. Centenary Edition. 10 vols. London, 1912.

Browning, Robert and Elizabeth Barrett Browning. *The Letters of Robert Browning and Elizabeth Barrett Barrett, 1845–1846,* ed. Elvan Kintner. 2 vols. Cambridge, Mass., 1969.

Browning, Robert and John Ruskin. 'Ruskin and the Brownings: Twenty-five Unpublished Letters', ed. David J. DeLaura. *Bulletin of the John Rylands Library,* 54 (spring 1972) 314–56.

Browning, Robert and Julia Wedgwood. *Robert Browning and Julia*

Wedgwood: A Broken Friendship as Revealed in their Letters, ed. Richard Curle. London, 1937.

Buckley, Jerome H. *Tennyson: The Growth of a Poet*. Boston, 1965.

Buckley Jerome H. *The Victorian Temper*. Cambridge, Mass., 1969.

Bullough, Geoffrey. *The Trend in Modern Poetry*. London, 1934.

Burnshaw, Stanley, ed. *The Poem Itself*. New York, 1967.

Burnshaw, Stanley. *The Seamless Web*. London, 1970.

Byron, George Gordon. *The Works of Lord Byron*, ed. Ernest H. Coleridge. Rev. ed. London, 1898.

Calderwood, James L. and Harold E. Toliver, eds. *Perspectives on Poetry*. New York, 1968.

Carroll, Lewis. *The Complete Works of Lewis Carroll*. London, 1939.

Catullus, C. Valerius. *Catullus: (Gai Valeri Catulli Veronensis Liber)*, trans. Celia and Louis Zukofsky. London, 1969.

Catullus, C. Valerius. *The Poems of Catullus*, ed. William A. Aiken. New York, 1950.

Chesterton, G. K. *Robert Browning*. London, 1936.

Collingwood, William G. *The Life and Work of John Ruskin*. 2 vols. London, 1893.

Collins, T. J. *Robert Browning's Moral–Aesthetic Theory, 1833–1855*. Lincoln, 1967.

Cooper, Philip. *The Autobiographical Myth of Robert Lowell*. Chapel Hill, 1970.

Corson, Hiram. *An Introduction to the Study of Robert Browning's Poetry*. Boston, 1896.

Cummings, Edward E. *Complete Poems*, ed. George James Firmage. 2 vols. London, 1968.

Cunningham, J. V., ed. *The Problem of Style*. New York, 1966.

Davie, Donald. *Ezra Pound: Poet as Sculptor*. London, 1965.

Davies, Hugh Sykes. *Browning and the Modern Novel*. St John's College Cambridge Lecture, 1961–2. Hull, 1962.

Deutsch, Babette. *Poetry in Our Time: A Critical Survey of Poetry in the English-Speaking World 1900 to 1960*. 2nd ed. New York, 1963.

Deutsch, Babette. *This Modern Poetry*. New York, 1935.

DeVane, William Clyde. *A Browning Handbook*. New York, 1935.

DeVane, William C. 'The Virgin and the Dragon', *Yale Review*, 37 (Sep 1947) 33–46.

Dijkstra, Bram. *The Hieroglyphics of a New Speech: Cubism, Stieglitz, and the Early Poetry of William Carlos Williams*. Princeton, N.J., 1969.

Donne, John. *The Complete Poems of John Donne, D.D.*, ed. Alexander B. Grosart. 2 vols. London, 1872.

Donne, John. *The Poems of John Donne*, ed. Herbert J. C. Grierson. 2 vols. Oxford, 1912.

Drew, Elizabeth and John L. Sweeney. *Directions in Modern Poetry.* New York, 1967.

Drew, Philip. *The Poetry of Browning: A Critical Introduction.* London, 1970.

Drinkwater, John. *Victorian Poetry.* London, 1923.

Dryden, John. *Of Dramatic Poesy and Other Critical Essays*, ed. George Watson. 2 vols. London and New York, 1962.

Duckworth, Francis R. G. *Browning's Background and Conflict.* London, 1931.

Duncan, Joseph E. *The Revival of Metaphysical Poetry: The History of a Style, 1800 to the Present.* Minneapolis, 1959.

Eliot, T. S. *After Strange Gods: A Primer of Modern Heresy.* London, 1934.

Eliot, T. S., trans. *Anabasis* by St- J. Perse. London, 1930.

Eliot, T. S. *The Complete Poems and Plays of T. S. Eliot.* London, 1969.

Eliot, T. S. *Dialogue on Poetic Drama* preceding *Of Dramatick Poesie: An Essay* (1668) by John Dryden. London, 1928.

Eliot, T. S. *Essays Ancient and Modern.* London, 1936.

Eliot, T. S. 'Milton', *Proceedings of the British Academy*, 33 (1947) 1–19.

Eliot, T. S. *The Music of Poetry.* Glasgow, 1942.

Eliot, T. S. *On Poetry and Poets.* London, 1957.

Eliot, T. S. *Poetry and Drama.* Cambridge, Mass., 1951.

Eliot, T. S. *The Sacred Wood: Essays on Poetry and Criticism.* 2nd ed. London, 1928.

Eliot, T. S. *Selected Essays.* 3rd ed. London, 1951.

Eliot, T. S. *The Three Voices of Poetry.* London, 1953.

Eliot, T. S. *To Criticize the Critic and other Writings.* London, 1965.

Eliot, T. S. preface to *Transit of Venus: Poems by Harry Crosby.* Paris, 1931.

Eliot, T. S. *The Use of Poetry and the Use of Criticism: Studies in the Relation of Criticism to Poetry in England.* London, 1933.

Faverty, Frederic E., ed. *The Victorian Poets: A Guide to Research.* Cambridge, Mass., 1956

Ford, Ford Madox. *The March of Literature: From Confucius to Modern Times*. London, 1939.

Ford, Ford Madox. *Thus to Revisit: Some Reminiscences*. New York, 1921.

Fowler, Roger, ed. *Essays on Style and Language*. London, 1966.

Frank, Joseph. *The Widening Gyre: Crisis and Mastery in Modern Literature*. New Brunswick, 1963.

Fuson, Benjamin W. *Browning and his English Predecessors in the Dramatic Monolog*. State University of Iowa Humanistic Studies, 8 (July 1942).

Fuson, Benjamin W. 'The Poet and his Mask', *Park College Faculty Lectures, Fifth Annual Series*, 1952–3. Parkville, 1954.

Gallup, Donald. *A Bibliography of Ezra Pound*. London, 1963.

Gardner, Helen. *Eliot and English Poetic Tradition*. 36th Byron Foundation Lecture, 22 Oct 1965.

Gardner, W. H. 'Introduction', *Poems and Prose of Gerard Manley Hopkins*. London and Baltimore, 1953.

Givens, Seon, ed. *James Joyce: Two Decades of Criticism*. New York, 1963.

Goodwin, K. L. *The Influence of Ezra Pound*. London, 1966.

Gridley, Roy E. *Browning*. Routledge Author Guides. London, 1972.

Griffin, W. Hall and Harry Christopher Minchin. *The Life of Robert Browning, with Notices of his Writings, his Family, and his Friends*. Rev. ed. London, 1910.

Groom, Bernard. *The Diction of Poetry from Spenser to Bridges*. London, 1955.

Gross, H. S. *Sound and Form in Modern Poetry: A Study of Prosody from Thomas Hardy to Robert Lowell*. Ann Arbor, 1964.

Hamilton, Ian, ed. *The Modern Poet: Essays from the Review*. London, 1968.

Hardy, Florence, *The Early Life of Thomas Hardy, 1840–1891*. London, 1928.

Hardy, Thomas. *The Collected Poems of Thomas Hardy*. London, 1960.

Hardy, Thomas. *Tess of the D'Urbervilles: A Pure Woman*. Vols 1 and 2 of the Mellstock Edition of *The Works of Thomas Hardy*. 37 vols. London, 1919.

Hardy, Thomas. *Thomas Hardy's Personal Writings: Prefaces, Literary Opinions, Reminiscences*, ed. Harold Orel. Lawrence, 1966.

Heisenberg, Werner. *The Physical Principles of the Quantum Theory*, trans. Carl Eckart and Frank C. Hoyt. Chicago, 1930.

Herford, C. H. *Robert Browning*. London, 1905.

Hesse, Eva, ed. *New Approaches to Ezra Pound: A Co-ordinated Investigation of Pound's Poetry and Ideas*. London, 1969.

Hill, Archibald. 'Pippa's Song', *University of Texas Studies in English*, 35 (1956) 51–6.

Honan, Park. *Browning's Characters: A Study in Poetic Technique*. New Haven, 1961.

Hopkins, Gerard Manley. *Poems of Gerard Manley Hopkins*, ed. W. H. Gardner. 3rd ed. London, 1948.

Hopkins, Gerard Manley and Richard Watson Dixon. *The Correspondence of Gerard Manley Hopkins and Richard Watson Dixon*, ed. Claude C. Abbott. London, 1935.

Hough, Graham. *Image and Experience: Studies in a Literary Revolution*. London, 1960.

Howarth, Herbert. *Notes on Some Figures Behind T. S. Eliot*. London, 1965.

Hughes, Glenn. *Imagism and the Imagists: A Study in Modern Poetry*. London, 1931.

Hulcoop, John F. 'Robert Browning, "Maker of Plays" and Poet: A Study of his Concepts and Practice of Drama and of their Relation to his Concepts and Practice of Poetry. With a Chronology of his Early Literary Career, 1832–1846'. Dissertation, University of London, 1960.

James, Henry. *The Art of Fiction and Other Essays*. New York, 1948.

James, Henry. 'The Novel in *The Ring and the Book*', *Notes on Novelists with Some Other Notes*. London, 1914.

James, Henry. *William Wetmore Story and His Friends: From Letters, Diaries and Recollections*. 2 vols. London, 1903.

Johnson, E. D. H. *The Alien Vision of Victorian Poetry: Sources of the Poetic Imagination in Tennyson, Browning, and Arnold*. Hamden, 1963.

Jones, A. R. 'Robert Browning and the Dramatic Monologue: The Impersonal Art', *Critical Quarterly*, 9 (winter 1967) 301–28.

Jones, Genesius. *Approach to the Purpose: A Study of the Poetry of T. S. Eliot*. London, 1964.

Jonson, Ben. *Three Comedies: Volpone, The Alchemist, Bartholomew Fair*, ed. Michael Jamieson. London, 1966.

Joyce, James. *Ulysses.* New York, 1934.

Jung, C. G. *Two Essays on Analytical Psychology.* Vol. VII of *Collected Works,* trans. R. F. C. Hull. London, 1953.

Keats, John. *The Poems of John Keats,* ed. Miriam Allott. London, 1970.

Kenmare, Dallas. *Browning and Modern Thought.* London, 1939.

Kenner, Hugh. *The Poetry of Ezra Pound,* London, 1951.

Kermode, Frank. *Romantic Image.* London, 1957.

King, Roma A. *The Bow and the Lyre: The Art of Robert Browning.* Ann Arbor, 1964.

King, Roma, A. 'Browning: "Mage" and "Maker" – a Study in Poetic Purpose and Method', *Victorian Newsletter* (autumn 1961) 21–5.

Knickerbocker, Kenneth L. 'Robert Browning: A Modern Appraisal', *Tennessee Studies in Literature,* 4 (1959) 1–11.

Langbaum, Robert. *The Modern Spirit: Essays on the Continuity of Nineteenth- and Twentieth-Century Literature.* London, 1970.

Langbaum, Robert. *The Poetry of Experience: The Dramatic Monologue in Modern Literary Tradition.* London, 1957.

Lawrence, D. H. *The Collected Letters of D. H. Lawrence,* ed. Harry T. Moore. 2 vols. London, 1962.

Lawrence, D. H. *The Complete Poems of D. H. Lawrence,* ed. Vivian de Sola Pinto and Warren Roberts. 2 vols. London, 1964.

Lawrence, D. H. *Women in Love.* London, 1921.

Leavis, F. R. *New Bearings in English Poetry: A Study of the Contemporary Situation.* London, 1932.

Litzinger, Boyd and Donald Smalley. *Browning: The Critical Heritage.* London, 1970.

Lounsbury, Thomas R. *The Early Literary Career of Robert Browning.* New York, 1911.

Lowell, Amy. *Tendencies in Modern American Poetry.* Boston, 1917.

Lowell, Robert. 'The Art of Poetry', III, interview in the *Paris Review,* 7, no. 25 (1961) 57–95.

Lowell, Robert. *Imitations.* London, 1962.

Lowell, Robert. *Life Studies.* 2nd ed. London, 1968.

MacLeish, Archibald. *The Collected Poems of Archibald MacLeish.* Boston, [1962].

MacNeice, Louis. *The Collected Poems of Louis MacNeice,* ed. E. R. Dodds. London, 1966.

MacNeice, Louis. *Modern Poetry: A Personal Essay.* London, 1938.

M[arsh], E[dward]. *Georgian Poetry, 1911–1912.* 3rd ed. London, 1913.

Marsh, Edward. *Georgian Poetry, 1920–1922.* London, 1922.

Martineau, Harriet. *Harriet Martineau's Autobiography.* 3 vols. London, 1877.

Matthiessen, F. O. *The Achievement of T. S. Eliot: An Essay on the Nature of Poetry.* 3rd ed. London and New York, 1958.

Melchiori, Barbara. *Browning's Poetry of Reticence.* London, 1968.

Melchiori, Giorgio. *The Tightrope Walkers: Studies of Mannerism in Modern English Literature.* London, 1956.

Mendl, R. W. S. 'Robert Browning, the Poet-Musician', *Music and Letters,* 42 (Apr 1961) 142–50.

Meredith, Owen. *Letters from Owen Meredith to Robert and Elizabeth Barrett Browning,* ed. Aurelia B. Harlan and J. Lee Harlan, Jr. Baylor, 1936.

Miller, Betty. *Robert Browning: A Portrait.* London, 1952.

Miller, Rosalind S. *Gertrude Stein: Form and Intelligibility.* New York, 1949.

Moore, Marianne. *Collected Poems.* London, 1951.

Musgrove, S. *T. S. Eliot and Walt Whitman.* Wellington, New Zealand, 1952.

Nemerov, Howard, ed. *Poets on Poetry.* New York, 1966.

Olson, Charles. *Projective Verse.* New York, 1959.

Orr, A. L. (Mrs Sutherland). *A Handbook to the Works of Robert Browning.* 6th ed. London, 1969.

Orr, A. L. (Mrs Sutherland). *Life and Letters of Robert Browning.* London, 1891.

Peckham, Morse. *Victorian Revolutionaries: Speculations on Some Heroes of a Culture Crisis.* New York, 1970.

Peterson, William S. *Interrogating the Oracle: A History of the London Browning Society.* Athens, Ohio, 1969.

Pinto, Vivian de Sola. *Crisis in English Poetry, 1880–1940.* London, 1951.

Plath, Sylvia. *Ariel.* London, 1965.

Plath, Sylvia. *Winter Trees.* London, 1971.

Poe, Edgar Allen. *The Centenary Poe: Tales, Poems, Criticism, Marginalia and Eureka by Edgar Allen Poe,* ed. Montagu Slater. London, 1949.

Pottle, Frederick. *The Idiom of Poetry.* Rev. ed. Ithaca, N.Y., 1946.

Pottle, Frederick. *Shelley and Browning: A Myth and Some Facts.* 1923 ed.; repr. Chicago, 1965.

Pound, Ezra. *ABC of Reading.* London, 1951.

Pound, Ezra. *The Cantos of Ezra Pound* [1–109]. London, 1964.

Pound, Ezra. *Ezra Pound: Translations.* Enlarged ed. London, 1963.

Pound, Ezra. *Gaudier-Brzeska: A Memoir.* London, 1916.

[Pound, Ezra]. *Des Imagistes: An Anthology.* London and New York, 1914.

Pound, Ezra. *The Letters of Ezra Pound, 1907–1941,* ed. D. D. Paige. London, 1951.

Pound, Ezra. *Literary Essays of Ezra Pound,* ed. T. S. Eliot. London, 1954.

Pound, Ezra. *Make it New: Essays by Ezra Pound.* London, 1934.

Pound, Ezra. *Pavannes and Divisions.* New York, 1918.

Pound, Ezra. *Personae: Collected Shorter Poems of Ezra Pound.* London, 1952.

Pound, Ezra. *Spirit of Romance.* Norfolk, Conn., 1952.

Pound, Ezra. 'Three Cantos – I', *Poetry,* 10 (June 1917) 113–21.

Pound, Ezra. 'Vorticism', *Fortnightly Review* 96 (1914) 461–71.

Press, John. *The Chequer'd Shade: Reflections on Obscurity in Poetry.* London, 1958.

Press, John. *A Map of Modern English Verse.* London, 1969.

Press, John. *Rule and Energy: Trends in British Poetry Since the Second World War.* London, 1963.

Puckett, S. M., Brother Walter Edward. 'The Nineteenth-Century Foundations of the Robert Browning–Ezra Pound Bridge to Modernity in Poetry'. Dissertation, St Louis University, 1961.

Quiller-Couch, Arthur, ed. *The Oxford Book of Ballads.* Oxford, 1910.

Ransom, John Crowe. *The World's Body.* New York and London, 1938.

Raymond, William O. *The Infinite Moment and Other Essays in Robert Browning.* 2nd ed. Toronto, 1965.

Richards, I. A. *Principles of Literary Criticism.* Rev. ed. London, 1960.

Roberts, Michael. *T. E. Hulme.* London, 1938.

Rossetti, William Michael. *Dante Gabriel Rossetti, His Family Letters: With a Memoir.* 2 vols. London, 1895.

Rossetti, William Michael, ed. *Præraphaelite Diaries and Letters.* London, 1900.

Rossetti, William Michael. *Some Reminiscences of William Michael Rossetti*. 2 vols. London, 1906.

Ruthven, K. K. *A Guide to Ezra Pound's Personae* (1926). Los Angeles, 1969.

Saintsbury, George. *From Blake to Swinburne*. Vol. 3 of *A History of English Prosody from the Twelfth Century to the Present Day*. London, 1910.

Schmiefsky, Marvel. 'Yeats and Browning: The Shock of Recognition', *Studies in English Literature*, 10 (autumn 1970) 701–21.

Scully, James, ed. *Modern Poets on Modern Poetry*. London, 1970.

Sewell, Elizabeth. *The Structure of Poetry*. London, 1951.

Sexton, Anne. *Selected Poems*. London, 1964.

Shakespeare, William. *Sonnets*, ed. C. Knox Pooler. The Arden Shakespeare. 2nd ed. London, 1931.

Sharp, William. *Life of Robert Browning*. London, 1890.

Shaw, W. D. *The Dialectical Temper: The Rhetorical Art of Robert Browning*. Ithaca, N.Y., 1968.

Shelley, Percy Bysshe. *The Complete Poetical Works of Percy Bysshe Shelley*, ed. Thomas Hutchinson. London, 1952.

Shelley, Percy Bysshe. 'A Defence of Poetry', *Peacock's Four Ages of Poetry, Shelley's Defence of Poetry, Browning's Essay on Shelley*. The Percy Reprints, no. 3, ed. H. F. B. Brett-Smith. Oxford, 1921.

Sitwell, Edith. *Collected Poems*. London, 1957.

Slatin, Myles. 'Mesmerism: a Study of Ezra Pound's Use of the Poetry of Robert Browning'. Dissertation, Yale University, 1957.

Some Imagist Poets, ed. anon. London, 1915, 1916.

Sparrow, John. *Sense and Poetry: Essays on the Place of Meaning in Contemporary Verse*. London, 1934.

Spears, Monroe K. *Dionysus and the City: Modernism in Twentieth-Century Poetry*. New York, 1970.

Speirs, John. *Poetry Towards Novel*. New York, 1971.

Spencer, Theodore, ed. *A Garland for John Donne*. London, 1931.

Spender, Stephen. 'Shades of Milk Wood', *Observer Review*, 6 June 1971.

Spender, Stephen. *World Within World: The Autobiography of Stephen Spender*. London, 1951.

Stange, G. Robert. 'Browning and Modern Poetry', *Pacific Spectator*, 8 (1954) 218–28.

Stead, C. K. *The New Poetic*. London, 1964.

Stein, Gertrude. *Bee Time Vine and Other Pieces* [1913–27]. Vol. 3 of Yale ed. of the unpublished writings of Gertrude Stein. New Haven, 1953.

Stevens, Wallace. *The Collected Poems of Wallace Stevens*. London, 1955.

Stevens, Wallace. *The Necessary Angel: Essays on Reality and the Imagination*. London, 1960.

Sullivan, John Patrick. *Ezra Pound and Sextus Propertius: A Study in Creative Translation*. London, 1965.

Symons, Arthur. 'Is Browning Dramatic?', *The Browning Society's Papers*, 1885–6, 2 (1885).

Sypher, Wylie. *Rococo to Cubism in Art and Literature*. New York, 1960.

Tennyson, Alfred. *The Poems of Tennyson*, ed. Christopher Ricks. London, 1969.

Tennyson, Hallam. *Alfred Lord Tennyson: A Memoir*. 2 vols. London, 1897.

Tennyson, Hallam, ed. *Tennyson and His Friends*. London, 1911.

Thomas, Dylan. *Collected Poems, 1934–1952*. London, 1952.

Tillotson, Geoffrey. 'A Word for Browning', *Sewanee Review*, 72 (1964) 389–97.

Tillotson, Geoffrey and Kathleen. *Mid-Victorian Studies*. London, 1965.

Tracy, Clarence, ed. *Browning's Mind and Art*. London, 1968.

Wagner, W. Richard. *Wagner on Music and Drama: A Compendium of Richard Wagner's Prose Works*, trans. H. Aston Ellis. New York, 1964.

Ward, Maisie. *Robert Browning and His World*. 2 vols. I. *The Private Face* (1812–1861). London, 1967. II. *Two Robert Brownings?* (1861–1889). London, 1969.

Warren, Alba H. *English Poetic Theory, 1825–1865*. New Jersey, 1950.

Welleck, René and Austin Warren. *Theory of Literature*. 3rd ed. London, 1963.

Wells, Henry W. *New Poets from Old: A Study in Literary Genetics*. New York, 1940.

Wheelwright, Philip. *Metaphor and Reality*. Bloomington, Ind., 1964.

Whiting, Lilian. *The Brownings: Their Life and Art*. Boston, 1911.

Whitman, Walt. *Leaves of Grass*. New York, 1954.

Wilde, Oscar. *The Works of Oscar Wilde*. London, 1963.

Williams, William Carlos. *The Autobiography of William Carlos Williams*. New York, 1951.

Williams, William Carlos. *The Collected Earlier Poems of William Carlos Williams*. London, [1967].

Williams, William Carlos. *The Collected Later Poems of William Carlos Williams*. London, 1965.

Williams, William Carlos. *I Wanted to Write a Poem: The Autobiography of the Works of a Poet*, ed. Edith Heal. Boston, 1958.

Williams, William Carlos. *Paterson*. New York, 1963.

Williams, William Carlos. *The Selected Letters of William Carlos Williams*, ed. John C. Thirlwall. New York, 1957.

Wilson, Edmund. *Axel's Castle*. New York, 1931.

Woolf, Virginia. *Collected Essays*. 4 vols. London, 1966–7.

Woolf, Virginia. *Granite and Rainbow: Essays by Virginia Woolf*. London, 1958.

Wordsworth, William. *The Poetical Works of William Wordsworth*, ed. E. de Selincourt and Helen Darbishire. 5 vols. Oxford, 1940–9.

Wordsworth, William. *Selected Poems and Prefaces*, ed. Jack Stillinger. Boston, 1965.

Wright, George T. *The Poet in the Poem: The Personae of Eliot, Yeats and Pound*. Berkeley, 1960.

Yeats, W. B. *Autobiographies*. London, 1955.

Yeats, W. B. *The Autobiography of William Butler Yeats*. New York, 1953.

Yeats, W. B. *Essays and Introductions*. London, 1961.

Yeats, W. B. *The Letters of W. B. Yeats*, ed. Allen Wade. London, 1954.

Yeats, W. B. *Letters to the New Island*, ed. Horace Reynolds. Cambridge, Mass., 1934.

Yeats, W. B. *Modern Poetry*. London, 1936.

Yeats, W. B., ed. *The Oxford Book of Modern Verse*. Oxford, 1936.

Yeats, W. B. *The Variorum Edition of the Poems of W. B. Yeats*, ed. Peter Allt and Russell K. Alspach. London and New York, 1957.

Yeats, W. B. *A Vision*. 2nd ed. London, 1937.

Zukofsky, Louis, ed. *An 'Objectivists' Anthology*. Le Beausset, Var, France, 1932.

Index

Fiction, and fact, 72–4
Film, 27, 157
Flaubert, Gustave, 161, 162
Ford, Ford Madox, 77, 121, 161
Form, and meaning, 152–3
Formal verse, 9; in Browning, 93–4
Free verse, 9, 167–8, 169
Frost, Robert, 98, 112
Furnivall, F. J., 34, 111, 113

Georgians, 16–19, 77
Grotesque, in Browning, 21, 49–50

Hardy, Thomas, 54–5, 66–7, 75, 169
Heisenberg, Werner, 58
Hemingway, Ernest, 169
Herbert, George, 11
Hopkins, Gerard Manley, 30, 80, 89, 144, 145, 162
Hugo, Victor, 42–3
Hulme, T. E., 35

Ideogram, 11, 27
Image, 71; abstract, 50, 92, 94; and characterisation, 68–71, 149–50; descriptive, 17–21; dream, 70; representational, 67–8; as structure, 140, 149; as vortex, 22, 25
Imagery, in Browning, 19–26, 50, 67–71, 94–5; colour, 14–16; in Tennyson, 67–70
Imagism, 7, 16, 19, 70, 73, 134
Imitation, and translation, 120–1, 124
Interior monologue, 169–70

James, Henry, 1, 104, 169–70, 171
Jerrold, Douglas, 33
Joyce, James, 161
Ulysses, 160, 172, 173–4
Jung, Carl Gustav, 115

Kean, Edmund, 117
Keats, John, 71, 77, 89, 94
Kipling, Rudyard, 139

Language, abstract, 50; archaic, in Browning, 86; concrete, 50; new, 37–8
Lawrence, D. H., 16, 29, 84–5, 168
Women in Love, 146
Lewis, Wyndham, 176–7
Life, and art, 47
Line, in modern poetry, 84–6, 163

Lowell, Amy, 167
Lowell, Robert, 63, 118, 162, 166; and Browning, 44, 164
Imitations, 124
Life Studies, 169
'Skunk Hour', 166
Lyric, 97, 137

MacLeish, Archibald, 27–8
MacNeice, Louis, 29, 50
Mallarmé, Stéphane, 137
Marsh, Edward, 16–18
Mask, 57, 107–8, 113–15, 132–3, 158, 171; and Browning, 107–8, 110–111, 126; and Eliot, 112, 114; and Frost, 112; and Pound, 112, 114, 120; and truth, 116, 117; and Williams, 112; and Yeats, 113, 117–18
Meredith, George, 167
Metrics, 83–6, 124, 152, 163, 174–5
Milton, John, 77, 89
Molière
Don Juan, 124–6
Montage, 156–7
Moore, Marianne, 10, 73, 85, 89–90
Morals, and literature, see Victorian readers and Browning
Myth, 171, 172, 174, 175

Narrative poetry, 97–8
Natorp, Gustave, 12
New criticism, 149
Novel, Browning and, 1

'Objective correlative', 25, 70, 71
Objective poet, 103, 108, 111–12; defined by Browning, 98; see also Objectivity, in poetry
Objectivity, and dramatic method, 103, 118–19, 132; in poetry, 29, 55, 158, 162; relation to facts, 57–58, 98, 113
Obscurity, 30–1, 140; in Browning, 22, 30, 33, 36, 50–1, 140–2; created by allusion, 31; created by elliptical construction, 30, 165–6; created by lack of common background, 63–4; created by psychological emphasis in poetry, 61; and Eliot, 30–1, 37; in Hopkins, 30; in Pound, 29–30; in Thomas, 30